The Art Signature File
2012 Edition

By G.B. David

DEDICATION

for Alex and Nicolas. . .
may your galaxies always be, visible,
with the knowledge to get there, obvious,
and the resources you need available!

Table of Contents

The Art Signature File
By G.B. David

I have found that sometimes you can just browse through the Art Signature File and discover the mark or signature of the artist you're trying to identify. Prices, Style, Medium, Nationality, Dates, and any other useful pertinent information we could find about the artist are listed also.

Data was compiled from information in public and private sales of art at over 500 fine art auction houses around the world. There are new collectors that are looking for different names of regional artists. In this new Art Signature File you will find the regional names of artists desired right now by most collectors

One area of art collecting is in the collector trying to find lost, or locating unknown art. I have discovered this art and a lot of the serious art collectors know what I am talking about. I have included the Degenerate artists that had so many works confiscated and lost in Germany, and a listing section for the WPA artists whose thousands of works were sold after the depression by the pound! Can you imagine, Fine Art by the pound! I hope this edition helps you to find, discover, identify and place your fine art.

Good Luck in your Art Adventures!

G.B. David

Artists starting with the letter "A"

1.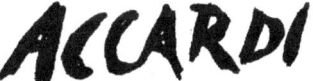

2. **NA**

NICCOLO ABBATE 1512-1670
Italian Painter $150,000

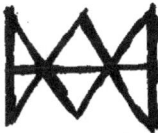

MARIO ABREU 1918-
Venezuala Painter $5,000

ACCARDI

CARLA ACCARDI 1924-
Italian Abstract, Genre, Portraits $71,000

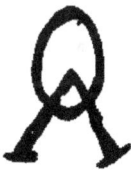

JOHANN (also Hans) ACHEN (also Aken, Aachen 1562-1615
German Portraits, Genre $450,000

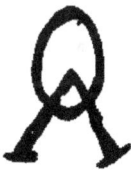

OSWALD ACHENBACH 1827-1905
German Landscape $50,000

LOUIS EMILE ADAN 1839-1937
French, Genre, Landscape $15,000

JANKEL ADLER 1895-1949
Polish Painter, Portraits, Nudes $100,000

SAMUEL ADLER 1898-1979
American Modern $1,000

EDMUND ADLER 1871-1957
Austrian Painter $10,000

MIKHAIL ADREENKO 1894-1982
Russian Painter $5,000

LUCIEN ADRION 1889-1953
French Painter $20,000

1. *Qv. Qv. aelst*

2. *Qv. Qv. aelst 1651*

3. **W. V. aelst**

WILLEM VAN AELST (also Aalst) 1625-1683
Netherlandish Still Life Painter $125,000

Fr. Aerni

FRANZ THEODOR AERNI 1853-1918
German Landscape $30,000

1. *JAertsen*

2. **Æ**

PIETER AERTSZEN 1507-1573
Dutch Genre, Portraits $150,000

afro

BASALDELLA AFRO 1912-1976
Italian Abstract $250,000

Agnes Aggerup

AGNES AGGERUP 1800's
Danish Floral $20,000

MAX AGOSTINI 1914-
French Painter $7,500

GEORGE W. AIKMAN 1830-1905
British Landscape, Genre $1,500

MAX EMANUEL AINMILLER (also Ainmuller) 1807-1870
German Painter, Architectural, $2,000

IVAN KONSTANTINOVICH AIVASOVSKY 1817-1900
Russian Landscape, Seascape $80,000

1.

2.

PAUL AIZPIRI 1919-
French Impressionist $20,000

FRANCESCO ALBANI 1578-1660
Italian Landscape $40,000

JOSEPH ALBERS 1888-1976
American Contemporary $275,000

JOS ALBERT 1886-1981
Belgian Painter, Landscape $40,000

RICHARD ALBITZ 1876-1954
German Painter, Landscape $1,500

ADAM EMORY ALBRIGHT 1862-1957
American N.A. Painter $55,000

HEINRICH ALDEGREVER 1502-1558
German, Allegory, Painter $6,000

FREDERICK JAMES ALDRIDGE 1850-1933
British Seascape $5,000

1.   2.
PIERRE ALECHINSKY 1927-
Belgian Abstract $2,000,000

1. *J.W.Alexander*

2. *John W. Alexander*

JOHN WHITE ALEXANDER 1856-1915
American N.A. Illustrator $400,000

Alfani

DOMENICO DI PAREDE ALFANI 1483-1553
French Painter $45,000

H,alken

SAMUEL HENRY ALKEN 1810-1894
British Animals, Genre, Horses $70,000

Marion Boyd Allen

MARION BOYD ALLEN 1862-1941
American Indians $5,000

Allievi

FERNANDO ALLIEVI 1954-
Argentina Genre, Painter $4,000

H.Allingham

HELEN ALLINGHAM 1848-1926
British Illustrator, Landscape, Genre $30,000

1. *A les A lori*

2. *A les A lori*

ALESSANDRO ALLORI 1535-1607
Italian Painter, Genre, Religious $100,000

Acas

CANO ALONSO 1601-1667
Spanish Painter

Alpuy

JULIO ALPUY 1919-
Mexican Painter, Landscape $7,000

R.Alt

RUDOLF VON ALT 1812-1905
Austrian Architecture Landscape $50,000

AALtdorfer

ALBRECHT ALTDORFER 1480-1538
German Landscape, Portraits $100,000

ABBEY ALTSON

ABBEY ALTSON 1864-1917
British Landscape, Portraits $20,000

Aman Jean

EDMOND FRANCOIS AMAN-JEAN 1860-1936
French Painter $150,000

Amat

JOSEP AMAT 1901-1991
Spain Painter $125,000

John Ambrose

JOHN AMBROSE 1900's
British Seascapes $1,800

Robert Wesley Amick

ROBERT WESLEY AMICK 1879-1969
American Illustrator $6,000

1. 2. CA (A CA 5.
C. Amiet   6.
3. 4. CA CA CA 7.

CUNO AMIET 1868-1961
Swiss Landscape $150,000

1. *Michael Ancher* *MA* 2.

MICHAEL ANCHER 1849-1927
Danish Painter, Landscape, Genre $120,000

a. ancher

ANNA ANCHER 1859-1935
Danish Painter, Genre, Landscape $35,000

J. B. Anderson

JAMES BELL ANDERSON 1886-1938
British Painter, Landscape $4,000

1.

Andreotti

2. *F Andreotti*

FEDERICO ANDREOTTI 1847-1930
Italian Painter $45,000

Nick Andrew

NICK ANDREW 1900's
British Landscape $1,000

**ANTHONY
ANGAROLA**

ANTHONY ANGAROLA 1893-1929
American Painter $1,500

CH ANGRAND

CHARLES ANGRAND 1854-1926
French Painter, Landscape $200,000

1. *Anker* 2. *Anker*

ALBERT ANKER 1831-1910
Swiss Landscape $250,000

Anjelmi

MICHELANGELO ANSELMI 1491-1554
Italian Painter, Nudes $80,000

Thos. Anshutz

THOMAS POLLOCK ANSHUTZ 1851-1912
American Genre Working People $1,000,000

Antes

HORST ANTES 1936-
German Painter $125,000

1. *LOSE* *AN TOLIN. P.*

2. *AN TOLIN.*
LOSE

JOSE ANTOLINEZ 1639-1676
Spain Genre $75,000

K. appel 5.

appel 1. *(K. appel* 2. 3.

4. *(K. appel*

KAREL APPEL 1921-
American Contemporary $300,000

CHARLES P. APPEL 1857-1928
American Landscape, Seascape $15,000

ANDREA APPIANI (elder) 1754-1817
Italian Fresco Painter, Allegory, Nudes $25,000

KRISHNA HAWLAJI ARA 1914-1984
India Painter, Nudes $5,000

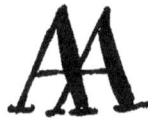

1.　　　　　　　2.

ALEXANDER
ARCHIPENKO 1887-1964
American Modern, Cubist, Sculpture, Abstract $2,667,000

MORDECAI ARDON 1896-1992
Israeli Painter, Landscape $120,000

JUAN DE ARELLANO 1614-1676
Spanish Still Life $1,100,000

Gonzalo Ariza

GONZALO ARIZA 1912-
Columbian Painter $25,000

Frank M. Armington

FRANK MILTON ARMINGTON 1878-1941
Canadian Etcher, Genre, Painter $7,500

MARY ARMOUR

MARY NICOL NEIL ARMOUR 1902-
British Painter, Landscape $60,000

G. D. ARMOUR

GEORGE DENHOLM ARMOUR 1864-1949 British Watercolour,
Landscape, Animals $10,000

ARMS

JOHN TAYLOR ARMS 1887-1953
American Painter, Seascape $7,500

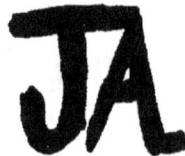

JOHN ARMSTRONG 1895-1973
British Painter, Allegory, Landscape $45,000

Boris Aronson

BORIS ARONSON 1902-
American Costume Stage Design $1,500

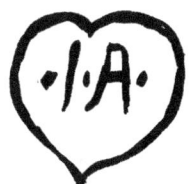

IVAR AROSENIUS 1878-1909
Swedish Painter $6,000

JACQUES D. ARTHOIS 1613-1684
Belgian Landscape, Genre $35,000

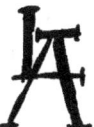

LOUIS ASHER 1804-1878
German Genre $3,500

JEAN JOSEPH ASIAUX 1764-1840
French Painter $0

HANS ASPER 1499-1571
German Portraits $5,000

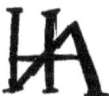

JAN ASSELIJN 1610-1652
Netherlandish Landscapes, Seascape $75,000

Assetto

FRANCO ASSETTO 1911-
Italian Painter $1,500

1. *B. vander: Ast fecit: e*

2. *B. vander: Ast*

BALTHASAR VAN DER AST 1590-1656
Netherlandish Still Life $2,800,000

N. ASTRUP

NIKOLAI ASTRUP 1880-1928
Norway Painter $600,000

Atamian

CHARLES-GARABED ATAMIAN 1872-1947
Turkish Beach Scenes $15,000

MAUD TINDAL ATKINSON 1900's
British Watercolour Animals Dogs $2,000

Dr. Atl

DR GERARDO MURILLO ATL 1875-1964
Mexican Painter $200,000

JEAN MICHEL ATLAN 1913-1960
French Abstract $650,000

1.

3.

2.

6.

4.

5.

7.

RENE AUBERJONOIS 1872-1957
French Painter, Genre, Animals $60,000

WILLIAM AUBERT 1856-1942
Swiss Painter $7,500

JEAN ERNEST AUBERT 1824-1906
French Genre, Still Life $15,000

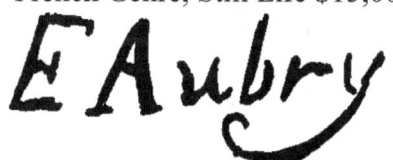

ETIENNE AUBRY 1745-1781
French Genre, Portraits $10,000

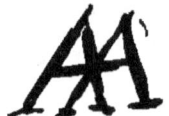

ABRAHAM AUBRY 1650-1682
French Painter $0

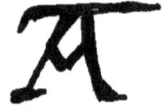

PETER AUDER 1500's
German Painter $0

GEORGE AULT 1891-1948
American Cubist $70,000

GIUSEPPE AURELI 1858-1929
Italian Genre $15,000

1.   2.   3.

HENDRIK (also Van Kampen, Hendrick) AVERCAMP 1584-1663
Dutch Landscape, Genre $8,688,000

1.

Milton Avery

2. *Milton Avery*

MILTON AVERY 1893-1964
American Painter $350,000

michael ayrton

MICHAEL AYRTON 1921-1975
British Painter $12,000

DAVID AZUZ

DAVID AZUZ 1942-
Israel Portrait $5,000

Artists starting with the letter "B"

KNUD BAADE 1808-1879
Danish Landscape, Seascape $7,500

EUGENE BABOULENE 1905-
French Painter $25,000

ALOIS BACH 1809-1893
German Genre, Landscape $10,000

JEAN JACQUES BACHELIER 1724-1806
French Floral, Animal Painter $50,000

JACOB ADRIAENSZ BACKER 1608-1651
Dutch Old Master $125,000

LOUIS D'ALBE BACKER 1762-1824
Swiss Landscape

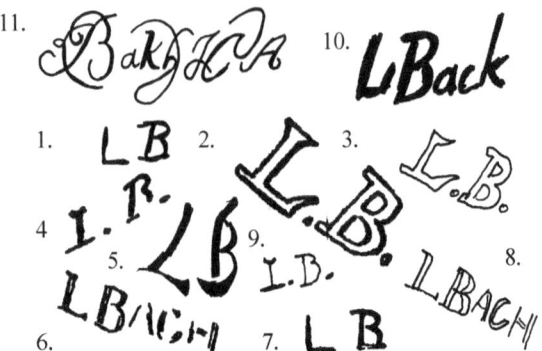

LUDOLF BACKHUIJSEN (also Backhuysen)1632-1708
Netherlandish Seascape, Old Master $450,000

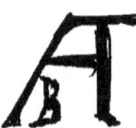

ANTONIO BADILE 1517-1560
Italian Painter, Genre $2,500

Baditz

OTTO VON BADITZ 1849-1908
Hungarian Genre, Portraits $1,000

Emile Baes

EMILE BAES 1879-1953
Belgian Painter $12,000

Walter A. Bailey

WALTER A. BAILEY 1894-
American Illustrator $1,500

Alice Bailly

ALICE BAILLY 1872-1938
Swiss Painter, Landscape $15,000

1. 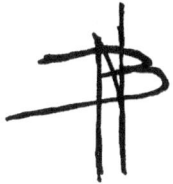 2.

DAVID BAILLY 1584-1657
Dutch, Genre, Still Life, Portraits $100,000

NATHANIEL HUGHES BAIRD 1865-1936
British Animals, Landscape $6,000

ENRICO BAJ 1922-
Italian Painter Sculptor $60,000

RALPH BAKSHI 1900's
American Genre, Portraits $1,000

1. BAKST 3. BAKST

2. BAKST

LEON BAKST 1866-1924
Russian Costume Stage Design $100,000

HANS GRIEN BALDUNG 1476-1545
German Portraits, Religious $150,000

1. **FB** 2. *U. V. Balen*

HENDRIK VAN (also Hendrick) BALEN (Elder) 1575-1632
Dutch Painter, Allegory $60,000

AB

ANTONIO BALESTRA 1666-1740
Italian Painter, Genre, Nudes $130,000

1. *FUTUR* 2. *BAYA FUTIBALA* 3. *BALLA FUTURISTA*

4. *BELYH FUTURISTA* 5. 6. *BALLA*

7. *RGFAM* 8. *BALLA* 9. *BALLA FUTURISTA* 10. *Balla*

~~~
FAENZA
DALDIS.BALLA

11. *Futurista Balla*

12. *BALLA* 13. *BALLA* 14. *BALLA FUTUR.AUSTIA*

15. *BALLA* 16. *BALLA* 17. *FUTUR BALLA*

GIACOMO BALLA 1871-1958
Italian Futurist $4,400,000

J. Ballavoine

JULES FREDERIC BALLAVOINE 1834-1901
French Nudes, Portraits, Allegory $50,000

MB

MOGENS BALLE 1921-1988
Scandinavian Painter $9,000

Ballesio

FEDERICO BALLESIO 1800's
Italian Painter $15,000

Niel Bally

NIEL BALLY 1900's
British Still Life $3,000

1. *Bs* 3. *Balthus* 2. *JB*

4. *Br.* 5. *Br.*

BALTUSZ KLOSSOWSKI DE ROLA BALTHUS 1908-
French Painter, Genre, Nudes $6,736,000

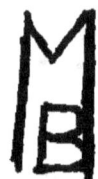

MIAIAHI BANDAC 1900's
Rumanian Painter

Bau Band.

BARTOLOMMEO BANDINELLI (also Baccio)1493-1560
Italian, Portraits, Genre, Religious $150,000

1. *By* 2. *B*

PIERRE CHARLES BAQUOY 1759-1829
French Painter, Engraver $1,000

N. Barabino

NICOLO BARABINO 1832-1891
Italian Painter, Landscape $20,000

F. Baratti

FILIPPO BARATTI 1900's
Italian Landscape $300,000

Barbari

JACOBO DE BARBARI 1440-1516
Italian Painter, Religious $10,000

Barbarigo

IDA BARBARIGO 1925-
Italian Abstract, Landscape $20,000

E. Barbarini

EMIL BARBARINI 1855-1930
Austrian Landscape $10,000

M. BARBASAN

MARIANO BARBASAN 1864-1924
Spanish Painter $100,000

**GEORGE
BARBIER**

GEORGE BARBIER 1881-1932
American Costume Stage Design $45,000

1. *B.f.*   2. *B*

(Il Guercino) G. F. BARBIERI 1591-1666
Italian Painter

Bargheer

EDUARD BARGHEER 1901-1979
German Landscape $20,000

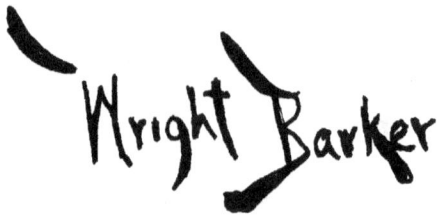

WRIGHT BARKER 1864-1941
British Landscape, Animals $30,000

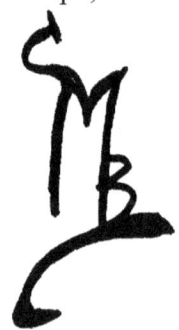

CICELY MARY BARKER 1895-1973
British Illustration $2,000

1. *E.B.*   2. *Barlach*

3. *El Barlach*

ERNST BARLACH 1870-1938
German Expressionist, Genre, Landscape $150,000

Barnabè

DUILIO BARNABE 1914-1961
Italian Abstract $15,000

L. Barrau

LAUREANO BARRAU 1864-1957
Spanish Genre $150,000

H. Barraud

HENRY BARRAUD 1811-1874
British Sporting $100,000

GV. Francois

GUSTAVE FRANCOIS BARRAUD 1883-1964
Swiss Painter, Landscape $3,000

Maurice Barraud

MAURICE BARRAUD 1884-1954
Swiss Landscape, Allegory $30,000

BARREDA

ERNESTO BARREDA 1927-
Chilean Painter, Landscape $10,000

P. Barth

PAUL BASILIUS BARTH 1881-1955
Swiss Landscape $20,000

Giov. Bartolena

GIOVANNI BARTOLENA 1866-1942
Italian Painter, Genre $25,000

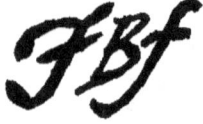

FRANCESCO BARTOLOZZI 1725-1815
Italian Portraits $2,500

LOREN BARTON 1893-1975
American Painter, Landscape, Illustration $1,000

ROSE MAYNARD BARTON 1856-1929
Irish Painter, Landscape, Genre $25,000

WILLIAM BARTRAM 1739-1823
British Painter $5,000

1.

2.

PIETRO BARUCCI 1845-1917
Italian Painter Landscape $30,000

BARYE

ANTOINE LOUIS BARYE 1796-1875
French Sclulptor, Animal $60,000

Marcuy Baxaiti

MARCO BASAITI (also Baxaiti) 1450-1520
Italian Painter, Religious $50,000

GB

GEORGE BASELITZ 1938-
German Painter, Abstract $1,100,000

JEAN MICHEL BASQVIAT

JEAN MICHEL BASQUIAT 1960-1988
American Compositions $5,509,500

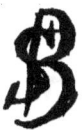

JACOPO BASSANO 1515-1592
Italian Genre $200,000

1. *B. Van Bassen*

2. *B Van Bassen*

BARTHOLOMEUS VAN BASSEN 1590-1652
Netherlandish Architecture Interiors, Landscape $70,000

1. *ABastien* 2. *A.BAstien.*

ALFRED THEODORE JOSEPH BASTIEN 1873-1955
Belgian Painter $20,000

HENRY MAYO BATEMAN 1887-1970
British Illustration Cartoonist $20,000

C. BOMPIANI BATTAGLIA
$1,200

ANDRE BAUCHANT 1873-1958
French Painter $45,000

FRANCOISE BAUDRU 1942-
French Genre, Abstract $1,500

GUSTAV BAUERN FEIND 1848-1904
Austrian Landscape, Arabs $60,000

MARCEL LOUIS BAUGNIET 1896-
Belgian Painter $7,000

PHILIPP BAUKNECHT 1884-1933
German Painter, Landscape $40,000

CHARLES BAUM 1812-1878
American Painter, Landscape $15,000

OTTO BAUMBERGER 1889-1961
Swiss Illustrator, Landscape $5,000

1. 2.

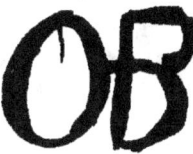

WILLI BAUMEISTER 1889-1955
German Painter, Landscape $300,000

1. 2.

WILLIAM A. BAZIOTES 1912-1963
American Painter, Abstract $300,000

LENARDO BAZZARO 1853-1937
Italian Landscape $25,000

GIFFORD BEAL 1879-1956
American N.A. Painter $75,000

REYNOLDS BEAL

REYNOLDS BEAL 1867-1951
American Seascapes, Genre, Landscape $30,000

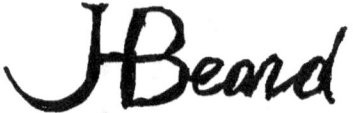

JAMES H. BEARD 1810-1893
American N.A. Landscape $10,000

W.H.Beard

WILLIAM HOLBROOK BEARD 1825-1900
American Landscape, Genre $75,000

AB

GEORGE BEARE 1700's
British Portraits $20,000

Begton

CECIL BEATON 1904-1980
British Costume Stage Design, Portraits $10,000

AB

ANDRE BEAUDIN 1895-1979
French Sculpture, Abstract, Nudes $60,000

Cecilia Beaux

CECILIA BEAUX 1855-1942
American Portrait, Genre, Castles $350,000

P.M.B.

PAULA MODERSON- BECKER 1876-1907
German Expressionist, Portraits $200,000

GEORGES BECKER

GEORGES BECKER 1845-
French Genre, Portraits $20,000

Beckman

1.   2. *cf*

MAX BECKMAN 1884-1950
German Portraits $22,560,000

FB Wenzell

ALBERT BECKWENZELL 1864-1917
American Genre, Illustrator $1,000

Carroll Beckwith

JAMES CARROLL BECKWITH 1852-1917
American Painter $55,000

GIOVANNI PAOLO BEDINI 1844-1924
Italian Portraits, Genre $15,000

1.

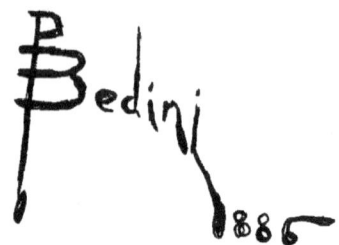

2.

JAN KAREL DONATUS VAN BEECQ 1638-1722
Netherlandish Ships Marines $35,000

CHRISTIAN BEEKMAN 1887-1964
Dutch Painter, Abstract $8,500

1.   2.

3.

MAX BEERBOHM 1872-1956
British Genre $7,000

J Beer Straten

JAN ABRAHAMSZ BEERSTRATEN 1622-1666
Netherlandish Marines, Landscape, Portraits $150,000

1.

B ciii straatin

2.

A. BEERSTRAET

ANTHONIE BEERSTRATEN Circa 1600's
Netherlandish Villages Landscapes Buildings $125,000

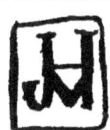

JACOBA VAN HEEMSKERCK VAN BEEST 1828-1894
Dutch Painter $7,500

C bEga

CORNELIS PIETERSZ BEGA 1620-1664
Dutch Old Master $45,000

CBF

KARL (also Carl, Joseph the Younger) BEGAS 1794-1854 German
Portraits, Landscape, Genre $20,000

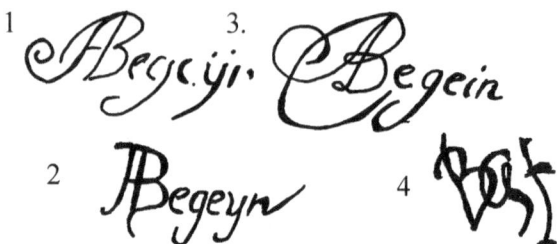

ABRAHAM JANSZ BEGEIJN (also Begeyn) 1621-1697
Netherlandish Landscape, Animals $200,000

1541

IsB

HANS SEBALD BEHAM 1500-1550
German Old Master $15,000

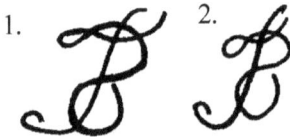

JOACHIM FRANZ BEICH 1665-1748
German, Religious, Genre, Landscape $8,500

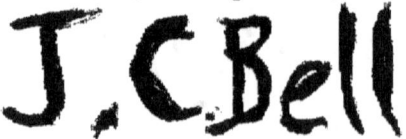

ABRAHAM HENDRICKSZ VAN BEIJEREN
(also Beyeren) 1621-1674 Netherlandish
Still Life, Seascape $125,000

J.C.Bell

J.C. BELL 1811-1895
British Painter, Animals, Landscape $80,000

S.D. Bella

STEFANO DELLA BELLA 1605-1664
Italian Landscape, Genre, Animals $15,000

1. *Bellange*   2. *Bellange*

JACQUES BELLANGE 1576-1638
French Engraver, Genre, Allegory $50,000

Bellei S.

GAETANO BELLEI 1857-1922
Italian Genre $50,000

Bellmer

HANS BELLMER 1902-1975
French Portraits, Nudes $10,000

B Belloto

BERNARDO BELLOTO 1720-1780
Italian Architectural Painter $1,500,000

1. *Geo. Bellows*   2. *GB*
2. *Geo Bellows*

GEORGE BELLOWS 1882-1925
American Painter, Genre, Portraits $27,500,000

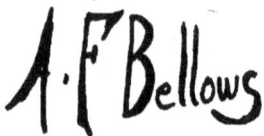

ALFRED FITCH BELLOWS 1829-1883
American Landscape, Still Life $45,000

1.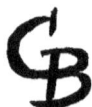

2.

ANTONIO BELLUCCI 1654-1726
Italian Painter, Allegory, Landscape $15,000

GABRIEL BELOT 1882-1962
French Landscape $2,500

LUDWIG BEMELMANS 1898-1962
American Illustrator, Genre $3,500

E.C. BENEZIT 1885-1975
French Landscape, Genre $1,500

BEN BENN 1884-1983
American Painter, Genre $2,000

GERRIT BENNER 1897-1981
Dutch Painter, Landscape $20,000

1.

2.   3.

ALEXANDRE BENOIS 1870-1960
Russian Costume Stage Design $15,000

1.

2.

NIKOLAI BENOIS 1900-
Russian Costume Stage Design $1,500

ALEXANDER VON BENSA 1820-1902
Austrian Landscape $15,000

FRANK WESTON BENSON 1862-1951
American N.A. Landscape $1,821,000

1.   2.

3.

THOMAS HART BENTON 1889-1975
American N.A. Painter $1,808,000

ETIENNE BEOTHY 1897-1961
Hungarian Portraits, Sculpture $15,000

1.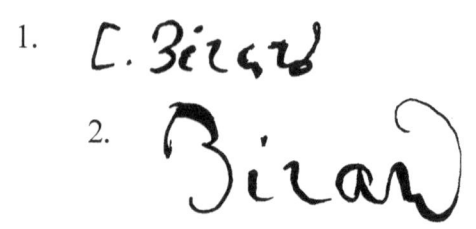

2.

CHRISTIAN BERARD 1902-1949
French Costume Stage Design $15,000

1. *Jean Beraud*,

2. *Jean Beraud*

JEAN BERAUD 1844-1935
French Paris Streets, Genre $2,000,000

1.   2.

3.   4.   NB

CLAES NICOLAES PIETERSZ BERCHEM 1620-1683
Netherlandish Horse, Landscapes, Seascape, Portraits $450,000

J Berck Heyde

JOB ANDRIAENSZ BERCK-HEYDE 1630-1693
Dutch Landscape, Genre $200,000

Gerrit · Berck · Heyde

GERRIT ADRIANSZ BERCKHEIJDE 1638-1698
Netherlandish Castles Landscape, Genre, Seascape $125,000

MBW

MARY BERESFORD-WILLIAMS 1931-
British Painter $1,000

H Berger

HANS BERGER 1882-1977
Swiss Landscape $7,500

1.

Louis Bergerot

2. *Louis Bergerot*

LOUIS BERGEROT 1925-
French Portraits $1,000

SVEN

SVEN BERLIN 1911-
British Painter, Sculptor $2,000

Lonid

LEONID BERMAN 1896-1976
Russian Painter $6,000

EUGENE BERMAN 1899-1972
American N.A.,Painter $10,000

1.

2.

3.

4.

EMILE BERNARD 1868-1941
French Impressionist $275,000

ETIENNE PROSPER BERNE-BELLECOUR 1838-1910
French Painter, Landscape, Genre $20,000

ANTONIO BERNI 1905-1981
Argentinian Painter $30,000

OSCAR E. BERNINGHAUS 1874-1952
American A.N.A. Illustrator $150,000

Louis Bérovd

LOUIS BEROUD 1852-1910
French Painter, Genre $190,000

A Berrugete

ALONSO (also Alonzo) BERRYGUETE
(also Berruguete) 1480-1561 Spanish Painter, Religious $75,000

Berserik

HERMAN BERSERIK 1921-
Dutch Painter $1500

Johann Berthelson

JOHANN BERTHELSON 1883-1969
American Paris Streets $5,000

JAMES BERTRAND

JAMES (also Jean Baptiste) BERTRAND 1825-1887
French Painter, History, Portraits $15,000

Ball Beschey

BALTHASAR BESCHEY 1708-1776
Dutch, Portraits

ALBERT BESNARD 1849-1934
French Painter, Genre, Portraits $20,000

HERMANN BETHKE 1825-1895
German Painter, Landscape $10,000

LOUIS BETTS 1873-1961
American Landscape, Portrait, Genre $20,000

1.

2.

JOSEPH BEUYS 1921-1986
German Abstract $100,000

BIKASH BHATTACHARJEE 1940-
India Modern, Genre $4,000

ANGELO DALL'OCA BIANCA 1858-1942
Italian Painter $25,000

FRANCOIS AUGUSTE BIARD 1799-1882
French Soldiers, Genre $170,000

GEORGE BIDDLE 1885-1973
American Illustrator, Landscape, Portrait $6,000

JOHANN JAKOB BIEDERMANN 1763-1830
Swiss Landscape, Genre $250,000

ERNEST BIELER 1863-1948
Swiss Landscape, Genre $150,000

1.

2.

ALBERT BIERSTADT 1830-1902
American N.A. Painter, Hudson River, Luminist $6,400,000

MARIE DE BIEVRE 1865-
Belgian Floral, Still Life $60,000

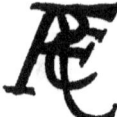

FRANCIA (also Francesco Di Cristofano) BIGIO 1482-1525
Italian Painter, Religious $85,000

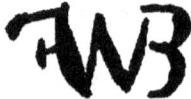

PIERRE BILLET 1837-1922
French Genre $50,000

FREDERICK WILLIAM BILLING 1835-1914
American Landscape $1,000

JACOBUS BILTIUS 1633-1681
Netherlandish Still Life $75,000

JULIEN BINFORD 1908-
American Painter $5,000

VICTOR JEAN BAPTISTE BINET 1849-1924
French, Animals, Landscape, Genre $15,000

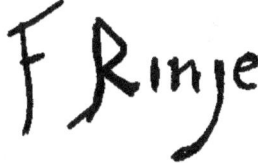

FRANZ (also Frans) BINJE 1835-1900
Belgian, Landscape $2,000

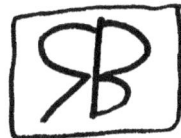

ROBERT BIRMELIN 1933-
American Modernist $1000

Franz A Bischoff

FRANZ A. BISCHOFF 1864-1929
American Plein Aire, California, Landscape $20,000

E.Biset

KAREL EMMANUEL (also Charles) BISET 1633-1680
Dutch Genre, Portraits $70,000

Label Bishop

ISABEL BISHOP 1902-1988
American Painter, Genre $10,000

Julius Bissier

JULIUS BISSIER 1893-1965
German Abstract, Landscape $50,000

HENRI BIVA 1848-1928
French Landscape $15,000

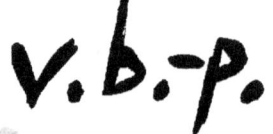

WILHELM BJERKE-PETERSEN 1909-1957
Danish Abstract $20,000

EUGEN DE BLAAS 1843-1932
Austrian Painter, Genre, Portrait $285,000

ELIZABETH BLACKADDER 1931-
British Watercolour, Genre $5,000

THOMAS BROMLEY BLACKLOCK 1863-1963
British Painter, Genre, Landscape $35,000

WILLIAM BLAKE 1757-1827
British Painter $3,928,000

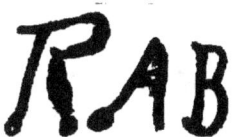

RALPH ALBERT BLAKELOCK 1848-1919
American N.A. Landscape $3,525,750

Blampied

EDMUND BLAMPIED 1886-1966
British Genre, Landscape, Seascape $15,000

Arnold Blanch

ARNOLD BLANCH 1896-1968
American Painter, Genre, Landscape $2,500

Antoine. Blanchard.

ANTOINE BLANCHARD 1910-1988
French Paris Streets $20,000

M.BLANCHARD   M B
1.   2.

MARIA BLANCHARD 1881-1932
Spanish Abstract, Portraits $400,000

J. E. Blanche

JACQUES EMILE BLANCHE 1861-1942
French Paris Scenes, Genre $75,000

E.H. BLASHFIELD

EDWIN HOWLAND BLASHFIELD 1848-1936
American Illustrator, Genre, Portraits $30,000

A. BLATAS

ARBIT BLATAS 1908-
French Painter, Genre, Landscape $5,500

Carle / Blenner

CARLE JOHN BLENNER 1864-1952
American Painter, Genre, Portraits $15,000

1. *D D. BLIECK D . D . B .* 2.

DANIEL DE BLIECK 1620-1673
Netherlandish Architecture Interiors, Landscape, Genre $25,000

1. 2. 3.

4. *Bloemaart*

5. *Bloemaert*

6. *A. Blommaert*

ABRAHAM BLOEMAERT 1564-1651
Dutch Old Master, Portraits, Landscape $350,000

1. **P.V.B** 2. (signature)

PIETER VAN BLOEMEN 1657-1720
Netherlandish Landscape, Old Master, Genre $70,000

A.BLOMME

ALPHONSE BLOMME 1889-1979
Belgian Painter, Lndscape $5,000

1. *Blommers,*

2. *Blommers*

BERNARDUS JOHANNES BLOMMERS 1845-1914
Dutch Painter, Genre $40,000

1. (monogram)

2. (signature)

LANCELOT BLONDEEL 1495-1561
Dutch Painter, Religious $10,000

E. Blondel

EMILE BLONDEL 1893-1970
French Paris Scenes $3,000

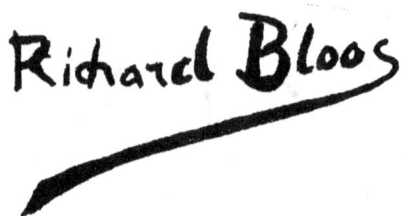

RICHARD BLOOS 1877-1956
German Landscape $15,000

1. 2. 3.

4.

OSCAR FLORIANUS BLUEMNER 1867-1938
American Painter, Landscape $350,000

LUDWIG BLUM 1891-1974
Israeli Painter, City Scenes, Landscape $10,000

1. 2.

ROBERT FREDERICK BLUM 1857-1903
American Samurai Oriental Geisha, Genre $200,000

Blythe

DAVID GILMOUR BLYTHE 1815-1865
American Painter, Genre $50,000

1. -U. Boccioni-

2. U. Boccioni

3. U.BOCCIONI

5. Boccioni

4. Boccioni

6. U. Boccioni

7. UB

8. UB

9. BOCCIONI

10. Boccioni

11. BOCCIONI

UMBERTO BOCCIONI 1882-1916
Italian Futurist $600,000

1. F. BOCION

2. FB

FRANCOIS BOCION 1828-1890
Swiss Landscape, Genre $90,000

HBH

JAN VAN (also Johann) BOCKHORST (also Bronckhorst)
1604-1668 Dutch Portraits, Religious $7,500

Joselin Bodley

JOSELIN BODLEY 1893-1974
British Landscape $3,500

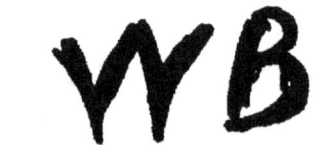

WALTER BODMER 1903-1983
Swiss Landscape, Genre $20,000

SANDOR BODO 1919-
American Portraits, Sculptor $1,000

HERBERT BOECKL 1894-1966
Austrian Painter, Genre, Landscape $150,000

BOELEMA

MAERTEN BOELEMA-1664
Netherlandish Still Life $65,000

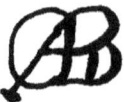

GUSTAV ADOLF (also Adolph) BOENISCH 1802-1887
German Landscape $1,500

THEODOR BOEYERMANS (also Boiermans, Boyermans)1620-1678
Dutch Portraits, Religious $15,000

J. Bogdani

JACOB BOGDANI 1660-1724 Hungarian Painter $50,000

А. Богданов

ALEXANDER BOGDANOV 1908-1989
Russian Genre $3,000

Богановбеі Балаckій

IVAN BOGDANOV-BIELSKI 1868-1945
Russian Painter $20,000

Bogen

CARLOS GONZALEZ BOGEN
Venezualan Painter $1,000

Boggio

EMILIO BOGGIO 1857-1920
Venezuelan Painter, Landscape, Portraits $45,000

1. *Boggs* 2. *Frank-Boggs*

FRANK MEYERS BOGGS 1855-1926
French Painter, Landscape, Seascape $35,000

HANS BOHLER 1884-1961
Austrian Painter, Genre $5,000

MAX BOHM 1868-1923
American N.A. Painter, Genre, Portraits $40,000

1.   2.

ADOLF BOHM 1861-1927
Austrian Secessionist, Abstract, Designer, Avant Garde $6,000

AARON BOHROD 1907-1992
American N.A.Painter, Landscape, Genre $7,000

1.   2.

LOUIS LEOPOLD BOILLY 1761-1845
French Landscape, Genre, Portraits $600,000

EDWARD DARLEY BOIT 1840-1916
American Landscape $5,000

1. **f8OL·F**   2. **NBoe**

HANS BOL 1534-1593
Netherlandish Castles, People, Landscape, Genre $60,000

1. *Bol*   3. *Bol*   5. *JB*
2. *F·Bol·Bol*   6. *f bol*
4.

FERDINAND BOL 1616-1680
Netherlandish Portraits $90,000

1. *Bve guin*   2. *Boldini*
3. *Boldini*

GIOVANNI BOLDINI 1844-1931
Italian Painter, Genre, Portraits $1,500,000

1. *David Bomberg*

2. *Bomberg*   3. *Bomberg*

DAVID BOMBERG 1891-1957
British Cubist $1,916,981

Bombois. C.ll

CAMILLE BOMBOIS 1883-1970
French Painter, Genre, landscape $100,000

M Bone

MUIRHEAD BONE 1876-1953
British Etcher, Landscape $3,000

1. **Rosa Bonheur**

RB **Rosa**
2.   3. **Bonheur**

ROSA BONHEUR 1822-1899
French Landscape $225,000

R. Bonin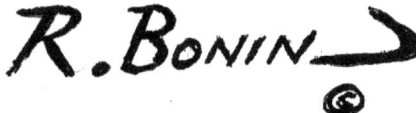

R. BONIN 1900's
American Painter, Genre, Landscape $1,000

1. **Bonnard**   **Bonnard**
2. **Bonnard**   5.
3. **Bonnard** **B** **Bonnard**
                    4.   6.

PIERRE BONNARD 1867-1947
French Post Impressionist $8,528,000

L. Bonnat.
1.   2.
              L. Bonnat

LEON BONNAT 1834-1922
French Painter, Genre, Portraits $45,000

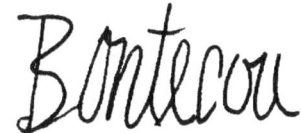

LEE BONTECOU 1931-
American Constructions $20,000

FRANCOIS BONVIN 1817-1887
French Genre, Impressionist, Landscape $50,000

ARNOLD VAN BOONEN 1669-1729
Dutch Genre, Portraits $12,000

RAYMOND BOOTH 1929-
British Painter, Animals $15,000

S. LAWSON BOOTH-1928
British Painter, Landscape $17,000

STAN BORACK 1900's
French Illustrator, Genre, Portraits $5,000

1. **O . PARIS**

2. *(signature monogram)*

PARIS BORDONE (also Bordon) 1500-1570
Italian Portraits, Religious $250,000

Edward Borein
1. *Edward . Borein* 2.

EDWARD BOREIN 1873-1953
American Cowboys $50,000

Bores

FRANCISCO BORES 1898-1972
Spanish Abstract $100,000

Carl Oscar Borg

CARL OSCAR BORG 1879-1947
American A.N.A. Cowboys $40,000

M. Borgeaud.

MARIUS BORGEAUD 1861-1924
Swiss Paris Streets, Genre $10,000

Jacobo Borges

JACOBO BORGES 1930-
Venezualan Landscape, Genre $30,000

Boras

NICHOLAS FRAY BORRAS 1530-1610
Spanish Painter $1,000

v: B.

ANTHONIE VAN BORSSOM 1630-1677
Netherlandish Landscape $40,000

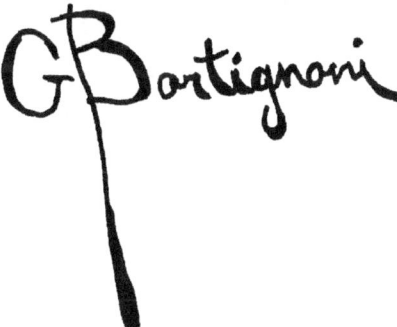

GIUSEPPE BORTIGNONI 1778-1860
Italian Genre $10,000

Bortnyik

ALEXANDER SANDOR BORTNYIK 1893-1977
Hungarian Abstract, Genre, Portraits $15,000

LOUIS BOSA 1905-1981
American Painter $2,000

ATUL BOSE 1898-
India Portraits $5,000

FREDERICK BOSLEY

FREDERICK ANDREW BOSLEY 1881-1941
American Painter, Portraits $30,000

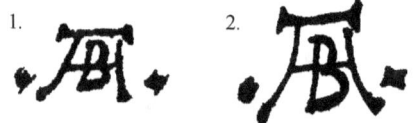

1.   2.

AMBROSIUS BOSSCHAERT 1569-1645
Netherlandish Still Life $2,400,000

BALTHASAR VAN DEN BOSSCHE (also Bos) 1681-1715
Dutch Genre, Portraits, Religious $25,000

RODOLPHE THEOPHILE BOSSHARD 1889-1960
French Landscape, Genre $55,000

CARLO BOSSOLI 1815-1884
Italian Painter, Landscape $30,000

JOSEPH H. BOSTON 1901-1955
American Landscape, Genre, Portrait $40,000

ANGEL BOTERO 1913-1986
Spanish Painter, Genre, Portrait $15,000

FERNANDO BOTERO 1932-
Latin Amer. Painter Sculptor $2,032,000

1.   2.   3.   4.

JAN DIRKSZ BOTH 1618-1652
Netherlandish Landscapes, Old Master, Portraits $120,000

HERBERT BOTTGER 1898-1954
German Painter, Landscape, Genre $10,000

I TALO BOTTI

ITALO BOTTI 1889-1974
Italian Painter, Genre, Landscape $9,000

Botticelli

ALESSANDRO (also Sandro) BOTTICELLI 1446-1510
Italian Painter, Genre, Portraits $16,000,000

Louis Bouche

LOUIS BOUCHE 1896-1969
American Painter, Genre, Landscape $3,000

f. Boucher

FRANCOIS BOUCHER 1703-1770
French Genre, Allegory $2,166,000

P. Boudet   P. Boudet

1.   2.

PIERRE BOUDET 1925-
French Paris Painter $7,000

E. Boudin G. Boudin

1.   2.

EUGENE BOUDIN 1824-1898
French Impressionist $1,600,000

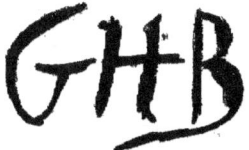

GEORGE HENRY BOUGHTON 1833-1905
American Watercolour, Landscape, Genre $30,000

W - BOVCVEREAV-

WILLIAM ADOLPHE BOUGUEREAU 1825-1905
French Painter, Portraits, Genre $3,526,500

q Rodo Boulanger

GRACIELA RODO BOULANGER 1936-
Latin American Painter, Portraits, Genre $20,000

G. BOVLANGER

GUSTAVE (also Clarence Rodolphe) BOULANGER 1824-1888
French Painter, Portraits, Nudes $35,000

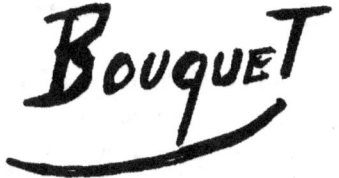

ANDRE BOUQUET 1897-
French Painter, Landscape $1,000

1. *Bourdon* [signature]

2. *Bourdon* [signature]

HENRI JACQUES (also Henry) BOURCE 1826-1899
Dutch Genre, Portraits, Landscape $2,000

Bourgeois [signature]

PETER FRANCIS BOURGEOIS 1756-1811
Swiss Painter, Landscape, Genre $1,500

Bourgonnier [signature]

CLAUDE CHARLES BOURGONNIER-1921
French Painter, Portrait $5,000

Bouvard [signature]

AUGUSTE BOUVARD 1800's
French Painter, Seascape $5,000

RUTHERFORD BOYD [signature]

RUTHERFORD BOYD 1882-1951
American Illustrator, Genre $20,000

ROBERT BRACKMAN 1898-1980
American N.A. Realist $6,000

1.

2.

WILLIAM BRADFORD 1830-1892
American A.N.A. Landscape $75,000

BASIL BRADLEY 1842-1904
British Watercolour, Genre, Landscape $4,500

FERDINANDUS DE (also Ferdinand) BRAEKELEER 1792-1883
German Genre $25,000

ANTON BRAITH 1836-1905
German Painter, Landscape $35,000

Braiton-Sala

ALBERT BRAITON-SALA 1885-1972
French Allegory, Portraits $30,000

B Bramantino

BARTOLOMEO SUARDI BRAMANTINO 1450-1530
Italian Painter, Religious, Portraits $40,000

2.

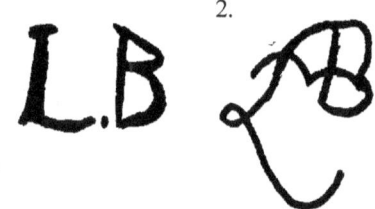

1.

LEONARD BRAMER 1596-1674
Dutch, Painter

Le Bramer

LEONARD (also Leonaert) BRAMER 1590-1667
Dutch Allegory, Genre $30,000

C. Brancaccio

CARLO BRANCACCIO 1861-1920
Italian Painter, Portrait, Landscape $100,000

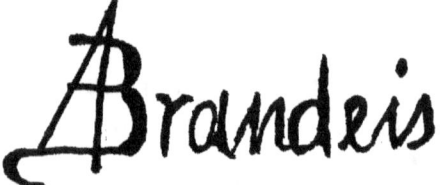

ANTONIETTA BRANDEIS 1849-1920
Austrian Landscape, City Scenes, Genre $15,000

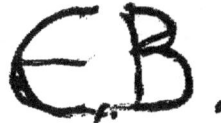

EUGENE BRANDS 1913-
Dutch Abstract, Landscape $40,000

JOSEF VON BRANDT 1841-1928
German Painter $20,000

SIR FRANK BRANGWYN 1867-1956
British R.A. Painter, Genre, Landscape $100,000

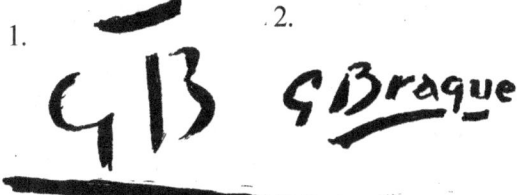

GEORGES BRAQUE 1882-1963
French Cubist $8,640,000

ANDRI BRASILIER 1929-
French Landscape, Portraits $220,000

BRAUER

ERICH BRAUER 1928-
Austrian Painter, Portrait, Paris $9,000

Maurice Braun

MAURICE BRAUN 1877-1941
American California Plein Aire $20,000

VICTOR BRAUNER

VICTOR BRAUNER 1903-1966
Rumanian Cubist $350,000

yves BRAYER

YVES BRAYER 1907-1990
French Painter, Landscape, Genre $30,000

JOHN LESLIE BRECK

JOHN LESLIE BRECK 1861-1899
American Landscape, Genre $125,000

JF Bredael

JAN FRANS BREDAEL (also Breda) 1683-1750
Dutch Landscape, Genre $90,000

1. *Breenberch*

2. *B*   3. *B*   5. *B*

4. *B*

BARTHOLOMEUS BREENBERGH 1599-1659
Netherlandish Genre, Old Master, Landscape, Mythology $125,000

RAYMOND BREININ 1910-
American Painter, WPA Artist $1,000

GEORGE HENDRIK BREITNER 1857-1923
Dutch Painter, Genre, Landscape $60,000

QUIRINGH (also Quiryn) GERRITZ BREKELENKAM
1620-1668 Netherlandish Genre, Old Master, Portraits $125,000

CO BREMEN 1865-1938
Dutch Painter, Landscape $20,000

JOHANN GEORG MEYER VON BREMEN 1813-1886
German Painter, Genre, Portraits $80,000

HANS ANDERS BRENDEKILDE 1857-1942
Danish Landscape, Genre $100,000

Isabelle Brent

ISABELLE BRENT 1961-
British Animals $1,000

1. *Jules Breton*

2. *Jules Breton Courrières*

JULES ADOLPHE AIME LOUIS BRETON 1827-1905
French Genre, Landscape $1,250,000

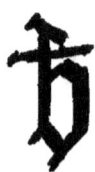

JORG I (elder) BREU 1475-1536
German Landscape, Religious, Genre $700,000

Franz De Breul

FRANZ DE BREUL 1800's
Belgian Painter, Landscape, Sheep $1,000

ARB

ANNA RICHARDS BREWSTER 1870-1952
American Illustrator, Landscape $2,000

1. *Brianchon*

2. *Brianchon* 3. *Brianchon*

MAURICE BRIANCHON 1899-1979
French Painter, Portrait, Genre $90,000

A.T.BRICHER.

3. *AB*

2. *ABRICHER*

1.

ALFRED THOMPSON BRICHER 1837-1908
American A.N.A. Seascape $100,000

1. *F.A Bridgman*

2. *F.A·Bridgman*

3. *F.A Bridgman*

FREDERICK ARTHUR BRIDGMAN 1848-1928
American N.A. Painter, Landscape, Genre $100,000

1. *[oo]*   2. **PAVOLO**

P BRIL   **BRILLI**

PAUWEL (also Paul, Paulo, Paulus) BRIL (also Brill) 1554-1626
Flemish Painter, Allegory, Genre, Landscape $125,000

Georges Brillouin

GEORGES BRILLOUIN 1817-1893
French Landscape, Genre $6,000

Brion

GUSTAVE BRION 1824-1877
German Genre, Portraits $60,000

F. D. Briscoe

FRANKLIN DULLIN BRISCOE 1844-1903
American Painter, Seascape, Landscape $6,000

Brodwolf

JURGEN BRODWOLF 1932-
Swiss Painter $10,000

W. Bromley

WILLIAM BROMLEY 1769-1842
British Painter, Genre $10,000

BRONZO FIORENTINO

AGNOLO (also Angelo) BRONZINO 1502-1572
Italian Painter, Religious $65,000

1. *alexander Brook*

2. *A. Brook*

ALEXANDER BROOK 1898-1980
American N.A. Painter, Landscape, Genre $5,000

J·Brooks

JAMES BROOKS 1906-1992
American Painter, WPA, Genre $30,000

N.A.BROOKS

NICHOLAS ALDEN BROOKS 1880-1904
American Painter, Genre, Seascape $20,000

1. *Brouwer* 2. *AB*

3. *A.Brauwer*

ADRIAEN BROUWER 1605-1638
Flemish Old Master, Portraits, Genre $40,000

CARLYLE BROWN

CARLYLE BROWN 1919-1964
American Painter $1,500

F.C.Brown.

FRED C. BROWN 1851-1941
British Painter, Farms $7,500

J.G. Brown N.A.

JOHN GEORGE BROWN 1831-1913
American N.A.Painter, Portraits, Genre $300,000

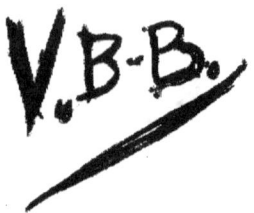

VINCENT R. BALFOUR BROWN 1901-
Australian Painter, Landscape, Genre $1,500

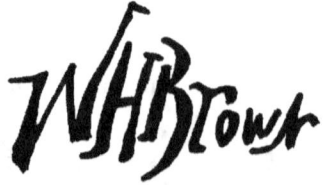

WILLIAM MARSHALL BROWN 1863-1935
British Painter, Genre, Seascape $25,000

WILLIAM MASON BROWN 1820-1890
American Painter, Landscape $40,000

BENJAMIN C. BROWN 1865-1942
American Landscape $25,000

W.H. BROWN 1800's
American Painter, Portraits $35,000

ROY H. BROWN 1879-1957
American A.N.A. Illustrator, Landscape $6,000

Byron Browne

BYRON BROWNE 1907-1961
American Abstract $20,000

Bruce

PATRICK HENRY BRUCE 1880-1937
American Cubist $1,215,750

BRVEGEL

PIETER (the elder) BRUEGHEL 1512-1569
Flemish Old Master, Religious, Genre $4,647,600

1. P·BRVEGHEL

2. BRVEGHEL·

PIETER (the younger) (also Peeter) BRUEGHEL 1564-1637
Netherlandish Religious, Genre, Old Master $3,000,000

1. *HBruncken*

2. HB

HENDRIK TER BRUGGEN 1588-1629
Dutch Old Master $100,000

Brugger

ARNOLD BRUGGER 1888-1975
British Landscape, Genre $7,000

HB

HANS BRUHLMANN 1878-1911
Swiss Still Life $30,000

1.

2.

FRANCOIS BRUNERY 1849-1926
Italian Genre, Portraits $60,000

MBrunswig

MARCELLE BRUNSWIG 1903-
French Portraits, landscape $1,000

GEORGE DE FOREST BRUSH 1855-1941
American Painter, Portrait $1,707,500

ALFRED BRYAN 1851-1899
British Painter, Horses $1,000

EVERETT LLOYD BRYANT 1864-1945
American Landscape, Genre $10,000

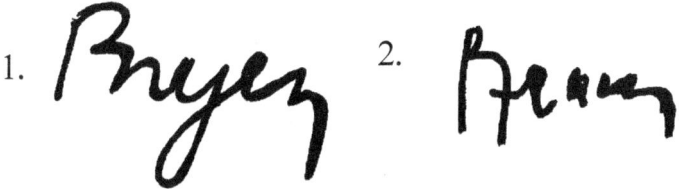

1. 2.

CAMILLE BRYEN 1907-1977
French Abstract $100,000

G. Buchet

GUSTAVE BUCHET 1888-1963
Swiss Cubist $40,000

Frank Buchser

FRANK BUCHSER 1828-1890
American Landscape, Genre $50,000

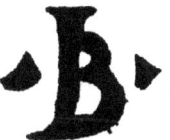

JOACHIM BUECKELEER 1535-1574
Netherlandish Religious, Genre $70,000

Conrad Buff

CONRAD BUFF 1886-1975
American Illustrator, Landscape $10,000

1. 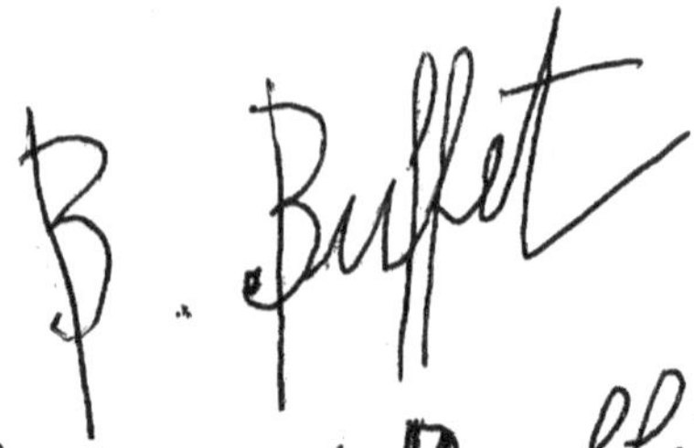 *B. Buffet*

2. 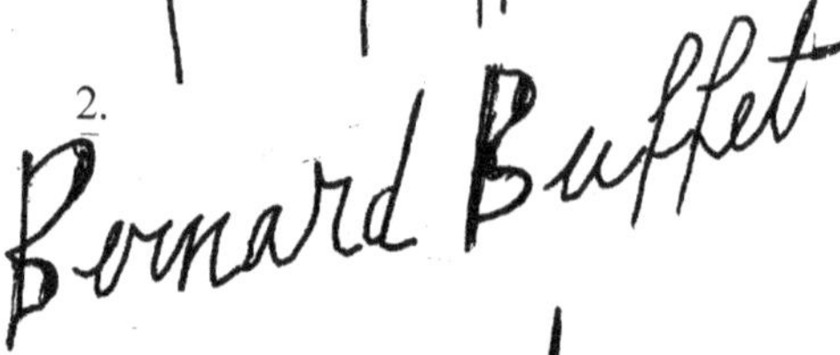 *Bernard Buffet*

3. 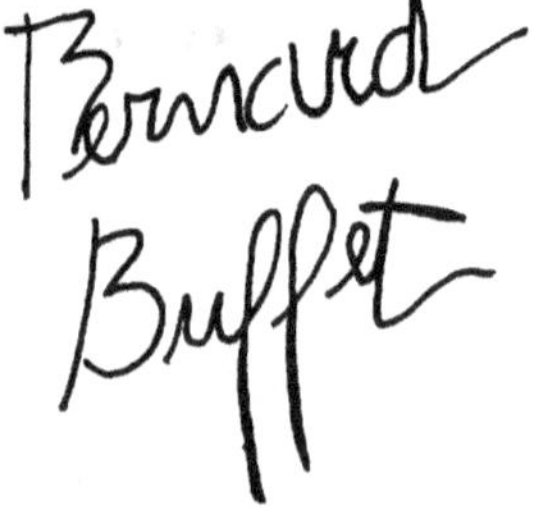 *Bernard Buffet*

BERNARD BUFFET 1928-
French Abstract $750,000

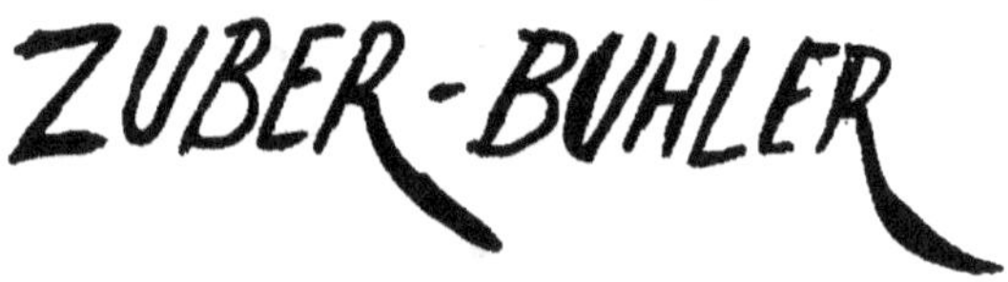

ZUBER-BUHLER

FRITZ ZUBER- BUHLER 1822-1896
German Painter, Genre, Portrait $4,000

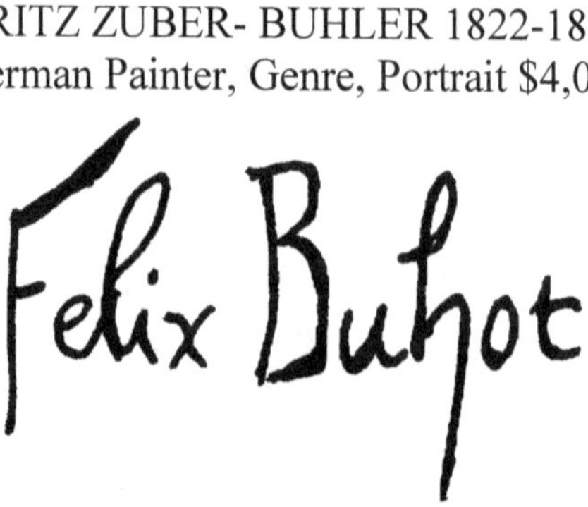

Felix Buhot

FELIX BUHOT 1846-1898
French Paris Streets, Genre, Landscape $10,000

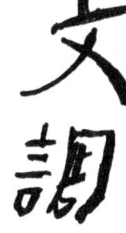

IPPITSUSAI BUNCHO 1725-1794
Japanese Woodblocks $20,000

RUPERT CHARLES WULSTEN BUNNY 1864-1947
Australian Landscape, Allegory $200,000

ELBRIDGE AYER BURBANK 1858-1949
American Cowboys, Indians, Portraits $5,000

1.

2.

CHARLES BURCHFIELD 1893-1967
American N.A. Watercolour, Landscape $90,000

HANS BURCKMAIR 1473-1531
German Portraits

COPELAND C. BURG 1895-
American Still Life $1,000

1.

2.

HBURKEL.

HEINRICH BURKEL 1802-1869
German Landscape, Genre $55,000

1.

2.

PAUL BURLIN 1886-1969
American Painter, Landscape $2,000

1. 2.

BURLIUK BURLIUK

DAVID BURLIUK 1882-1967
Russian Futurist $55,000

BA. BYPЛIUK

VLADIMIR DAVIDOVITCH BURLIUK 1886-1917
Russian Painter, Landscape $50,000

Fritz Bürmann

FRITZ BURMANN 1892-1945
German Painter, Portrait, Landscape $5,000

Burns

MILTON J. BURNS 1853-1933
American Painter, Genre $5,000

J.Burr

JOHN P. BURR 1831-1892
British Painter, Genre $15,000

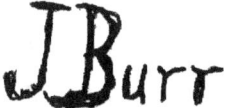

ALBERTO BURRI 1915-
Italian Abstract $2,666,000

W.B.

WILHELM BUSCH 1832-1908
German Painter, Genre, Landscape $10,000

1.
N.Bush   2. **NBush**

NORTON BUSH 1834-1894
American Painter, Landscape $30,000

Gaston Bussière

GASTON BUSSIERE 1862-1929
French Genre, Allegory $20,000

M.BUSSON

MARCEL BUSSON 1913-
French Painter, City Views $4,500

ULysse . Butin

ULYSSE LOUIS AUGUSTE BUTIN 1838-1883
French Genre, Animals $4,000

T. E. Butler

THEODORE EARL BUTLER 1876-1937
American Painter, Landscape, Genre $50,000

Büttner

HANS BUTTNER 1850-
German Painter, Genre, Landscape $15,000

WMB

WILLEM PIETERZ BUYTEWECH 1590-1630
Dutch Old Master $90,000

Byzantios

CONSTANTIN BYZANTIOS 1924-
Rumanian Painter, Landscape $15,000

Artists starting with the letter "C"

Alex Cabanel

ALEXANDER CABANEL 1823-1889
French Genre, Portraits, Arabs $400,000

M. Cabre

MANUEL CABRE 1890-
Venezualan Painter, Genre $20,000

F.C.B. Cadell

FRANCIS CAMPBELL BOILEAU CADELL 1883-1937
British Painter, Portrait, Landscape $200,000

Paul Cadmus

PAUL CADMUS 1904-
American Painter $100,000

Cadoret

MICHEL CADORET 1912-1985
French Painter, Genre $8,000

WALTER WALLOR CAFFYN 1845-1898
British Landscape, Genre $5,000

CARLO (also Carletto) CAGLIARI 1570-1596
Italian Painter $1,000

GUIDO CANLASSI CAGNACCI 1601-1681
Italian Painter, Religious, Allegory $200,000

MARCELLE CAHN 1895-1981
French Painter, Portrait $15,000

GUSTAVE CAILLEBOTTE 1848-1894
French Painter, Portrait, Landscape $14,300,000

ALEXANDRE CALAME 1810-1864
Swiss Landscape $30,000

LETTERIO CALAPAI 1902-
American Painter, Lithographer $1,000

1.

2.

3.

4.

ALEXANDER MILNE CALDER 1898-1977
American Mobiles $4,185,750

MARCO CALDERINI 1850-1941
Italian Painter, Landscape, Genre $70,000

FRANCOIS CLAUDIUS COMPTE (also Comte) CALIX
1813-1880 French Genre, Portraits $25,000

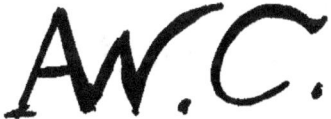

AUGUSTUS WALL CALLCOTT 1779-1844
British Portraits, Landscapes $50,000

Callot

JACQUES CALLOT 1592-1635
French Engravings, Genre, Landscape $300,000

ABRAHAM CALRAET 1642-1722
Netherlandish Genre, Landscape, Old Master, Still Life $30,000

Calzada

HUMBERTO CALZADA 1944-
Cuban Painter, Genre $5,000

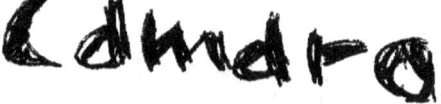

HERMENE GILD ANGLADA CAMARASA 1873-1959
French, Painter, Paris Scenes $3,701,000

Camara

ALEXANDER CAMARO 1901-
German Painter, Genre, Portraits $20,000

L Cambiasi

LUCA CAMBIASO 1527-1585
Italian Painter, Religious, Portraits $20,000

SIR DAVID YOUNG CAMERON 1865-1945
British Watercolour, Genre, Landscapes $15,000

HUGH CAMERON 1835-1918
British Painter, Genre, Landscape $20,000

KATHERINE CAMERON 1874-1965
British Painter, Landscape, Genre $5,000

GIANFREDO CAMESI 1940-
Swiss Genre $1,000

CHARLES CAMOIN 1879-1965
French Painter, Genre, Landscape $100,000

HEINRICH CAMPENDONK 1889-1957
German Blau Reiter $300,000

P. Camphuijsen.

GOVERT CAMPHUIJSEN 1624-1672
Netherlandish Genre, Landscape $40,000

AN . CAM .

ANTONIO CAMPI 1523-1591
Italian Painter, Religious, Portraits $7,500

Campo

FEDERICO DEL CAMPO 1800's
Peruvian Painter Venice Scenes $200,000

F. Molina Campos

FLORENCIO MOLINA CAMPOS 1900's
Latin American Portraits, Genre $8,000

1.
RAC

2.
RAC.

de la Canal

3.

RAMON ALVA DE LA CANAL
Painter

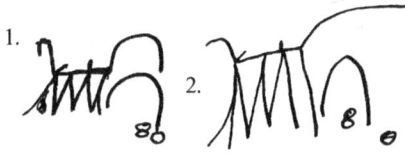

BENJAMIN CANAS 1933-
Latin American Painter $7,500

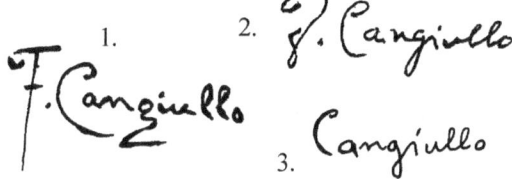

FRANCESCO CANGIULLO 1884-1977
Italian Genre $25,000

YVONNE CANU 1920-
French Landscape, Portraits $10,000

NOEMIE CAPAMAGIAN
$3,000

JOZEF (also Joseph) CAPEK 1887-1945
Czechoslavakian Landscape, Cubism, Avant Garde $10,000

JAN VAN DER CAPELLE (also Cappelle) 1624-1679 Dutch
Seascape $6,242,000

Capogrossi

GIUSEPPE CAPOGROSSI 1900-1972
Italian Abstract $125,000

Capoletti

JOSE MANUEL CAPULETTI 1925-
Spanish Allegory $5,000

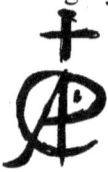

POLIDORODA CARAVAGGIO 1490-1543
Italian Painter, Religious $2,500

Cardona

JOAN CARDONA 1877-1958
Spanish Painter, Portraits $20,000

**VINCENT
CARDVCH**

VINCENZO (also Vincente) CARDUCHO (also Carducci) 1578-1638
Spanish Painter, Genre, Religious $20,000

G.CARELLI

CONSALVE CARELLI 1818-1906
Italian Landscape, Genre $20,000

A.C

ALOIS CARIGIET 1902-1985
Swiss Watercolour, Genre, Landscape $25,000

CARLES

ARTHUR B. CARLES 1882-1952
American Abstract $50,000

ACarletti

ALICIA CARLETTI 1946-
Argentinian Painter, Genre $2,000

Carlin

JOHN CARLIN 1813-1891
American Landscape, Genre $3,000

J.B Carloni

GIAMBATTISTA CARLONI 1594-1680
Italian Painter $2,000

1. **Emil Carlsen**
2. **S. Emil. Carlsen**

SOREN EMIL CARLSEN 1853-1932
American Plein Aire, Genre, Landscape $45,000

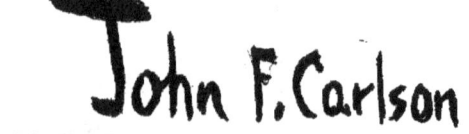

JOHN FABIAN CARLSON 1875-1945
American Watercolour, Landscape $40,000

JEAN CAROLUS-1872
Belgian Painter $10,000

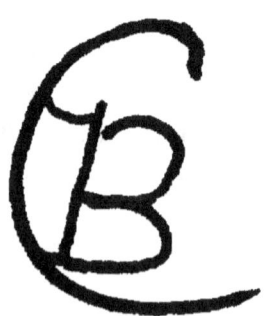

CHARLES EMILE AUGUSTE CAROLUS-DURAN 1838-1917
French Painter, Nudes, Portraits $350,000

JEAN BAPTISTE CARPEAUX 1826-1875
French Painter, Landscapes $35,000

SAMUEL S. CARR 1837-1908
American Painter, Landscape, Genre $75,000

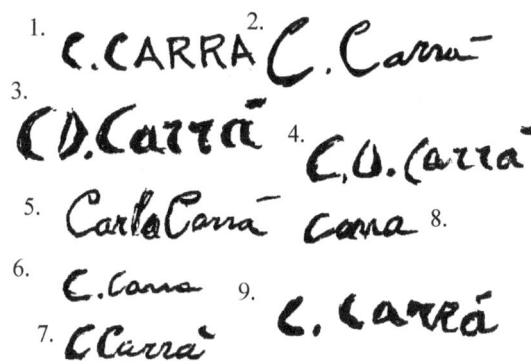

CARLO DELMAZZO CARRA 1881-1966
Italian Futurist, Landscapes, Compositions $350,000

AGOSTINO CARRACCI 1557-1602
Italian Painter, Religious, Allegory $125,000

ANNIBALE CARRACCI 1560-1609
Italian Painter, Religious, Allegory $5,227,500

LUDOVICO (also Lodovico) CARRACCI 1555-1619
Italian Painter, Religious, Genre $13,703,000

MARIO CARRENO 1913-
Cuban Illustrator, Seascape, Genre $275,000

103

J.M.Carrick

JOHN MULCASTER CARRICK-1878
British Landscape, Genre $45,000

Louis Carrier-Belleuse

LOUIS ROBERT CARRIER-BELLEUSE 1848-1913
French Allegory, Genre $30,000

ROSALBA CARRIERA 1675-1757
Italian Painter, Landscape, Allegory $30,000

Eugène Carrière

EUGENE CARRIERE 1849-1906
French Painter, Genre $30,000

1.

2. *Leonora Carrington*

LEONORA CARRINGTON 1917-
British Painter, Genre, Landscape $300,000

JOHN CARROLL 1892-1959
American Illustrator $2,500

WILLIAM JAMES CARROLL 1900's
British Portraits, Genre $7,500

A. DUNCAN CARSE-1938
British Watercolour, Landscape, Genre $5,000

ENRICO CARUSO 1873-1921
Italian Stage Costume Design $2,000

JEAN CARZOU 1907-
French Landscape $20,000

FRANCESCO CASANOVA 1727-1805
Italian Allegory, Landscape, Battle $17,000

VICTOR CASNELLI 1867-1961
American Cowboys, Genre, Landscape $2,500

FELICE CASORATI 1883-1963
Italian Portraits, Landscape $450,000

1.   2.

MARY CASSATT 1855-1926
American Impressionist $4,072,000

GERALD I. CASSIDY 1879-1934
American Cowboys, Genre, Landscape $20,000

JEAN PIERRE CASSIGNEUL 1935-
French Painter, Genre, Portraits $150,000

ALFRED JOSEPH CASSON 1898-1992
Canadian Painter, Landscape, Portraits $35,000

SIR HUGH CASSON 1909-
British Watercolour, Genre, Portraits $1,000

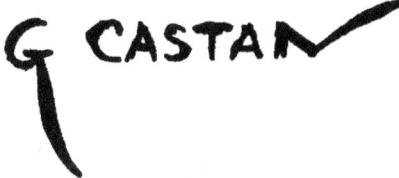

GABRIELE CASTAGNOLA 1828-1883
Italian Painter, Genre, Portraits $8,500

GUSTAVE CASTAN 1832-1892
Swiss Genre, Landscape $17,000

1.   2.

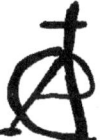

BERNARDO CASTELLO (Castelli) 1557-1629
Italian Painter, Religious $15,000

CLAUDIO CASTELUCHO 1870-1927
Spanish Painter, Genre, Portraits $7,000

GIOVANNI BENEDETTO CASTIGLIONE 1616-1670
Italian Painter, Religious, Landscape $90,000

VINCENZO CATENA 1465-1531
Italian Painter, Religious $200,000

1.

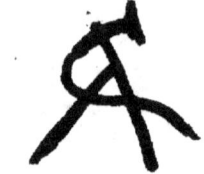

2.

EUGENE-HENRI CAUCHOIS 1850-1911
French Landscape $30,000

PETER CAULITZ 1650-1719
German Landscape, Animals $1,000

ROLF CAVAEL 1897-1980
German Abstract $20,000

EMILIANO DI CAVALCANTI 1897-1967
Latin American Painter, Genre, Landscape $150,000

VITTORIO CAVALLERI 1860-1938
Italian Painter, Landscape $5,000

GIACOMO CAVEDONE 1577-1660
Italian Painter, Religious, Portraits $30,000

EUGENIO CAXES 1577-1642
Spanish Religious $10,000

F.A. CAZALS 1865-1941
Italian Genre $1,000

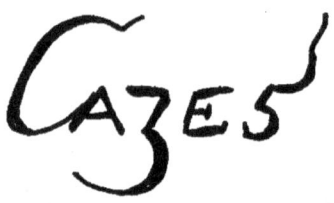

PIERRE JACQUES CAZES 1676-1754
French Painter, Religious, Genre $15,000

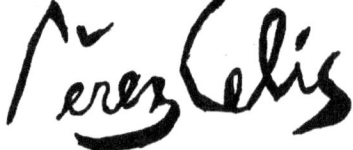 DI PIETRO CECCO
1370-1402
Italian Religious, Genre $40,000

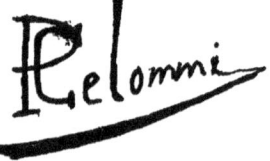

PEREZ CELIS 1939-
Argentinian Painter, Landscape $10,000

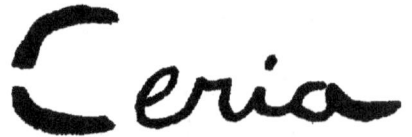

PASQUALE CELOMMI 1860-1928
Italian Painter, Landscape, Genre $10,000

M Cerezo

MATEO CEREZO (also Zerezo) 1635-1675
Spanish Painter, Religious $10,000

Ceria

EDMOND CERIA 1884-1955
French Landscape $12,000

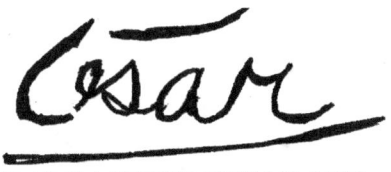

BALDACCINI CESAR 1921-
French Sculptor $60,000

GIUSEPPE CESARI 1568-1640
Italian Painter, Religious, Portraits $50,000

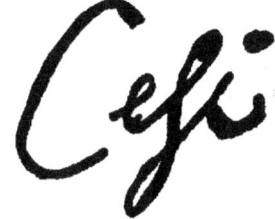

BARTOLOMEO CESI 1583-1649
Italian Old Master $25,000

PABLO DE CESPEDES 1538-1608
Spanish Painter, Sculpter $1,000

1. 2.

PAUL CEZANNE 1839-1906
French, Landscape, Nudes, Impressionist, Watercolors $60,500,000

Chadwick

LYNN CHADWICK 1914-
British Painter, Portraits $1,860,000

W. CHADWICK

WILLIAM CHADWICK 1879-1962
American Lyme Painter, Landscapes $20,000

Marc Chagall

MARC CHAGALL 1887-1985
Russian Painter, Genre, Portraits $13,500,000

CHAISSAC
Chaissac

GASTON CHAISSAC 1910-1964
French Abstract Collage $70,000

J.D. Chalfant

JEFFERSON DAVID CHALFANT 1856-1931
American Painter, Genre $25,000

BORIS CHALIAPIN 1904-1979
Russian Illustrator, Portraits $1,500

JEAN-LAURENT CHALLIE 1880-1945
French Landscape $10,000

ALFRED EDWARD CHALON 1780-1860
British, Genre, Portraits, Landscape $10,000

GEORGE CHAMBERS 1803-1840
British, Genre, Landscape, Seascape $15,000

1. PHI. CHAMPAIGNE

2. Phil de Champaigne

PHILIPPE DE CHAMPAIGNE (also Champagne) 1602-1674 Flemish
Portraits, Religious $150,000

JAMES WELLS CHAMPNEY 1843-1903
American Illustrator, Genre, Portraits $40,000

Chapelain Midy

ROGER CHAPELAIN-MIDY 1904-1992
French Seascapes, Landscape $9,000

James Chapin

JAMES CHAPIN 1887-1975
American Painter, Portraits, Genre $4500

BRYANT CHAPIN

BRYANT CHAPIN 1859-1927
American Landscape $10,000

1. *Ch Chaplim* 2. *Chaplin*

CHARLES CHAPLIN 1829-1891
French Landscape, Genre $45,000

Charchoune

SERGE CHARCHOUNE 1888-1975
Russian Painter, Portraits, Landscape $100,000

J·chardin

JEAN BAPTISTE SIMEON CHARDIN 1699-1779
French Painter, Genre, Portraits $2,400,000

JEAN CHARLOT 1898-1979
Mexican Illustrator, Genre, Portraits $20,000

1.

2.

3.

WILLIAM MERRITT CHASE 1849-1916
American Painter, Portraits, Landscape $10,000,000

THEODORE CHASSERIAU 1819-1856
French Painter, Genre, Portraits $1,029,000

SHIAVAX CHAVDA 1914-
India Painter $4,500

GEORGE CHENARD HUCHE 1864-1937
French Landscape, Seascapes $9,000

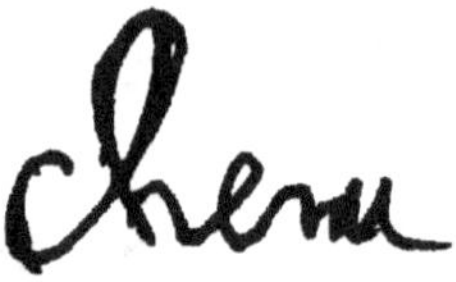

DIDIER CHENU 1956-
French Genre, Painter, Portraits $2,000

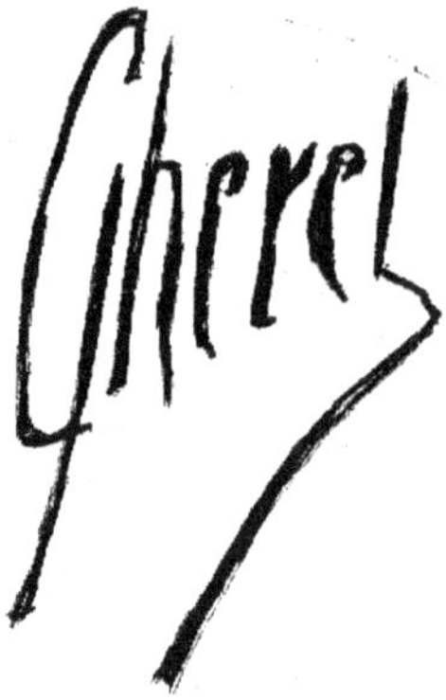

JULES CHERET 1836-1932
French Illustrator, Genre, Seascapes $25,000

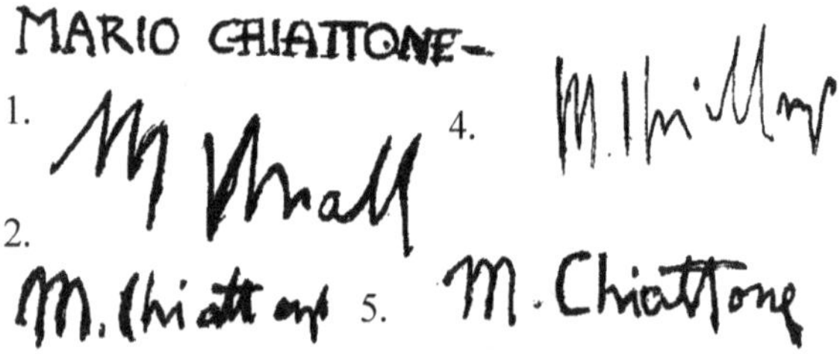

MARIO CHIATTONE-

1.

4.

2.

3.

5.

MARIO CHIATTONE
Painter

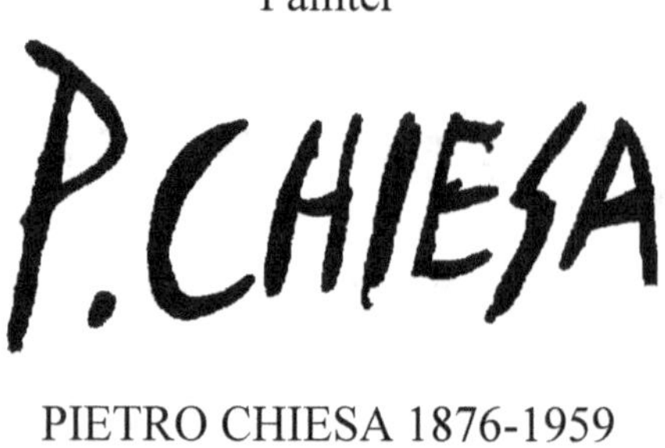

PIETRO CHIESA 1876-1959
Swiss Landscape, Genre $9,000

IVAN F. CHOULTSE 1876-1932
American Painter, Landscapes $10,000

JAMES ELDER CHRISTIE 1847-1914
British Painter, Portraits, Genre $10,000

JAVACHEFF CHRISTO 1935-
Bulgarian Assemblage $125,000

HOWARD CHANDLER CHRISTY 1873-1952
American Illustrator, Genre $90,000

1.

2.

LEON CHWISTEK
Painter

CESARE CIANI 1854-1925
Italian Engraver, Landscapes, Portraits $15,000

RAFAEL CIDONCHA 1952-
Spain Genre, Painter $3,000

1.

2.   3.

CARLO CIGNANI 1628-1719
Italian Painter, Religious, Allegory $35,000

NICOLAI CIKOVSKY 1894-1934
Russian Painter, Genre, Landscape $30,000

PIETER CLAESZ 1596-1660
Dutch Old Master $1,000,000

1.

2.

GEORGES CLAIRIN 1843-1919
French Painter, Genre, Landscape $50,000

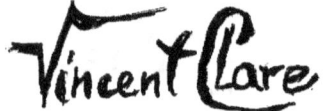

VINCENT CLARE 1855-1930
British Painter, Landscape, Still Life $7,500

1. *Alson Clark*

3. *Alson Clark*

ALSON SKINNER CLARK 1876-1949
American Landscape, Genre $10,000

Gahm Clarke

GRAHAM CLARKE 1941-
British Watercolour $2,500

E. Clarkson

EDWARD CLARKSON 1855-1860
American Painter, Genre $1,000

R CLAROT

RENE CLAROT 1882-1972
Belgian Painter, Landscape $7,500

J. Clausell

JOAQUIN CLAUSELL 1886-1935
Mexican Landscape $75,000

G. CLAUSEN

SIR GEORGE CLAUSEN 1852-1944
British Painter, Landscape, Genre $1,200,000

1.

2.

ANTONIO CLAVE 1913-
Spanish Stage Costume Design $150,000

JAMES HUGHES CLAYTON 1900's
British Genre, Landscape $3,500

ROBERT CLEMINSON -1868
British Painter, Genre, Landscape $5,000

JAMES GOODWYN CLONNEY 1812-1867
American Genre $100,000

WILLIAM BAXTER PALMERCLOSSON 1848-1926
American Engraver, Genre, Landscape $5,000

JOHN FORD CLYMER 1907-1989
American Illustrator, Landscape, Genre $75,000

1.

3.

2.

JEAN COCTEAU 1889-1963
French Illustrator, Allegory, Portraits $150,000

1.

2.

PIETER J. (also Kodde) CODDE 1599-1678
Netherlandish Genre, Portraits $125,000

JAN COELENBIER 1600-1677
Netherlandish Landscapes $10,000

CLAUDIO COELLO 1635-1693
Spanish Painter, Religious $4,000

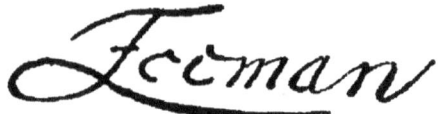

JACOB COEMAN Circa 1600's
Netherlandish Genre $10,000

1.   2.   3.

JOSEPH COGELS 1786-1831
German Landscape, Seascape $6,000

R. COGGHE

REMY COGGHE 1854-1935
Belgian Painter, Portraits, Genre $5,000

Elanor Colburn

ELANOR COLBURN 1866-1939
American Indians $3,000

T. Cole

THOMAS COLE 1801-1848
American Luminist, Hudson River, Landscapes $1,000,000

J. Foxcroft Cole

JOSEPH FOXCROFT COLE 1837-1892
American Landscape $3,000

JAMES COLE 1800's
British Painter, Genre, Landscape $10,000

CHARLES CARYL COLEMAN 1840-1928
American Watercolour, Genre, Landscape $80,000

1.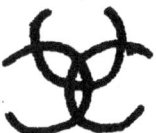

2.

SAMUEL COLEMAN 1832-1920
American N.A., Landscape, Hudson River, Genre $30,000

PAUL COLIN 1892-1985
French Painter, Landscape, Genre $15,000

1.

2.

FRANCISCO COLLANTES 1599-1656
Spanish Religious, Genre, Landscape, Still Life $10,000

John Collier

JOHN COLLIER 1850-1934
British Genre, Landscape $25,000

A Colunga

ALEJANDRO COLUNGA 1948-
Mexican Painter, Sculptor, Genre $25,000

Combas

ROBERT COMBAS 1957-
French Contemporary, Genre $80,000

1. *Léon Comerre*

2. *Leon Comerre*

LEON FRANCOIS COMERRE (also Commere) 1850-1916
French Allegory, Genre $30,000

J. T. Kompe

JAN TEN COMPE 1713-1761
Netherlandish Estates Landscapes $10,000

P. C . COMTE

PIERRE CHARLES COMTE 1823-1895
French Painter, Genre,Portraits $25,000

Conca

SEBASTIANO CONCA 1679-1764
Italian Painter, Religious, Genre $50,000

George Condo

GEORGE CONDO 1957-
American Painter, Genre, Portraits $80,000

MARVIN CONE

MARVIN D. CONE 1891-1964
American Painter, Landscape, Genre $25,000

Congnet

GILLIS (also Vlet) CONGNET 1575-1599
Flemish Portraits, Mythology $30,000

F.O. Conrad

F.O. CONRAD 1800's
German Painter, Genre $1,000

CONSTANT A. NIEUVENHUYS CONSTANT 1920-
Dutch Painter, Genre, Portraits $100,000

BENJAMIN CONSTANT 1845-1902
French Painter, Portraits, Allegory $30,000

GIOVANNI CONTARINI 1549-1605
Italian Portraits, Religious $6,500

TITO CONTI 1842-1924
Italian Genre, Portraits $40,000

HOWARD COOK 1901-1980
American Abstract, Landscape, Genre $20,000

BERYL COOK 1926-
British Children, Genre, Portraits $10,000

ASTLEY D. M. COOPER 1856-1924
American Illustrator, Genre, Landscape $5,000

ALFRED EGERTON COOPER 1883-1974
British Painter, Horses, Genre, Portraits $8,000

1. 2.

ABRAHAM COOPER 1787-1868
British Military, Animals. Landscape $150,000

ALEXANDER COOSEMANS 1627-1689
Netherlandish Still Life, Old Master, Landscapes $50,000

GEORGE COPE 1855-1929
American Landscape, Still Life $200,000

WILLIAM COPLEY 1920-
American Painter, Genre $10,000

Horbellini

LUIGI CORBELLINI 1900-1968
Italian Landscapes, Portraits $10,000

Jon Corbino

JON CORBINO 1905-1964
American Painter, Genre, Landscape $5,000

Aster Corbould

ASTER R.C. CORBOULD-1920
British Painter, Genre, Landscape $6,500

L-C

CHARLES LE CORBUSIER 1887-1965
French Abstract, Genre $250,000

LOVIS CORINTH

LOVIS CORINTH 1858-1925
German Expressionist, Landscape, Genre $250,000

F. Cormon

FERNAND (also Ferdinand) CORMAN (also Cormon) 1845-1924
French Portraits, Religious, Landscape $25,000

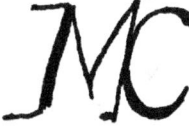

MICHEL CORNEILLE (the elder) 1601-1664
French Old Master, Landscape $6,500

M Corneille

MICHEL CORNEILLE (the younger) 1642-1708
French Painter, Religious, Mythology $30,000

G.F.

GOUDA VAN CORNELIS 1500's
Dutch, Painter

1. **CH** 2. **CH.**

CORNELIS VAN HAARLEM CORNELISZ 1562-1638
Netherlandish Genre Portraits, Allegorical, Old Master $60000

1. *Mrph Cornall*

2. *Joseph Cornell*

JOSEPH CORNELL 1903-1972
American Shadow Boxes $400,000

PAUL CORNOYER

PAUL CORNOYER 1864-1923
American A.N.A. Painter $80,000

129

P. CORNU

PIERRE CORNU 1895-
French Landscape, Portraits $6,000

RAFAEL CORONEL

RAFAEL CORONEL 1932-
Mexican Painter, Genre $150,000

COROT

JEAN BAPTISTE CAMILLE COROT 1796-1875
French Romanticist, Genre, Landscape $3,000,000

Corpora

ANTONIO CORPORA 1910-
Italian Abstract, Landscape $20,000

1. *Corregio* 2. *Re♡gio*

3. *ANTONIVS DE ALLEGRIS*

ANTONIO ALLEGRI CORREGGIO 1494-1534
Italian Painter, Religious, Mythology $350,000

1.　2.

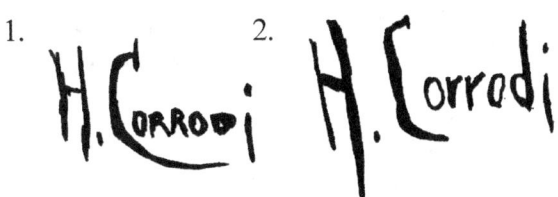

HERMANN DAVID SALOMON CORRODI 1844-1905
Italian Landscape, Genre $25,000

EDOVARD CORTÉS

EDOUARD CORTES 1884-1969
French Paris Streets, Genre $45,000

2.

1.

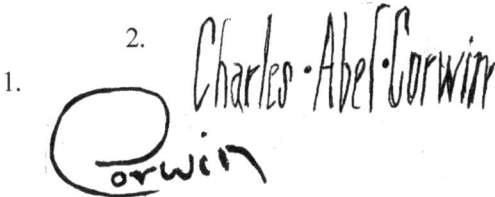

CHARLES ABEL CORWIN 1857-1938
American Cowboys & Indians $15,000

Cossiers

JAN COSSIERS (also Causiers, Cotsiers) 1600-1671
Flemish Portraits, Genre $60,000

2.

1. Cosson COSSON

MARCEL COSSON 1878-1956
French Painter, Genre, Portraits $20,000

Costa

ORESTE COSTA 1851-1900
Italian Allegory, Genre $10,000

LAVRENTIVS COSTA

LARENZO I COSTA (the elder) 1460-1535
Italian Painter, Religious, Genre $150,000

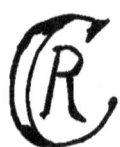

1. *John E. Costigan*

2. **V.E. COSTIGAN**

JOHN E. COSTIGAN 1888-1972
American N.A., Painter, Landscape, Genre $15,000

RICHARD COSWAY 1740-1821
British Miniature Painter, Genre, Landscape $25,000

P+A+COT

PIERRE AUGUST COT 1837-1883
French Portrait, Genre, Portraits $90,000

J.S.Cotman

JOHN SELL COTMAN 1782-1842
British Landscape, Genre, Seascape $30,000

Alan Cotton

ALAN COTTON 1900's
British Painter $2,500

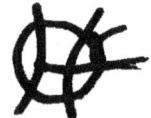

HORATIO HENRY COULDREY 1832-1893
British Animals, Genre $10,000

1. *G Courbet*

2. *G. Courbet*

GUSTAVE COURBET 1819-1877
French Impressionist $8,460,000

1. *L.-Courtat*   *L.Courtat* 2.

LOUIS COURTAT-1909
French Allegory, Genre $8,500

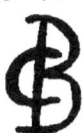

JACQUES COURTOIS 1621-1676
French Battle Painter $65,000

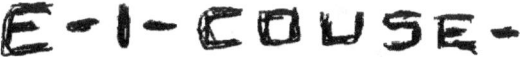

GUSTAVE COURTOIS 1852-1924
French Portraits, Genre $30,000

E-I-COUSE-

EANGER IRVING COUSE 1866-1936
American N.A. Cowboys & Indians $150,000

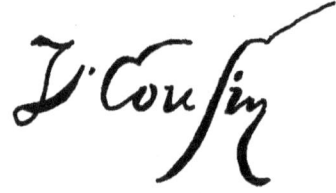

JEAN COUSIN 1500-1589
French Miniature Painter $1,000

COVARRUBIAS

MIGUEL COVARRUBIAS 1904-1957
American Illustrator, Portraits $20,000

R.M.G. COVENTRY

ROBERT MCGOWEN COVENTRY 1855-1914
British Watercolour, Genre $3,000

RUSSELL COWLES 1887-1979
American Painter, Landscape, Genre $2,500

KENYON COX

KENYON COX 1856-1919
American Illustrator, Genre, Portraits $5,000

DAVID (the younger) COX 1809-1885
British Landscape $10,000

DAVID (the elder) COX 1783-1859
British Landscape, Genre $30,000

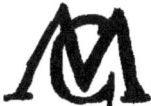

MICHIEL VAN (also Fiamingo) COXCUEN
(also Coxie) 1499-1592 Flemish Painter, Allegory $30,000

1. *A CoYPE*   3. *Coypel*

2. *A.C.*

CHARLES ANTOINE COYPEL 1694-1752
French Portraits, Genre, Allegory $100,000

Noypel

NOEL COYPEL (the Elder) 1628-1707
French Painter, Religious $500,000

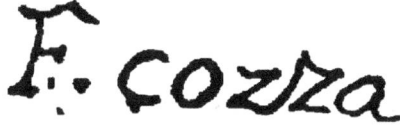

FRANCESCO COZZA 1605-1682
Italian Landscape, Religious, Genre $70,000

JOOST VAN (also Joos) CRAESBECKE (also Craesbeeck)
1606-1662 French Genre, $30,000

1.   2.

CASPAR DE (also Gaspard) CRAEYER (also Krayer) 1584-1669
Flemish Painter $2,000

1.

2.

EDWARD GORDON CRAIG 1872-1966
British Costume Stage Design $1,000

THOMAS BIGELOW CRAIG 1849-1924
American N.A. Landscape $5,000

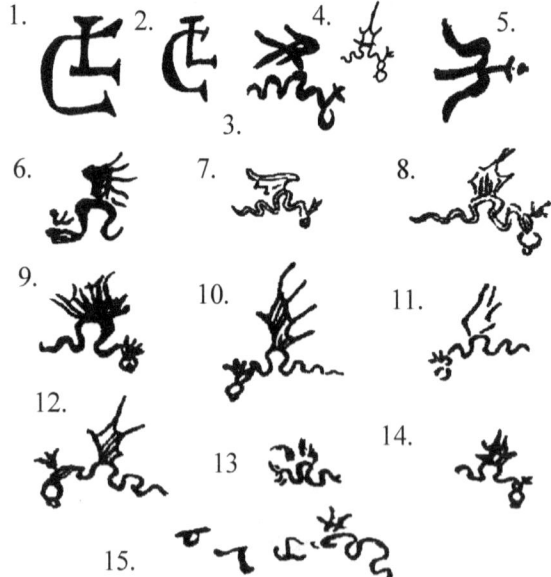

1. 2. 4. 5.

3.

6. 7. 8.

9. 10. 11.

12. 14.

13.

15.

LUCAS (the elder) CRANACH 1472-1553
German Religious, Portraits, Allegory $7,920,000

1. 2.

R. BRUCE CRANE 1857-1937
American N.A. Landscape $40,000

RALSTON CRAWFORD 1906-1977
American Illustrator, landscape, Still Life $100,000

LORENZO DI (also Barducci) CREDI 1459-1537
Italian Painter, Portraits, Religious $1,000,000

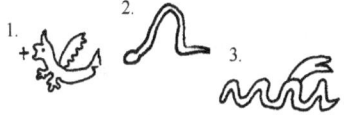

GIOVANNI BATTISTA CRESPI 1557-1633
Italian Painter, Religious, Genre $100,000

DANIELE CRESPI 1590-1630
Italian Painter, Allegory, Religious $20,000

FRANCIS CRISS 1901-1973
American Painter, Genre $15,000

GEORGES CROEGAERT 1848-1923
French Genre, Portraits $75,000

WILLIAM CROSBIE 1915-
British Watercolour, Genre, Landscape $20,000

HENRY EDMOND CROSS 1856-1910
French Impressionist $700,000

JEAN CROTTI 1878-1958
French Abstract $100,000

EDWARD CUCUEL 1879-1951
American Illustrator, Genre, Landscape $25,000

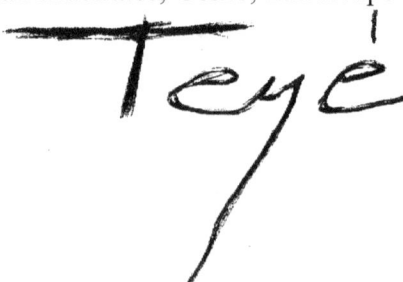

TERESA CUELLAR (TEYE) 1934-
Latin American Painter, Still Life, Landscape $10,000

2.

1.

DIRCK VAN CUERENHERT 1522-1590
Dutch

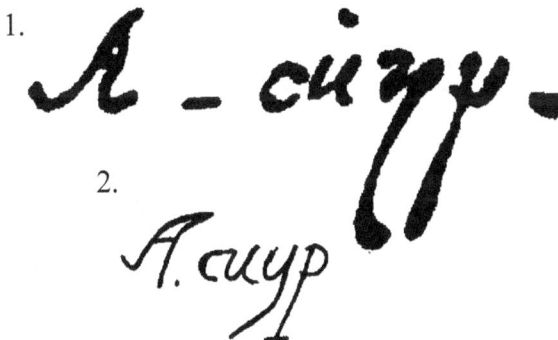

JOSE LUIS CUEVAS 1934-
Mexican Illustrator, Genre $9,000

FRANS VAN CUIJCK 1640-1689
Netherlandish Still Life $10,000

AELBERT CUIJP 1620-1691
Netherlandish Sheep, Genre, Landscape, Old Master $250,000

FRED CUMING 1930-
British Landscape, Seascape $6,000

JOSE CUNEO 1887-1977
Latin American Landscape, Genre $40,000

TRINH CUNG 1939-
British Painter $5,000

CHARLES COURTNEY CURRAN 1861-1942
American Landscape, Genre $100,000

1.

2.

3.

JOHN STEUART CURRY 1897-1946
American Painter, Landscape $80,000

LOUIS CURTI 1900's
French Genre $1,000

J. Cusenier

JEANIE CUSENIER 1900's
French Genre $1,000

M. Cusi

MANUEL CUSI Y FERRET 1857-1922
Italian Painter, Genre $15,000

Aeny len borch

ABRAHAM VAN CUYLENBORCH(also Kuylenburg,
Cuylenberg) Dutch Landscape, Animals $7,500

J.G. cuyp

JACOB GERRITSZ (also Jakob) CUYP 1575-1649
Dutch Animals, Landscape $300,000

Jaroslav Čermak

JAROSLAV CZERMAK 1831-1878
Polish Genre $1,000

Tytus Czyzewski

TYTUS CZYZEWSKI 1880-1945
Polish Landscapes, Portraits $7,000

Artists starting with the letter "D"

CARAN D'ACHE 1858-1909
Russian Cartoonist $2,500

CHARLES BERTRAND D'ENTRAYGUES 1850-
French Painter, Genre $75,000

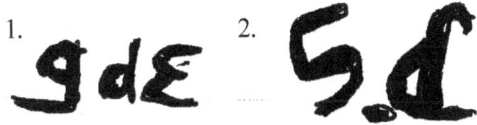

GEORGES D'ESPAGNAT 1870-1950
French Painter, Landscape $150,000

GIJSBERT d'HONDECOETER 1604-1653
Netherlandish Animals, Landscapes $25,000

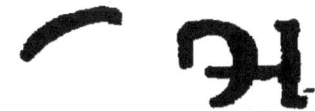

MELCHIOR d'HONDECOETER 1636-1695
Netherlandish Animals, Landscapes $200,000

1.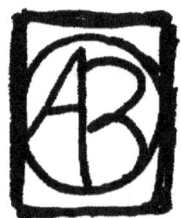

LEONARDO DA VINCI 1452-1519
Italian Genre, Portraits, Religious $31,800,000

LEON DABO 1868-1960
American Painter, Portraits, Landscapes $45,000

HELEN DAHM 1878-1978
Swiss Painter, Genre, Portraits $5,000

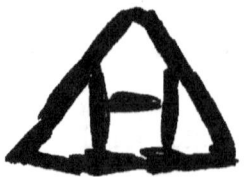

EDOARDO DALBONO 1841-1915
Italian Painter, Landscape, Genre $50,000

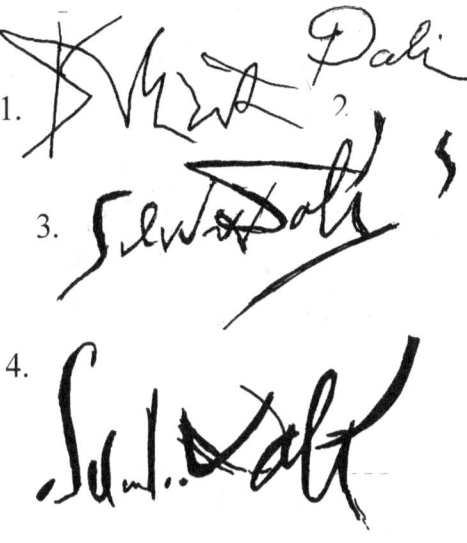

1.
2.
3.
4.

SALVADOR DALI 1904-1989
Spanish Surrealist $4,126,680

LEON DALLEMAGNE 1800's
French Painter, City Views, Towns $1,000

EUGENIA DANERI 1881-1970
Argentina Genre, Landscape $8,000

HENRI PIERRE DANLOUX 1753-1809
French Portraits, Genre $200,000

W·T·DANNAT

WILLIAM TURNER DANNAT 1853-1929
American Painter, Portraits, Genre $7,500

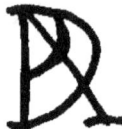

PIERRE DARDANI 1677-1735
Italian, Painter, Genre $1,500

G, DAREL

GEORGE DAREL 1892-1942
Swiss Landscape, Genre $5,000

1.　　　　2.

EDUARD DARGE 1805-1883
German Painter

Darpelus

ANDRE HENRI DARGELAS 1828-1906
French Painter, Genre $15,000

Sunil Das

SUNIL DAS 1939-
India Genre $4,500

Dasburg

ANDREW MICHAEL DASBURG 1887-1979
Landscape, Cubist, Still Life $120,000

Georgi Dathan

JOHANN GEORG DATHAN 1703-1748
German Portraits $10,000

Daubigny

CHARLES FRANCOIS DAUBIGNY 1817-1878
French Etcher, Landscape, Animals $80,000

JAMES DAUGHERTY

JAMES HENRY DAUGHERTY 1886-1974
American Indians, Genre $20,000

1. *Daumier*

2. *h.D.* 3. *h.D*

HONORE DAUMIER 1810-1879
French Cartoonist, Genre, Portraits $2,248,800

Davain-lesage

PIERRE DAVAIN-LESAGE 1800's
French Beach Scenes $1,000

RANDALL DAVEY 1887-1964
American Modernist, Genre $30,000

1. 2.

5. 6.

3. 4.

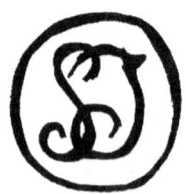

JACQUES LOUIS DAVID 1748-1825
French Modernist, Genre, Allegory $6,250,000

GERARD DAVID 1460-1523
Dutch Old Master $1,000,000

STANLEY S. DAVID 1847-1898
American Genre, Still Life $15,000

ARTHUR B. DAVIES 1862-1928
American Cubist, Landscape $30,000

JA Davila

JOSE ANTONIO DAVILA 1935-
Venezualan Painter, Landscape, Genre $20,000

Gladys Rockmore Davis

GLADYS ROCKMORE DAVIS 1901-1967
American Painter, Genre, Landscape $5,000

1. *Stuart Davis*

2. *Stuart Davis*

STUART DAVIS 1894-1964
American Abstract $2,422,500

Wm. M. DAVIS

WILLIAM M. DAVIS 1829-1920
American Landscape $50,000

C. H. Davis

CHARLES HAROLD DAVIS 1856-1933
American N.A. Landscape $20,000

1. *J·A·D*

2. *J.A.Davis*

JANE ANTHONY DAVIS 1821-1854
American Primitive, Portraits $10,000

M.Dewson

MANIERRE DAWSON 1887-1969
American Villages $12,000

E Dayes

EDWARD DAYES 1763-1804
British Landscape, Genre $12,000

de Belay

PIERRE DE BELAY 1890-1947
French Portraits, Seascapes $40,000

Henri De Braekeleer

HENRI DE BRAEKELEER 1840-1888
Belgian Painter, Genre $50,000

A·F·de·Bréanski

ALFRED FONTVILLE DE BREANSKI-1893
British Landscape $15,000

Alfred de Bréanski

ALFRED DE BREANSKI SNR. 1852-1928
British Landscape $55,000

P. Puvis de Chavannes

PIERRE PUVIS DE CHAVANNES 1824-1898
French Genre, Portraits $350,000

1. G. de Chirico

2. Gede chi

GIORGIO DE CHIRICO 1888-1978
Italian Painter, Allegory, Portraits $4,000,000

de Diego

JULIO DE DIEGO 1900-1966
American Landscape $1,000

JEAN DE DINA 1870-1955
European Genre, Seascape $6,000

ADELAIDE MILTON DE GROOT 1891-
Dutch Painter, Landscape, Seascape $1,000

CORNELIS DE HEEM 1631-1695
Dutch Still Life $500,000

WILLEM DE KOONING 1904-1997
American Abstract, Compositions $63,500,000

NARCISSE VIRGILE DIAZ DE LA PENA 1807-1876
French Barbizon, Landscape, Genre $100,000

FERNAND DE LAUNAY 1800's
French Portraits, Genre, Landscape $10,000

KAREL DE MOOR also Carel (see Moor) 1656-1738
Dutch Genre, Religious $60,000

1.

2.

3.

FREDERIK DE MOUCHERON 1633-1686
Dutch Landscape, Genre $35,000

ISAAK DE MOUCHERON 1670-1744
Dutch Landscape, Genre $30,000

CLOTILDE B. DE NIGRIS 1900's
American, Painter, $1,000

PIETER FRANCOIS (also Pierre Frans) DE NOTER 1779-1842
Dutch Landscape, Seascape, Animals $35,000

A. de Pereda

ANTONIO DE PAREDA 1599-1669
Spanish Painter

LEON DE SMET

LEON DE SMET 1881-1966
Belgian Landscape, Still Life $80,000

Nicolas

NICOLAS DE STAEL 1914-1955
Russian Contemporary $1,500,000

1.

Vlaminck

2.

Vlaminck

MAURICE DE VLAMINCK 1876-1958
French Landscape, Still Life, Portraits $6,500,000

E. DEBAT-PONSAN

EDOUARD BERNARD DEBAT-PONSON 1847-1913
French Painter, Landscape, Genre $25,000

Decaisne

HENRI DECAISNE 1799-1852
Belgian Portraits, Genre, Religious $2,500

J. Decker

JOSEPH DECKER 1853-1924
American Painter, Genre, Still Life $650,000

1. *C.D.* 2. *Decker*

CORNELIS GERRITSZ DECKER 1600-1678
Netherlandish Landscape, Genre, Portrait $50,000

A. Defaux

ALEXANDRE DEFAUX 1826-1900
French Animals, Landscape, Genre $8,000

1. *Defregger*

2. *F. Defregger*

FRANZ VON DEFREGGER 1835-1921
German Painter, Genre $100,000

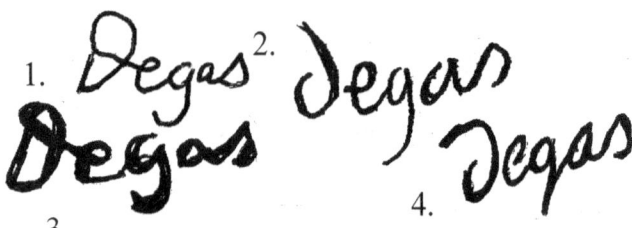

1. 2. 3. 4.

EDGAR DEGAS 1834-1917
French Impressionist $28,000,000

JEAN DEGOTTEX 1918-1988
French Abstract $20,000

ADOLF DEHN 1895-1968
American N.A. Illustrator $7,500

GIOVANNI DEL RE 1829-1915
Italian Painter, Genre, Portraits $7,500

LEON DELACHAUX 1850-1919
French Painter, Genre, Landscapes $6,500

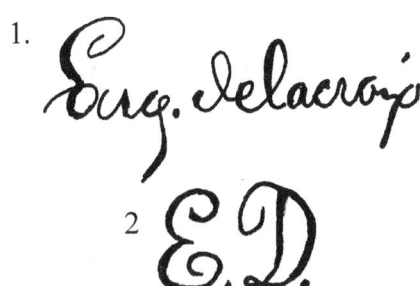

EUGENE DELACROIX 1798-1863
French Painter, Allegory $1,000,000

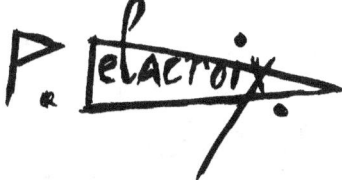

PAULINE DELACROIX GARNIER 1863-1912
French Painter $7,500

Delapierre

ROGER DELAPIERRE 1935-
Swiss Painter, Landscape $3,500

ROBERT DELAUNAY 1885-1941
French Orphism $5,170,000

SONIA DELAUNAY 1885-1979
French Abstract $325,000

Delaunay

JULES ELIE DELAUNAY 1828-1891
French Genre $10,000

DVDELEN
D VAN DELEN 1636

DIRK VAN DELEN 1605-1671
Netherlandish Architectural, Genre, Landscape $75,000

Delleani

LORENZO DELLEANI 1840-1908
Italian Landscape $25,000

T. m. D.

FELIX DELMARLE

A. Delobbe

ALFRED DELOBBE 1835-1920
French Genre, Still Life, Portraits $20,000

C. Delort

CHARLES EDOUARD DELORT 1841-1895
French Landscape $15,000

1. *H·C·Delpy*

2. *H.C.Delpy* 3. *H.C.Delpy*

HIPPOLYTE CAMILLE DELPY 1842-1910
French Landscape $20,000

P. Delvaux

PAUL DELVAUX 1897-1994
Belgian Painter, Genre, Landscape $1,250,000

[D]

GILLES DEMARTEAU 1722-1778
Dutch, Genre, Portraits, Mythology $1,000

MEWDEMING

EDWIN W. DEMING 1860-1942
American Indians, Landscape $5,000

C. Slemuth 1.

C. Demuth 2.

CHARLES DEMUTH 1883-1935
American Watercolour, Genre, Allegory $800,000

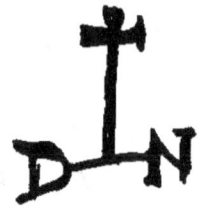

FRANCESCO DENANTO 2500's
Italian, Painter $1,000

1. *MAU·DENIS*
2. **MAUD**   3.
4. *maurice Denis*

MAURICE DENIS 1870-1943
French, Landscape, Portraits, Nabis $385,000

1. *Blenner*   3. *Denner*
2. *Denner*   4. *Denner*

BALTHASAR DENNER 1685-1749
German Portraits, Genre $6,500

Depen   1. *DEPERO*
2.   3. *DEPERO*   4.
5. *Depen*   6. *F.Depero*   *F.Depero*

FORTUNATO DEPERO 1892-1960
Italian Abstract, Futurist $50,000

160

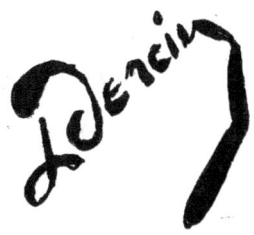

ANDRE DERAIN 1880-1954
French Landscape $1,000,000

MARCELLIN DESBOUTIN 1823-1902
French Painter, Portraits $10,000

F. DESHAYES

FREDERIC-LEON DESHAYES 1883-1970
French Painter, Still Life, Genre $1,500

H.D. JEAN BAPTISTE DESHAYS 1729-1765
French Painter, Allegory $45,000

ALEXANDER FRANCOIS DESPORTES 1661-1743
French Still Life, Animals, Landscape $400,000

EDOUARD DETAILLE

EDOUARD DETAILLE 1848-1912
French Military $50,000

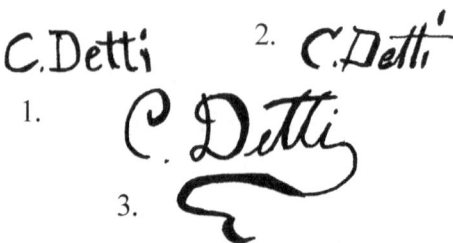

1. C.Detti
2. C.Detti
3. C. Detti

CESARE AUGUSTE DETTI 1847-1914
Italian Painter, Genre, Portraits $50,000

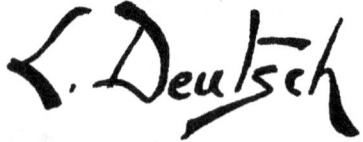

A.DEUSSER

AUGUST DEUSSER 1870-1942
German Painter, Genre, Land $5,000

L. Deutsch

LUDWIG DEUTSCH 1856-1935
Austrian Landscape, Genre $200,000

L. Devedeux

LOUIS DEVEDEUX 1820-1874
French Painter, Landscape, Genre $15,000

E. Deveria

EUGENE DEVERIA 1805-1865
French Portraits, Genre $20,000

T.W Dewing

THOMAS W. DEWING 1851-1938
American Portraits $500,000

W. DEXEL

WALTER DEXEL 1890-1973
German Abstract $15,000

Angelo di Benedetto

ANGELO DI BENEDETTO 1913-
American Painter $1,000

L. g. di Palma

LEON JEAN GIORDANO DI PALMA 1881-
Italian City Streets $1,000

Dickinson

PRESTON DICKINSON 1891-1930
American Abstract, Portraits, Landscapes $300,000

1. RD 2. RD

RICHARD DIEBENKORN 1922-1993
American Abstract $1,700,000

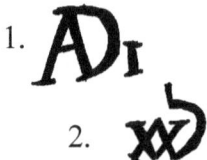

1.
2.
3.

ABRAHAM VAN DIEPENBEECK (also Diepenbeck) 1596-1675
Flemish Portraits, Genre Allegory $65,000

PIERRE DIERCKX 1871-1947
Belgian Painter, Genre $5,000

JOHANN FRIEDRICH DIETLER 1804-1874
Swiss Landscape, Portraits, Genre $15,000

ADELHEID DIETRICH 1827-
German Painter, Still Life $50,000

ADOLF DIETRICH 1877-1957
Swiss Landscape $100,000

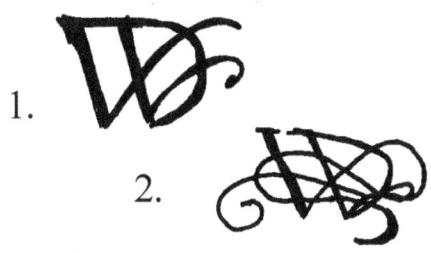

1.

2.

WENDEL DIETTERLEIN 1550-1599
German Painter, Landscape $2,500

1. *d.*   2. *diller*

BURGOYNE DILLER 1906-1965
American Abstract $105,000

JIM DINE 1935-
American Contemporary $250,000

1. *E. DINET*

2. *E. DINET*

ETIENNE DINET 1861-1929
French Painter, Genre $100,000

J. Dismorr

JESSICA S. DISMORR (also Dismoor) 1885-1939
British Landscape, Abstract, Composoitions $5,000

DIVLGHEROFF

NICOLA (also Nicholay, Nicholas) DIULGHEROFF 1901-1982
Italian Landscapes, Abstract Compositions $7,500

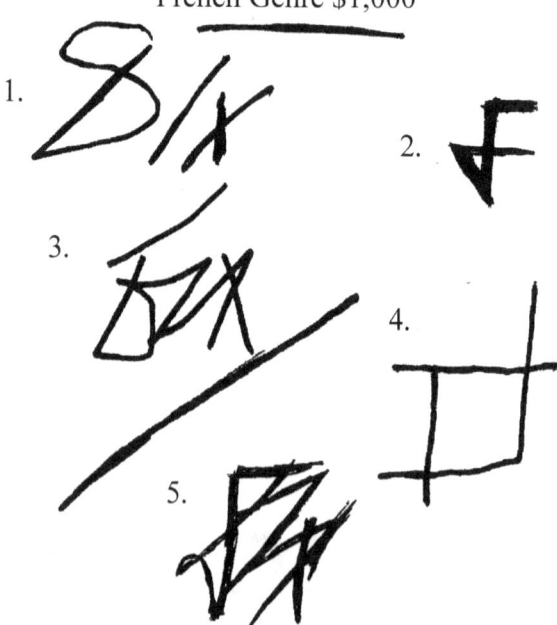

ELIANE DIVERLY 1914-
French Genre $1,000

OTTO DIX 1891-1969
German Expressionist, Genre $5,400,000

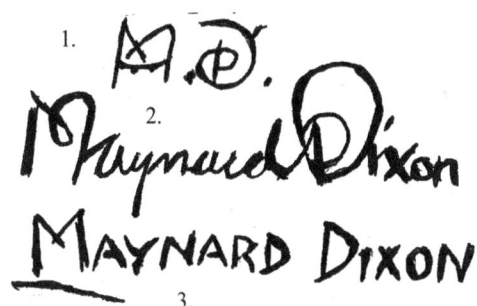

MAYNARD DIXON 1875-1946
American Cowboys & Indians $100,000

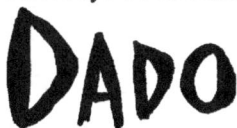

MIO DRAG DJURIK 1933-
Yugoslavian Genre, Allegory, Abstract $20,000

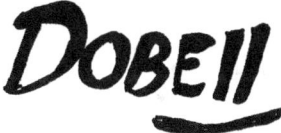

SIR WILLIAM DOBELL 1899-1970
Australian Painter, Landscape $175,000

MSTISLAV DOBOUJINSKY 1875-1957
Russian Costume Stage Design $10,000

JACOB VAN DER DOES 1623-1673
Netherlandish Sheep, Pastures $10,000

1. *S · van der Does*
2. *5.VDoes*
3. *SVDoes*
4. *V does*

SIMON VAN DER DOES 1653-1719
Netherlandish Sheep, Landscapes $10,000

Stevan Dohanos

STEVAN DOHANOS 1907-1994
American Illustrator, Genre $16,000

1. *Carl Dlc*

2. *CDolci*

CARLO DOLCI 1616-1686
Italian Painter $2,500

1. *Dominguez*

2. *Dominguez*

OSCAR DOMINGUEZ 1906-1958
Spanish Abstract $1,149,000

CORNELIS CHRISTIAAN DOMMELSHUIZEN 1842-1928
Dutch Painter, Genre $15,000

MARTHE DONAS 1885-1967
Belgian Painter, Abstract $170,000

1.
2.
3.
4.
5.
6.

KEES VAN DONGEN 1877-1968
Dutch Sculptor, Landscape, Expressionist $1,500,000

LAMBERT DOOMER 1622-1700
Netherlandish Landscape Genre $30,000

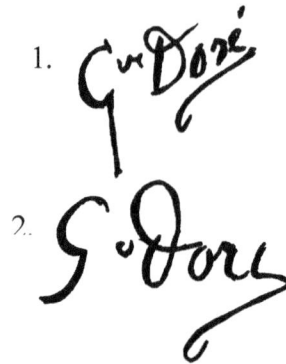

PAUL GUSTAVE DORE 1832-1883
French Landscape Genre $150,000

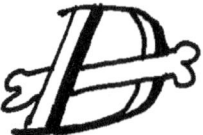

GIOVANNI DI NICOLO DOSSI (also Dosso) 1479-1542
Italian Landscape, Allegorical Painter $3,500,000

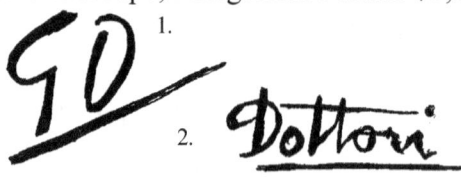

GERARDO DOTTORI 1884-1977
Italian Genre, Abstract Compositions $35,000

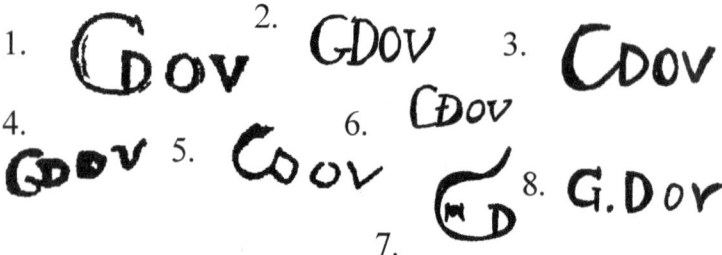

GERRIT (also Gerard) DOU (also Dow, Douw) 1613-1675
Netherlandish Genre, Portraits, Religious $2,042,000

PAUL DOUGHERTY 1877-1947
American N.A., Painter, Landscape, Seascape $10,000

EDWIN DOUGLAS 1848-1914
British Engraver, Painter, Genre $25,000

JAN FRANS VAN (also Johannes Franciscus) DOUVEN 1655-1727
French Portraits, Allegory $22,000

ARTHUR GARFIELD DOVE 1880-1946
American Modernist, Landscape, Abstract $400,000

PATRICK DOWNIE 1871-1945
British Painter, Landscape $4,500

GABRIEL FRANCOIS DOYEN 1726-1806
French Painter, Religious, Allegory $60,000

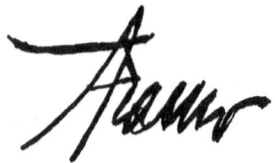

JULES-RESNARD (also Isnard, Renard) DRANER 1833-1926
French Military, Genre $5,000

GEORGE W. DREW 1875-1968
American Landscape $2,000

MARTIN DROLLING 1752-1827
Dutch Genre, Landscape, Mountains $160,000

JOOST CORNELISZ the Elder DROOCH-SLOOT
(also Drooghsloot) Dutch Religious, Landscape, Genre $75,000

WILLIAM DRUMMOND 1800's
British Costume Stage Design $3,000

GUY PENE DU BOIS 1884-1958
American Painter, Landscape, Genre $90,000

HANS FABER DU FAUR 1863-1944
German Painter $30,000

FRANCOIS DU MONT 1752-1833
French Pastels, Genre, Portraits $2,500

1.

3.

2.

4.

HENDRICK JACOBSZ (also Jacobs, Hendrik) DUBBELS
1621-1676 Netherlandish Boats, Seascape, Landscape $250,000

GUILLIAM DUBOIS 1609-1680
Netherlandish Landscapes $25,000

AMBROISE DUBOIS 1543-1614
Flemish Painter, Portraits $45,000

GUILLAUME DUBUFFE 1853-1909
French Allegory, Genre $5,000

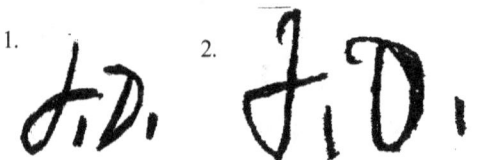

JEAN DUBUFFET 1901-1985
French Abstract $5,000,000

MARCEL VILLON DUCHAMP 1887-1968
French Modernist Cubist $1,762,500

FRANS (also Francois) DUCHATEL 1616-1694
Flemish Genre, Landscape $20,000

JOSEPH DUCREUX 1737-1802
French Portraits $15,000

LEONARDO DUDREVILLE 1885-1976
Italian Portraits, Landscape $30,000

EDOUARD DUFEU 1840-1900
French Landscape $4,500

JEAN DUFY 1888-1964
French Painter, Genre, Landscape $100,000

1.   2.

RAOUL DUFY 1880-1953
French Painter, Portraits, Landscape $6,000,000

1.

2.

GASPARD (also Poussin) DUGHET 1613-1675
French Landscapes, Allegory $18,000

1.

2.

3.

KAREL DUJARDIN 1622-1678
Netherlandish Allegorical $500,000

EDMUND DULAC 1882-1953
French Genre, Portraits $50,000

PIERRE DUMONT 1884-1936
French Landscapes $20,000

ANDRE DUNOYER DE SEGONZAC 1884-1974
French Illustrator, Landscape $50,000

WILLIAM HERBERT (BUCK) DUNTON 1878-1936
American Illustrator, Genre, Landscape $40,000

JOSEPH SIFFRED DUPLESSIS 1725-1802
French Painter, Landscape, Portraits $15,000

JULES DUPRE 1811-1889
French Painter, Genre, Landscape $30,000

JULIEN DUPRE

JULIEN DUPRE 1851-1910
French Landscape, Genre $50,000

Dupressoir

JOSEPH DUPRESSOIR 1800-1959
French Landscape $1,000

ABDurand

ASHER BROWN DURAND 1796-1886
American Landscapes, Genre $300,000

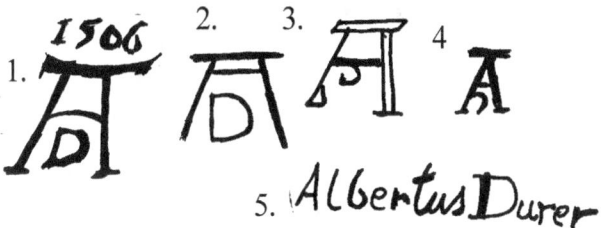

ALBRECHT DURER 1471-1528
German Old Master, Portraits, Allegory $400,000

ISABELLE DURET-DUJARRIC 1949-
French Painter, Genre, Landscape $20,000

G.H.DURRIE

GEORGE HENRY DURRIE 1820-1863
American Landscapes $225,000

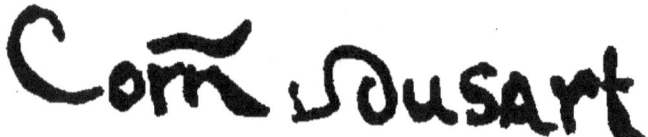

CORNELIS DUSART 1660-1704
Dutch Genre, Portraits $100,000

Duval

ETIENNE DUVAL 1824-1914
Swiss Landscape $7,000

DUVERGER

THEOPHILE EMMANUEL DUVERGER 1821-1900
French Painter, Genre, Portraits $20,000

E.DWURNIK

EDWARD DWURNIK 1900's
Polish Villages $1,000

Charlie Dye

CHARLIE DYE 1906-1972
American Illustrator, Genre, Cowboys $40,000

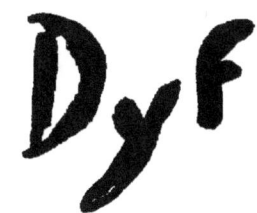

MARCEL DYF 1894-1985
French Landscape, Genre $15,000

Artists starting with the letter "E"

EAKINS

THOMAS EAKINS 1844-1916
American Impressionist, Genre $68,000,000

JOAN EARDLEY

JOAN KATHLEEN HARDING EARDLEY 1921-1963
British Landscapes $35,000

Maud Earl

MAUD EARL 1865-1943
British Landscape, Genre $20,000

R. EARL

RALPH EARL 1751-1801
American Landscape $30,000

ALFRED EAST

SIR ALFRED EAST 1849-1913
British R.A. Watercolour, Landscape $5,000

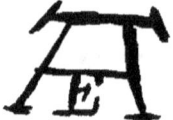

ADAM EBERLE 1805-1830
Italian Painter, Religious $2,500

1. Ëbert 2. CHEbert

CHARLES EBERT 1873-1959
American Landscape $20,000

1. CE 2. CE

KARL EBERT 1821-1885
German Landscape $40,000

1. ℬ 2. *JHBEibuschitz*

HEDWIG EIBUSCHITZ 1880-
Austrian, Landscape, Rivers $1,000

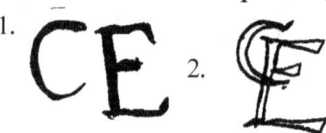

ALBERT GUSTAF ARISTIDES EDELFELT 1854-1905
Finland Painter, Landscape, Genre $1,000,000

1. *G. V. Eckbout.*

2. *GV. Eerkout*

GERBRAND VAN DEN EECKHOUT 1621-1674
Netherlandish Genre, Portraits $200,000

Eekman (signature)

NICOLAS EEKMAN 1889-1973
British Painter, Genre, Portraits $15,000

_SE_ (monogram)

STAN EGERTON 1900's
British Landscape $1,000

1.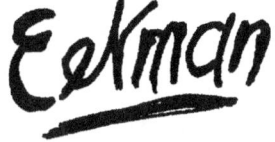

2. _N. EGGEN-HOFER_ (signature)

NICK EGGENHOFFER 1897-1976
American Cowboys, Genre $25,000

1. _EGGER-LIENZ_ (signature)

2.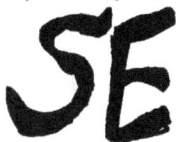

ALBIN EGGER-LIENZ 1868-1926
Swiss Painter, Genre, Portraits $250,000

1. 2. 3. (monograms)

ADOLF (also Carl, Karl Ludwig) EHRHARDT 1813-1899
German Painter $5,000

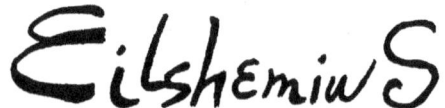

LOUIS MICHEL EILSHEMIUS 1864-1941
American Abstract, Landscape $5,000

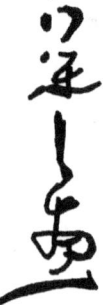

HOSODA EISHI 1756-1829
Japanese Woodblocks, Genre $5,000

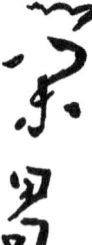

CHOKOSAI EISHO 1700's
Japanese Woodblocks, Portraits $20,000

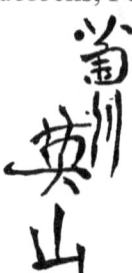

KIKUKANA EIZAN 1787-1868
Japanese Woodblocks $15,000

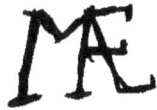

GEORGE SAMUEL ELGOOD 1851-1943
British Landscape $15,000

MARIE ELLENRIEDER 1791-1863
German Genre, Portrait $5,000

OTTOMAR I (also Ottmar) (the elder) ELLIGER 1633-1679
German Still Life, Genre, Religious $100,000

OTTMAR II (the younger) ELLIGER 1666-1732
Dutch Allegory, Painter $25,000

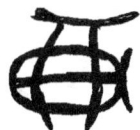

JAMES SANFORD ELLSWORTH 1802-1874
American Painter, Portraits $2,000

ALFRED ELMORE 1815-1881
British Painter, Allegory, Genre $5,500

ᗅRTᕼᑌᖇ J. ELSLEY

ARTHUR JOHN ELSEY 1843-1919
British Painter, Genre $100,000

1. Æ   2. ÆI
        Elseimer
3.

ADAM ELSHEIMER 1578-1620
German Landscape $4,450,000

J. EMMS

JOHN EMMS 1843-1912
British Horses, Landscape $75,000

Empoli

JACOPO C.D. EMPOLI 1554-1640
Italian Religious Painter $20,000

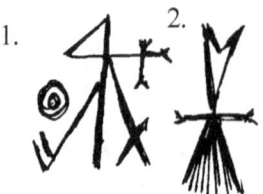

1.   2.

CORNELIS ENGELBRECHTSEN (also Engelberts) 1468-1533
Dutch Painter, Genre, Religious $50,000

1. *K. v. E.*

2. *K v E*

KARL VON ENHUBER 1811-1867
German Genre $10,000

DELPHIN ENJOLRAS 1857-1945
French Genre, Portraits $25,000

ENNEKING

JOHN JOSEPH ENNEKING 1838-1916
American Landscapes, Genre $100,000

1. *J Ensor*

2. ENSOR

JAMES ENSOR 1860-1949
Belgian Impressionist $300,000

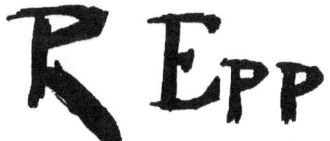

RUDOLF EPP 1834-1910
German Painter, Genre, Landscape $30,000

SIR JACOB EPSTEIN 1880-1959
British Sculptor, Portraits, Landscape $60,000

ULRICH ERBEN 1940-
German Painter $7,500

FRITZ ERLER 1868-1940
German Painter, Allegory, Genre, Landscape $7,500

HANS ERNI 1909-
Swiss Genre, Portraits, Nudes $25,000

MAX ERNST 1891-1976
American Surrealist $2,429,500

1. *R.Ernst*

2. *R.Ernst*

RUDOLF ERNST 1854-1932
Austrian Genre, Painter, Landscape $125,000

Erte

ROMAIN DE TERTOFF ERTE 1892-1990
Russian Stage Costume Bronze $30,000

E. ERTz

EDWARD ERTZ 1862-1954
American Watercolour, Landscape $5,000

E. ESBENS

EMILE ETIENNE ESBENS 1821-
French Genre, Portraits $1,000

Escalante

JUAN ANTONIO ESCALANTE 1630-1670
Spanish Religious Painter $1,500

A. Escher

ALBERT VON ESCHER 1839-1905
Swiss Painter $1,500

h. J Espinosa

JACINTO ESPINOSA 1600-1680
Spanish Painter, Religious, Portraits, Genre $30,000

C. J. Esselens.

JACOB ESSELENS 1626-1687
Netherlandish Marines, Boats, Landscape $30,000

iV. Es

JACOB VAN ESSEN 1606-1666
Dutch Still Life, Painter $150,000

B. Estense

BALDASSARE ESTENSE 1500's
Italian Portraits

E Stéve

MAURICE ESTEVE 1904-
French Abstract Compositions $200,000

Etchells

FREDERICK ETCHELLS 1886-1973
British Watercolour, Genre, Portraits $35,000

S.S. David

DE SCOTT EVANS 1847-1898
American Painter, Genre, Still Life $20,000

1. 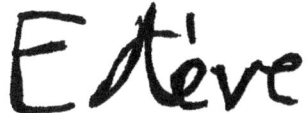   2. *Ab*

3. *A:V EVERDINCEN*
A.v. Everdingen.

4.
EH. v) Everdingen   5.

ALLART.VAN 6.
EVERDINGEN   7. *Everdinge*

A: EVERDINGEN 8.

ALLAERT VAN (also Allart) EVERDINGEN 1621-1675
Dutch Old Master, Landscape $150,000

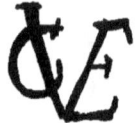

CESARE BOETIUS VAN EVERDINGEN 1606-1679
Dutch Genre, Portraits $250,000

1.

2.

PHILIP EVERGOOD 1901-1973
American Illustrator, Genre, Portrait $40,000

1.   2.

ANTON CLEMENS EVERS 1802-1848
German Genre, Portraits $2,500

ADRIANUS EVERSEN 1818-1897
Dutch Painter, Genre $30,000

JOHANNES HENDRIK (also Jan) EVERSEN 1906-
Dutch Painter, Genre, Still Life $15,000

HANS EWOUTSZ 1515-1574
Netherlandish Allegorical, Portraits $85,000

1.

2.

ALEXANDRIA EXTER 1882-1949
Russian Stage, Costume Design, Abstract $1,000,000

CHARLES VAN DEN EYCKEN 1859-1923
Belgian Landscape, Genre $50,000

Artists starting with the letter "F"

CAREL (also Karel) FABRITIUS 1622-1654
Dutch Old Master, Allegory, Landscape $700,000

BARENT FABRITIUS 1624-1673
Netherlandish Religious, Genre $20,000

THOMAS FAED 1826-1900
British Watercolour, Genre $125,000

LOUIS FAEHNLEIN -1930
French Painter, Genre $12,000

MILES FAIRHURST 1900's
British Landscape $1,200

ABEL FAIVRE 1867-1945
French Painter, Genre, Landscape $10,000

THEODOR FALCKEISEN 1765-1814
Swiss Painter, Religious $4,500

1.

2.

3.

GIOVANNI FALCONNETTO 1458-1534
Italian Architectural Painter $1,500

KAREL VAN (also Carel) FALENS (also Valens) 1683-1733
Dutch Landscape, Genre $12,000

LUIS RICCARDO FALERO 1851-1896
Spanish Genre, Portraits $30,000

JOHN FALTER

JOHN FALTER 1910-1982
American Illustrator, Genre, Cowboys $20,000

Fantin

HENRI FANTIN LATOUR 1836-1904
French Painter, Floral, Landscape, Impressionist $10,000,000

VDoubourg

VICTORIA FANTIN-LATOUR (Doubourg) 1800's
French, Painter

PAOLO FARINATI 1524-1606
Italian Painter, Genre, Religious $120,000

Jerry Farnsworth

JERRY FARNSWORTH 1895-1983
American Painter, Genre, Portraits $5,000

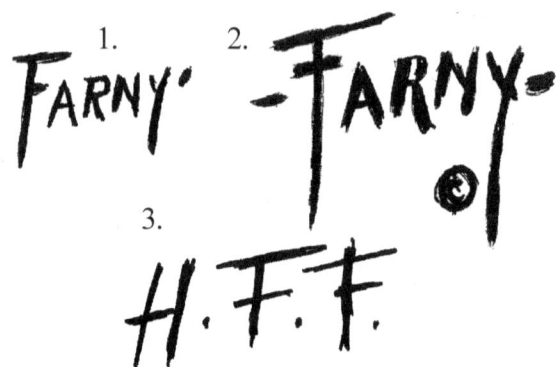

1. 2. 3.

HENRY F. FARNY 1847-1916
American Cowboys $1,212,000

JOSEPH FARQUHARSON 1846-1935
British Painter, Landscape, Genre $80,000

DAVID FARQUHARSON A.R.A. 1840-1907
British Watercolour, Landscape $15,000

HENRI FARRE 1871-1934
American Painter, Portrait $10,000

LORENZO FASOLO -1520
Italian Painter

JOSEPH FASSBENDER 1902-1974
German Abstract $5,000

1. 2.

GIOVANNI FATTORI 1825-1908
Italian Etcher, Genre, Landscape $300,000

HENRI V. GABRIEL LE FAUCONNIER 1881-1946
French Landscape, Cubism, Genre, Portraits $40,000

JEAN FAUTRIER 1897-1964
French Landscape, Portrait $2,500,000

A . FAVORY
ANDRE FAVORY 1889-1937
French Painter, Cubist, Genre, Landscape $4,000

NICOLAI FECHIN 1881-1955
American Cowboys $150,000

ADOLPHE FEDER 1886-1943
French Cubist, Genre, Landscape $9,000

1. 2.

PIETER VAN HARLINGEN FEDDES (also Petrus) 1586—1634
Dutch, Portraits, Religious $10,000

ILSE FEHLING (Witting) 1896-1982
German, Portraits, Sculpture $2,500

FRIEDRICH FEIGL 1884-1965
German Landscape $1,500

1.

2.

3.

LYONEL FEININGER 1871-1956
German Expressionist, Cubist $7,688,000

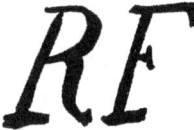

ROBERT FEKE 1707-1752
American Painter, Portraits $3,500

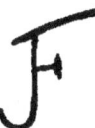

CONRAD FELIXMULLER 1897-1977
German Painter, Portraits, Genre $75,000

JOSEPH FELON 1818-1896
French Painter, Genre $6,000

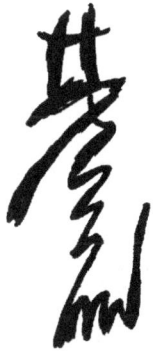

LIN FENGMIAN 1900-1991
Chinese Fans, Landscape $3,500

SERGE FERAT 1881-1958
French Abstract, Landscape, Genre $15,000

Claude L. Ferneley

CLAUDE LORRAINE FERNELEY 1822-1891
British Sporting, Landscape $15,000

Fernhout

EDGAR FERNHOUT 1912-1974
Dutch Painter, Portrait, Landscape $25,000

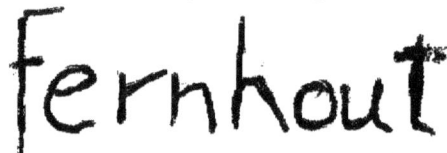

JESUS REYES FERREIRA (CHUCHO) 1882-1977
Mexican Animals $1,000

Ferren

JOHN FERREN 1905-1970
American Abstract $10,000

C. FERRIER

GABRIEL JOSEPH M. A. FERRIER 1847-1914
French Portraits, Nudes $50,000

FERRONI S.A.

GIAN FRANCO FERRONI 1927-
Italian Landscape, Genre $15,000

ROBERT FERRUZZI 1927-
Italian Still Life Landscape $7,500

MELCHIOR FESELEN (also Feselein)-1538
German Painter $2,000

DOMENICO FETI 1589-1624
Italian Painter, Portraits, Allegory $80,000

H. FEWSMITH 1821-1846
American Painter $1,000

BRIAN DAVIS FFOLKES 1900's
British Cartoonist $1,000

O.F.F.

ORLANDO FIACCO 1550-
Italian Portraits, Religious $3,500

1.　　　2.

ODOARDO FIALETTI 1573-1638
Italian Painter, Landscape, Portraits $15,000

E. FICHEL

BENJAMIN EUGENE FICHEL 1826-1895
French Painter, Genre, Portraits $10,000

ERNEST FIENE 1894-1965
American N.A. Painter, genre, Portraits $25,000

P.Figari-

PEDRO FIGARI 1861-1938
Latin American Painter, Genre $500,000

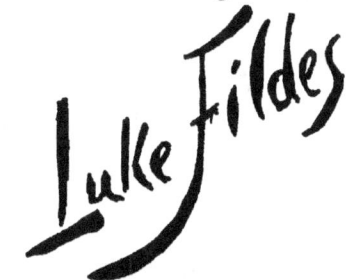

JAN FIJT 1611-1661
Netherlandish Hunting Genre $10,000

SAMUEL LUKE FILDES 1844-1927
British Genre, Landscape $125,000

FILLIA

LUIGI COLUMBO FILLIA 1904-1936
Italian Cubist Compositions $35,000

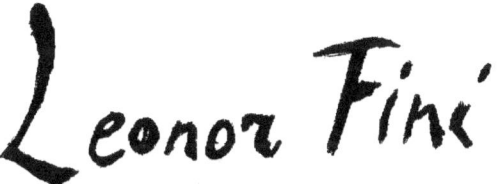

LEONOR FINI 1885-1996
Argentinian Painter, Genre, Landscape $150,000

FIRMIN-GIRARD

MARIE FRANCOIS FIRMIN-GIRARD 1838-1921
French Paris Streets, Genre, Landscape $100,000

ANTON OTTO FISCHER 1882-1962
American Illustrator, Genre, Seascape $7,000

JOSEPH FISCHER 1769-1822
Austrian

PAUL FISCHER 1860-1934
Danish Landscape, Genre $230,000

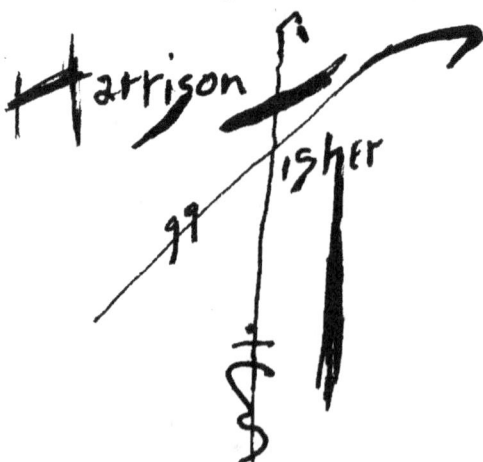

HARRISON FISHER 1875-1934
American Illustrator, Genre, Landscape $20,000

1.

2.

KAI FJELL 1907-1989
Norwegian Painter, Genre, Landscape $375,000

JAMES MONTGOMERY FLAGG 1877-1960
American Caricature Illustration, Genre $10,000

ADOLF FLEISHMANN 1892-1969
German Painter, Abstract $50,000

BARTHOLET FLEMAEL 1614-1675
Dutch Portraits, Mythology $50,000

NICOLAS ROBERT FLEURY 1797-1890
French Genre $2,000

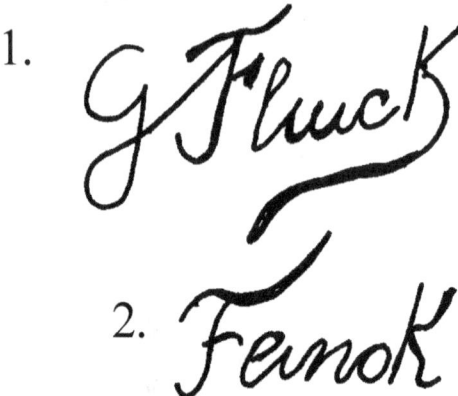

1. *G Fluuck*

2. *Femok*

GOVAERT FLINCK 1615-1666
Dutch Portraits, Landscape, Religious $400,000

J. Floch

JOSEPH FLOCH 1894-1966
Australian Painter, Genre, Landscape $3,000

DE Flynn

DIANNE FLYNN 1900's
British Genre $3,500

J. Folchi

FERDINAND FOLCHI 1822-1883
Italian Painter, Genre $10,000

Follini

CARLO FOLLINI 1848-1938
Italian Painter, Landscape $15,000

Fonseca

GONZALO FONSECA 1922-
Latin American Landscape, Sculpture, Genre $100,000

REYNALDO

REYNALDO (also Reinaldo) FONSECA 1925-
Latin American Painter, Genre, Portraits $10,000

-Fontaine

JOE FONTAINE 1900's
French Paris Streets $1,000

1. *L LavFon*

2. LAVINIA

LAVINIA FONTANA 1552-1614
Italian Painter, Religious, Mythology $100,000

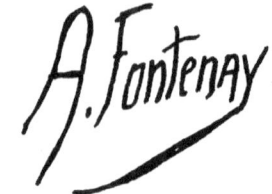

ANDRE FONTENAY 1913-
French Paris Streets, Landscape, Portraits $1,000

JEAN LOUIS FORAIN 1852-1931
French Illustrator, Genre, Portraits $90,000

1. **Stanhope A. Forbes**

Stanhope a. Forbes
2.

STANHOPE ALEXANDER FORBES 1857-1947
British Landscape, Genre $150,000

P. FOREST

PIERRE FOREST 1881-1971
French Still Life, Seascape, Genre $3,500

ACHILLE B. FORMIS 1832-1906
Italian Landscape $40,000

R.Forner

RAQUEL FORNER 1902-1988
Argentinian Painter, Genre $12,000

Fornerod

RUDOLPHE FORNEROD 1882-1953
Swiss Painter, Genre, Landscape $2,500

FF

ERNST JOACHIM FORSTER 1800-1885
German Portraits $2,000

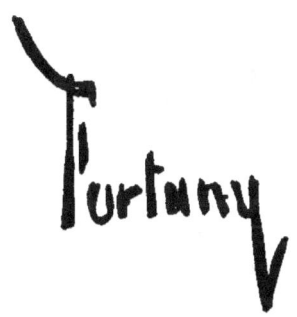

MARIANO FORTUNY Y CARBO 1838-1874
Spanish Genre, Landscape, Portraits $200,000

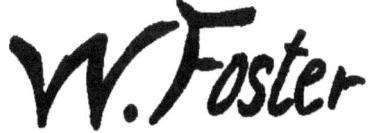

WILLIAM FOSTER 1853-1924
British Birds Watercolour, Landscape $5,000

E. FOUGERAT

EMMANUEL FOUGERAT 1869-1945
French Painter, Genre $2,000

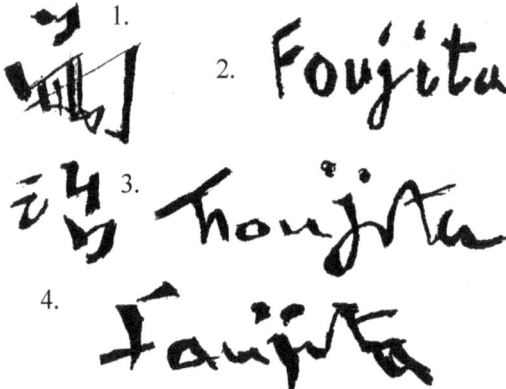

1.
2. *Foujita*
3. *Foujita*
4. *Foujita*

TSUGOUHARU FOUJITA 1886-1968
Japanese Painter, Genre $5,000,000

1. **D** 2. **D• CH F•**

CHARLES FOUQUERAY

D. CHARLES FOUQUERAY 1872-1956
French Painter, Genre $15,000

A.M.Fowerker

A. MOULTON FOWERAKER 1873-1942
British Landscape $3,000

1. *Fragonard* 2. *Fragonard*

JEAN-HONORE FRAGONARD 1732-1806
French Allegory, Genre, Landscape $8,000,000

G·FRAIPONT

GEORGES FRAIPONT 1873-1912
French Painter, Genre $35,000

I·FRANCIA

GIACOMA FRANCIA 1485-1557
Italian Painter, Religious, Allegory $100,000

Francia

FRANCESCO FRANCIA 1450-1517
Italian Painter, Religious $350,000

J. F. Francis

JOHN F. FRANCIS 1810-1885
American Landscape, Portrait, Genre $250,000

J. Bond Francisco

JOHN BOND FRANCISCO 1863-1931
American Plein Aire, Landscape, California $4,000

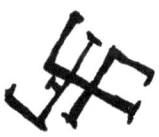

FRANZ(also Franz Friedrich) FRANCK (also Frank)
1627-1687 German Painter, Still Life $1,200,000

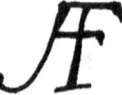

AMBROSIUS (also Franck) FRANCKEN (The Elder) 1544-1618
Dutch Portraits, Religious, Landscape $50,000

1.

2.

FRANS (also Franck) FRANCKEN (The Younger) 1581-1642
Dutch Landscape, Religious, Allegory $150,000

1.

2.

HELEN FRANKENTHALER 1928-1988
American Abstract Compositions $800,000

JEAN FRANQUELIN 1798-1839
French Genre, Children, Portraits $90,000

ETTORE ROESLER FRANZ 1845-1907
Italian Landscape $7,500

AUGUST FRANZEN 1863-1938
American Painter, Genre, Portraits $5,000

1. *[signature: Frasconi]*   2. *[monogram: AF]*

ANTONIO FRASCONI 1919-
American, Illustrator, Woodblocks $1,000

[signature: Fraser. A]

ALEXANDER FRASER (also Frazer) 1786-1865
Scottish Genre, Landscape, Children $5,000

[signature: WM Frazer]

WILLIAM MILLER FRAZER 1864-1961
British Landscape, Genre $5,000

1. *[signature: M Fre]* 2. *[signature: EREMIN]*

MARTIN DE FREMINET (also Freminel) 1567-1619
French Painter $70,000

[signature: P. FRENZENY]

P. FRENZENY 1840-1902
American Indians, Genre $10,000

[signature: TK. FRÈRE]

THEODORE CHARLES FRERE 1814-1888
French Painter, Genre, Landscape $70,000

EDOUARD PIERRE FRERE 1819-1886
French Genre, Portraits, Landscape $25,000

1.   2.   3.

WILLIAM CHARLES ANTHONY FRERICHS 1829-1905
American Indians, Genre $15,000

ROGER DE LA FRESNAYE 1885-1925
French Abstract Cubist $200,000

1.   2.

OTTO FREUNDLICH 1878-1943
German Painter, Expressionist $200,000

EUGENE H. FREY 1864-1930
French Painter, Still Life, Genre, $6,000

EMILE FRIANT 1863-1932
French Painter, Landscape $12,000

JOHNNY FRIEDLAENDER 1912-1992
German Illustrator, Genre $20,000

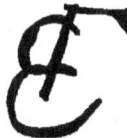

ERNST FRIES 1801-1833
German Landscape, Portraits $15,000

ACHILLE EMILE OTHON FRIESZ 1879-1949
French Painter, Landscape, Still Life $1,000,000

JOHANNE NICOLINE LOUISE FRIMODT 1861-1920
Danish Painter, Genre $25,000

DAME ELIZABETH FRINK 1930-1993
British Genre Allegorical $20,000

NIELS FRISTRUP 1837-1909
Danish Landscape $15,000

Eug Fromentin

EUGENE SAMUEL A. FROMENTIN 1820-1876
French Arab Genre $100,000

1. **A.B. FROST**

2. **A. B. FROST**

ARTHUR BURDETT FROST 1851-1928
American Cowboys, Genre $60,000

Louis Agassiz Fuertes

LOUIS AGASSIZ FUERTES 1874-1927
American Illustrator, Genre, Landscape $20,000

Fullarton

JAMES FULLARTON 1900's
British Landscapes $3,000

DAVID FULTON • R.S.W.

DAVID FULTON 1850-1930
British Painter, Genre, Landscape $15,000

furini

FRANCESCO FURINI 1600-1649
Italian Portraits, Landscape, Genre, Religious $30,000

Fussli

JOHANN HEINRICH FUSSLI 1741-1825
Swiss Genre, Portraits, Illustration $100,000

1. *J.Fy*   2. *Joh.Fyt*

JAN FYT 1611-1661
Dutch Still Life, Landscape, Animals $350,000

Artists starting with the letter "G"

PAUL JOSEPH CONSTANTIN GABRIEL 1828-1903
Dutch Painter, Landscape $30,000

GUILIAM GABRON 1619-1678
Dutch Still Life, Animals $80,000

TADDEO (also Agnolo, Angelo) GADDI 1300-1366
Italian Painter, Religious $900,000

1. 2.

BAREND (also Barent) GAEL (also Gaal) 1620-1703
Dutch Landscape, Animals, Genre $20,000

ALEXANDER GAELEN 1670-1728
Dutch Painter, Battles, Landscape $20,000

LOUIS GAIDAN 1847-1925
French Painter, Genre $17,000

FRANS GAILLIARD 1861-1932
French Painter, Genre $75,000

1. 2.

DEMETRIUS EMMANUEL GALANIS 1882-1966
American Engraver, Still Life, Landscape $5,000

EUGENE GALIEN-LALOUE 1854-1954
French Paris Streets, Landscape $50,000

FRANCOIS GALL 1912-1945
French Painter, Portraits, Genre $20,000

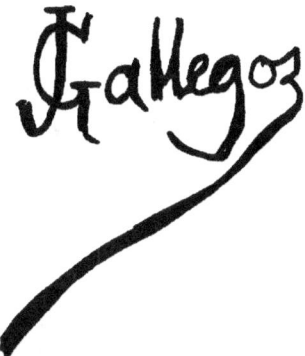

JOSE GALLEGOS Y ARNOSA 1859-1902
Spanish Painter, Genre $175,000

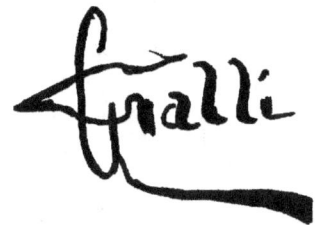

GIUSEPPE GALLI 1866-1953
Italian Watercolour, Genre $10,000

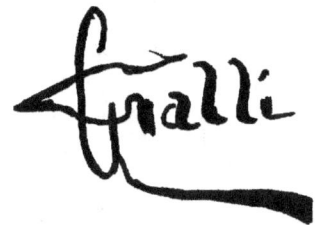

LOUIS GALLOCHE 1670-1761
French Painter, Genre, Religious $45,000

E. Gallois

EMILE GALLOIS 1882-1965
Belgian Painter, Landscape, Genre $1,500

Gamba

ENRICO GAMBA 1831-1883
Italian Landscape, Genre $8,000

Gampenrieder

KARL GAMPENRIEDER 1860-1930
German Painter, Portraits, Genre $25,000

1. *JTG*

2. *J. Torces. SARCIA*

JOAQUIN TORRES GARCIA 1874-1949
Latin American Sculptor, Landscape, Genre $500,000

G. GARDET

GEORGES GARDET 1863-1939
French Animals $60,000

B. Garofolo

IL BENVENUTO GAROFALO 1481-1559
Italian Painter, Religious $15,000

GIOVANNA GARZONI 1600-1679
Italian, Floral, Still Life $90,000

LEON GASPARD 1882-1964
American Taos Painter, Genre, Landscape $250,000

LUCAS HELMONT VAN GASSEL 1500-1550
Dutch Painter, Religious, Landscape $30,000

JEAN BRUNO GASSIES (also Gassier) 1786-1832
French Genre $4,000

LEE GATCH 1902-1968
American Abstract $10,000

Léon GAUD

LEON GAUD 1844-1908
Swiss Landscape $10,000

L P Gaudin

LUIS PASCUAL GAUDIN 1566-1621
Italian Painter $2,000

1. *L. Gauffier*   2. *L. Gauffier*

LOUIS GAUFFIER 1761-1801
French Painter, Portraits, Mythology $250,000

I.M.GAUGENGIGL.

1.

2. *GGGCL*

INGNAZ MARCEL GAUGENGIGL 1855-1932
American Etcher, Genre, Portraits $75,000

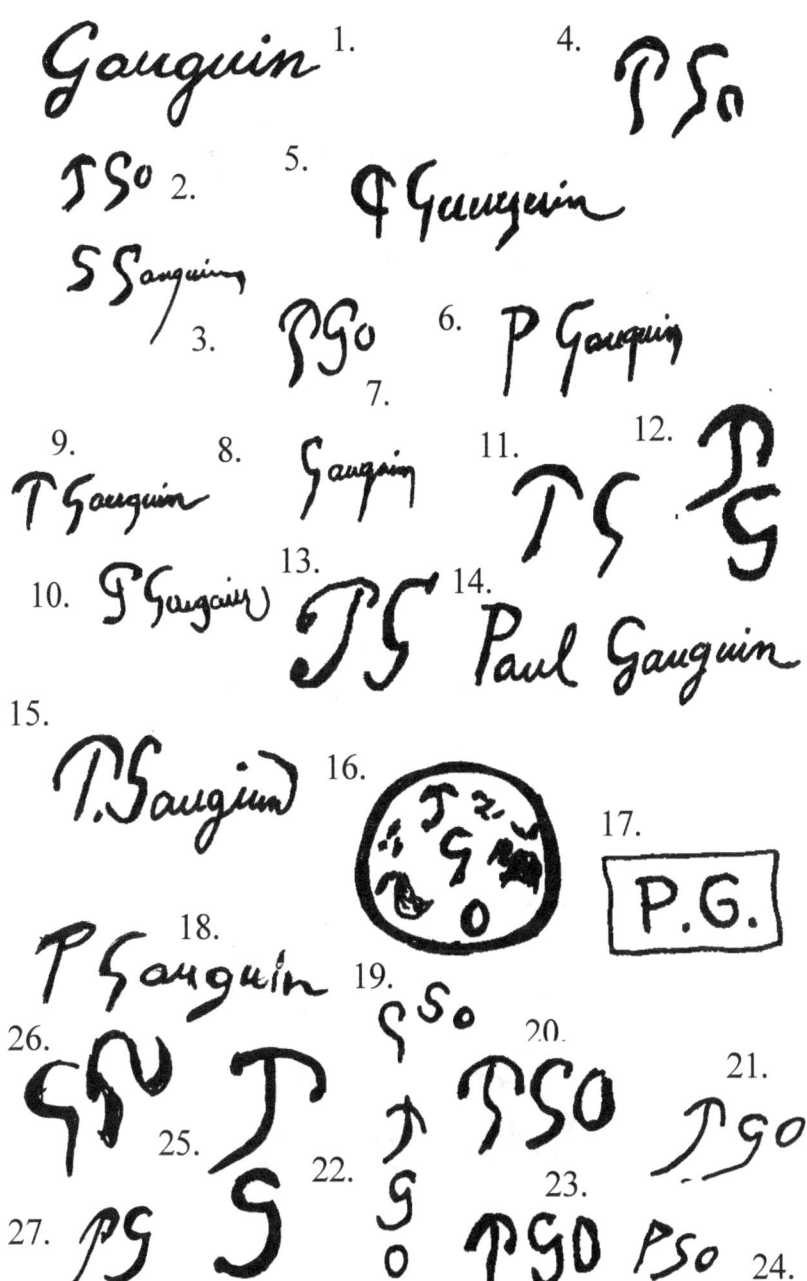

PAUL GAUGUIN 1848-1903
French Painter, Portraits Genre, Post Impressionist $40,330,000

1.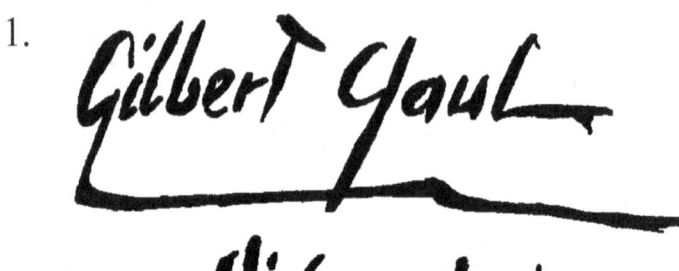

2.

WILLIAM GILBERT GAUL 1854-1919
American N.A. Cowboys $15,000

DAVID GAULD 1866-1936
British R.S.A. Painter, Genre $15,000

ARMAND-DESIRE GAUTIER 1825-1894
French Painter, Genre $1,000

WALTER GAY 1856-1937
American Painter, Genre, Portraits $50,000

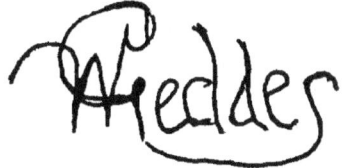

WILLIAM GEDDES 1841-1884
British Painter, Genre, Still Life $10,000

1.

2.

ANDREW GEDDES 1789-1844
Scottish Portraits $20,000

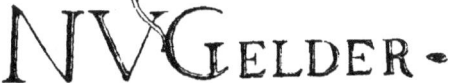

JACOB VAN GEEL 1585-1635
Netherlandish Landscapes $10,000

JOOST VAN GEEL 1631-1698
Dutch Genre, Portraits $10,000

NICOLAES VAN GELDER 1636-1678
Netherlandish Still Life $25,000

1.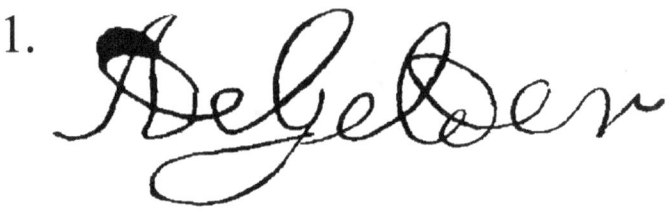

2.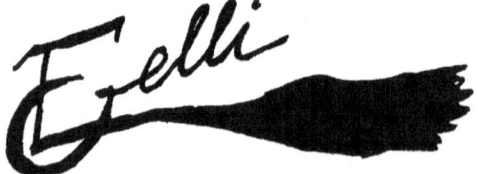

ARENT DE GELDER 1645-1727
Netherlandish Portraits, Genre $25,000

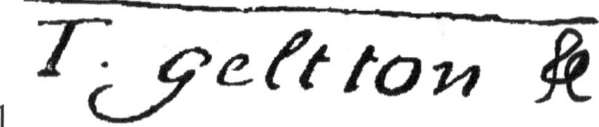

MAXIMILLIAN LAMBERT GELISSEN 1786-1867
Belgian Landscape, Genre $4,000

EDOARDO GELLI 1852-1933
Italian Painter, Genre, Portraits $7,500

1.

2.

TOUSSAINT GELTON 1629-1680
Netherlandish Allegorical $2,000

lucengenin

LUCIEN GENIN 1894-1958
French Painter, Portraits, Genre $40,000

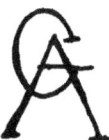

ABRAHAM GENOELS (also Genaels Archimedes) 1640-1723
Dutch Landscape, Animals $5,500

Gentleschi

ORAZIO GENTILESCHI 1562-1647
Italian Painter, Portraits, Religious, Genre $7,500

B^{ron} Gerard

FRANCOIS GERARD 1770-1837
Italian Portraits, Mythology, Genre $1,875,000

G Gericault

JEAN LOUIS GERICAULT 1791-1824
French Animals, Genre, Landscape $5,249,000

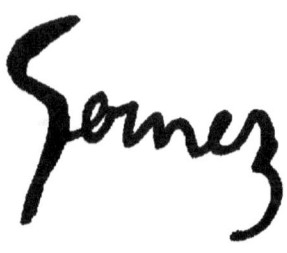

PAUL ELIE GERNEZ 1888-1948
French Cubist, Nudes $20,000

J.L.GEROME **J.L.GEROME**
1.   2.
JEAN LEON GEROME 1824-1904
French Allegory, Landscape, Genre, Animals $3,083,000

GERZSO
GUNTHER GERZSO 1915-
Mexican Painter, Genre, Landscape $550,000

LEO GESTEL
LEO GESTEL 1881-1941
Dutch Painter, Genre, Allegory $350,000

I. GETZ
ILSE GETZ 1917-
German Assemblage $1,000

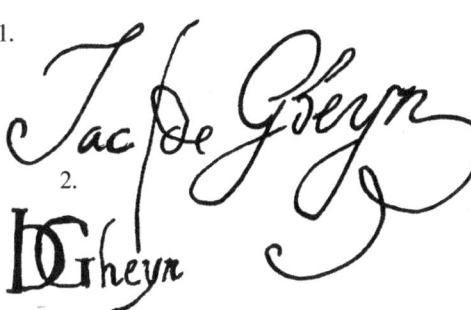

JACQUES DE GHEYN THE YOUNGER 1565-1629
Flemish Old Master $75,000

Ghiglion-Green

MAURICE GHIGLION-GREEN 1913-
French Landscape, Genre $2,500

Alberto Giacometti

ALBERTO GIACOMETTI 1906-1966
Italian Cubist, Genre $103,900,000

1.   2.

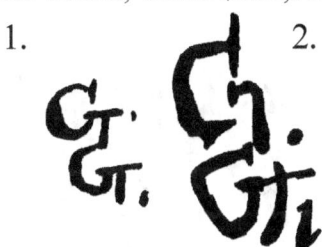

GIOVANNI GIACOMETTI 1868-1933
Swiss Painter, Landscape $100,000

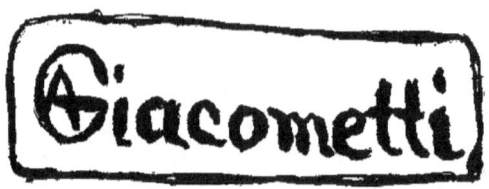

AUGUSTO GIACOMETTI 1877-1947
Swiss Religious, Landscape, Portraits $500,000

F. Giacomotti

FELIX HENRI GIACOMOTTI 1828-1909
French Painter, Genre $8,500

W.A. Gibson

WILLIAM ALFRED GIBSON 1866-1931
British Painter, Landscape $9,000

S.R. Gifford

SANFORD ROBINSON GIFFORD 1823-1880
American Luminist, Hudson River, Painter $500,000

C.N. Gysbrechts.

1.

Cornelius Gysbrechts

2.

CORNELIS NORBERTUS GIJSBRECHTS Circa 1600's
Netherlandish Still Life $3,500

P. GEYSEL

PEETER (also Pieter) GIJSELS 1621-1691
Netherlandish Still Life, Genre $30,000

1.
Victor Silbert

2.
Victor Silbert

VICTOR GILBERT 1847-1933
French Landscapes, Genre $200,000

Dennis Gilbert

DENNIS GILBERT 1922-
British Genre $1,000

GILES

CARL RONALD GILES 1916-
British Cartoonist $2,000

Tom Gilfillan

TOM GILFILLAN -1940
British Painter $1,500

SIR WILLIAM GEORGE GILLIES 1898-1973
British Painter, Genre, Landscape $25,000

1.

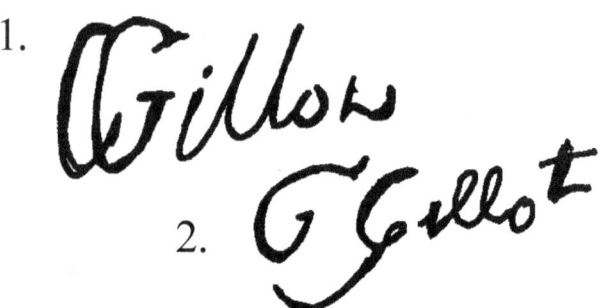

2.

CLAUDE GILLOT 1673-1722
French Genre, Portraits $50,000

GIACINTO GIMIGNANI 1611-1681
Italian Painter, Religious, Genre, Mythology $40,000

WILHELM GIMMI 1886-1965
Swiss Paris Streets, Landscape $20,000

FRANCESCO GIOLI 1846-1922
Italian Painter, Genre, Portraits $20,000

1. *L. Giordano*

2. *L. Giordano*

LUCA GIORDANO 1632-1705
Italian Painter, Religious, Genre, Allegory $100,000

FIRMIN · GIRARD

FIRMIN FRANCOIS (also Francis) GIRARD 1838-1921
French Genre, Landscape $120,000

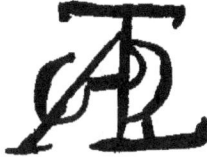

ANNE LOUIS GIRODET DE ROUSSY 1766-1824
French Portraits, Mythology, Landscape $300,000

E. Giroux

ERNEST GIROUX 1851-
French Portraits $25,000

A. Gisbert

ANTONIO GISBERT 1835-1901
Spanish Painter, Genre, Portraits $50,000

1.

2.

WILLIAM J. GLACKENS 1870-1938
American N.A. Ashcan School $600,000

P.P. LEON GLAIZE

PIERRE PAUL LEON GLAIZE 1842-1932
French Genre, Portraits $20,000

FRITZ GLARNER 1899-1972
American, Abstract $125,000

MARSHALL GLASIER 1902-
American Painter $1,000

HG

2.

1.

HG

HANS HEINRICH GLASER -1673
Swiss, Mythological Painter $5,000

W.M.G

WILLIAM MERVYN GLASS 1885-1965
British, Landscape $4,500

ALBERT GLEIZES

1.

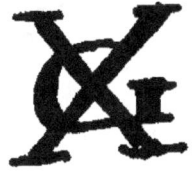

2.

3.

ALBERT GLEIZES 1881-1953
French Cubist, Landscape $650,000

FRANZ XAVIER GLINK 1795-1873
German Painter $1,000

EUG. GLUCK

LOUIS THEODORE EUGENE GLUCK 1820-1898
French Painter $2,000

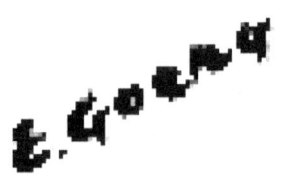

ÉDOUARD JOSEPH GOERG 1893-1969
$4380

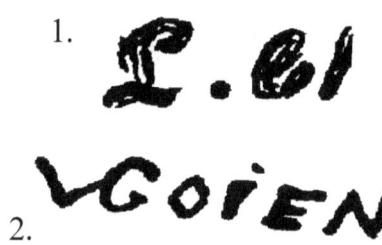

JAN VAN GOIJEN 1596-1656
Netherlandish Landscape $4,500

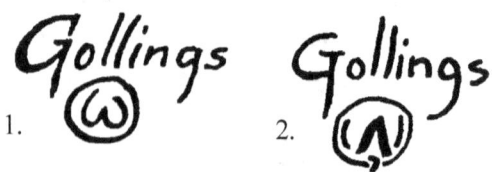

WILLIAM GOLLINGS 1878-1932
American Cowboys $8,500

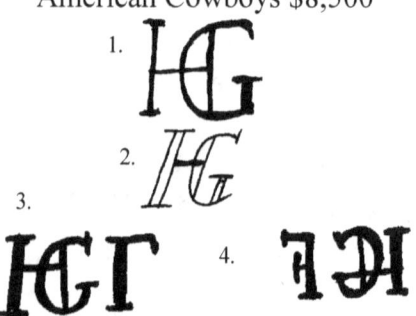

HENDRIK GOLTZIUS 1588-1617
Dutch Old Master, Allegory, Genre $1,500,000

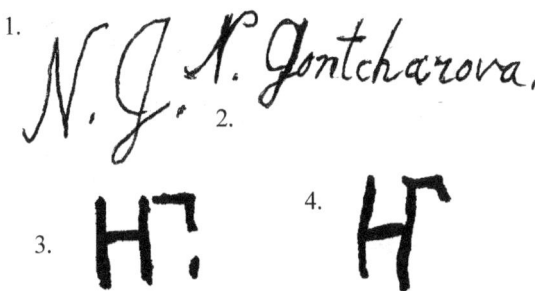

1.

2.

3.

4.

NATALIA (also Nathalie Sergeevna) GONTCHAROVA
1881-1962 Russian Abstract, Compositions $10,900,000

PEDRO ANGEL
GONZALEZ

PEDRO ANGEL GONZALEZ 1929-
Latin American Painter, Genre $1,000

1.

2.

JOHN STRICKLAND GOODALL 1908-
British, Seascapes, Genre $3,000

goodnough

ROBERT GOODNOUGH 1917-
American Abstract $7,500

Albert Goodwin

ALBERT GOODWIN
$6,000

1.

2.

ARTHUR CLIFTON GOODWIN 1866-1929
American Impressionist, Landscape $20,000

MICHELE GORDIGIANI 1835-1909
Italian Painter, Genre, Landscape $10,000

1.

2.

ARSHILLE (also Vosdanig Manoog Adoian) GORKY 1904-1948
American Abstract, Portraits, Compositions $3,962,500

AARON HENRY GORSON 1872-1933
American Painter, Portraits $30,000

1.

2.

FRIEDRICH KARL GOTSCH 1900-1984
German, Painter, Landscape, genre $45,000

LEOPOLD GOTTLIEB 1883-1930
Polish Painter, Genre $5,000

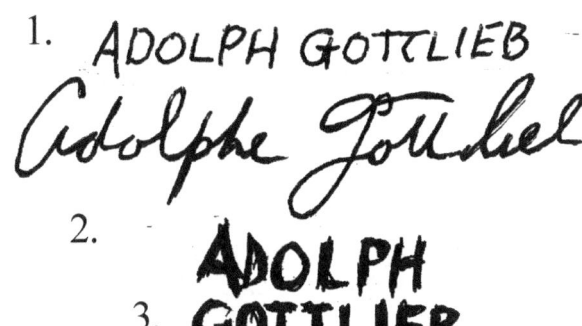

1. ADOLPH GOTTLIEB

Adolphe Gottlieb

2. **ADOLPH**

3. **GOTTLIEB**

ADOLPHE GOTTLIEB 1903-1974
American Abstract $150,000

R. Goubie

JEAN RICHARD GOUBIE 1842-1899
French, Painter, Genre, Landscape $70,000

1. *Jules Goupil*

2. *Jules Goupil*

JULES ADOLPHE GOUPIL 1839-1883
French Genre, Portraits $20,000

P. GourDault

PIERRE GOURDAULT 1880-1915
French, Landscapes $5,000

GOUVRANT

GERARD GOUVRANT 1946-
French Painter, Genre $20,000

JEAN LEAON HEMRI GOUWELOOS 1865-1943
Belgian Nudes, Genre $25,000

JAN VAN GOYEN (also Goijen) 1596-1656
Dutch Painter, Landscape, Genre $1,875,000

BENOZZO GOZZOLI 1424-1498
Italian Painter, Religious, Genre $325,000

COLIN GRAEME 1858-1910
British Painter, Landscape, Animals $10,000

URS GRAF 1485-1528
Swiss, Old Master, Genre $3,000

GRAHAM

JOHN GRAHAM 1890-1961
American, Painter, Portraits, Still Life $225,000

Peter Graham

PETER GRAHAM 1836-1921
British Watercolour, Landscape $15,000

D. Gran

DANIEL GRAN 1694-1757
German Painter, Religious $10,000

F Granacci

FRANCESCO (also Francisco) GRANACCI 1477-1543
Italian Painter, Religious, Genre $150,000

M.Grandi

ERCOLE DI GIULIO GRANDI 1462-1531
Italian Painter $2,000

L Graner

LUIS GRANER Y ARRUFI 1867-1929
Spanish Seascapes, Genre, Landscape $40,000

GRANET

FRANCOIS MARIUS GRANET 1775-1849
Italian Architectural, Landscape $60,000

C R GRANT

CLEMENT R. GRANT 1849-1893
American, Landscape $8,000

Grant

DUNCAN GRANT 1885-1978
British Landscape, Genre $50,000

1.   A GRASS-Mick 2.

AUGUSTIN GRASS-MICK 1873-1963
French Landscape $5,000

Jessie D Gray

JESSIE DIXON GRAY-1893
British Genre, Portraits $1,000

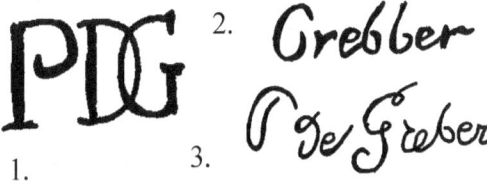

WALTER GREAVES 1841-1930
British Landscape $10,000

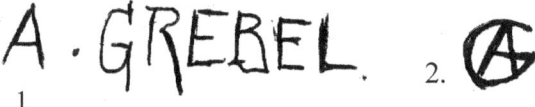

PIETER DE FRANZ (also Pieterz) GREBBER 1600-1665
Dutch Portraits, Religious $60,000

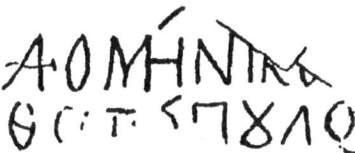

ALPHONSE GREBEL 1885-
American Painter $1,000

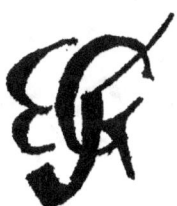

DOMENICO THEOTOCOPULI GRECO (El Greco) 1541-1614
Spanish Portraits $2,000,000

EDWARD JOHN GREGORY 1850-1909
British, R.A. Watercolour, Seascape $10,000

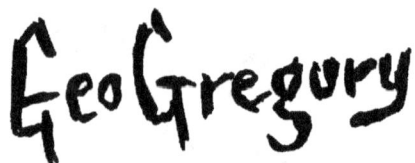

GEORGE GREGORY 1849-1938
British Seascapes $4,500

JEAN BAPTISTE GREUZE 1725-1805
French Genre, Portraits $450,000

HENRI PIERRE GREVEDON 1776-1860
French Portraits, Genre $3,500

HEINRICH ALDE GREVER 1502-1558
German Allegory $6,000

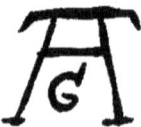

HANS BALDUNG GRIEN 1484-1545
German Old Master $150,000

ROBERT GRIFFIER 1688-1750
Dutch Seascape, Military Painter $25,000

1. *J GRIFFIER*

2. *J. GRIFFIER*

JAN GRIFFIER (the Elder) 1656-1718
Dutch Landscape, Genre $125,000

1. **WALTER GRIFFIN**

2. **GRIFIN**

WALTER GRIFFIN 1861-1935
American Impressionist $10,000

1. 2. *Boris Dugnuly Grigoriev*

BORIS D. GRIGORIEFF 1886-1939
Russian Painter, Genre, Landscape $12,000

grilley

ROBERT GRILLEY 1920-
American Genre $1,000

I.GRIMMER

HANS (also Johannes) GRIMMER 1500's
German Portraits $1,000

Atkinson Grimshaw

ATKINSON GRIMSHAW 1836-1893
British, Landscape, Portraits $70,000

1. *Juan Gris* 2. *Juan Gris*

3. *Juan Gris*

4. *Juan Gris* 5. *JS* 6. *JS*

JUAN GRIS 1887-1927
Spanish, painter, Genre $8,479,000

Ernest Griset

ERNEST HENRY GRISET 1844-1907
British Watercolour, Indians $5,000

Georges Croegaert

GEORGES GROEGAERT 1848-
German Painter $1,000

ADRIANUS JOHANNES GROENEWEGEN 1874-1963
Dutch, Landscape, Genre $2,000

MARCEL GROMAIRE 1892-1971
French Abstract $300,000

RED GROOMS 1937-
American Painter $65,000

WILLIAM GROPPER 1897-1977
American Painter, Genre $40,000

ANTOINE JEAN BARON GROS 1771-1835
French Portraits $600,000

RUDOLF GROSSMAN 1882-1941
German Painter, Genre $3,000

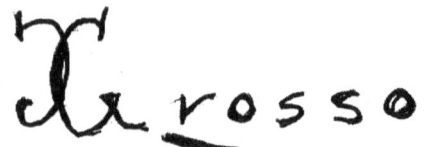

GIACOMO GROSSO 1860-1938
Italian, painter, Allegory $6,000

1.

GEORGE GROSZ 1893-1959
German Expressionist $150,000

2.

3.

JULES ALEXANDRE GRUN 1868-1934
French Painter, Allegory $25,000

ISAAC GRUNEWALD 1889-1946
Swedish Painter, Portraits, Landscape $65,000

ADRIAAN DE GRYEFF (also Grif, Grief) 1670-1715
Flemish Landscape, Still Life, Genre $20,000

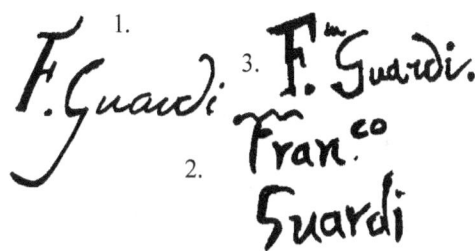

1.
3.
2.

FRANCESCO GUARDI 1712-1793
Italian Old Master, Landscape $13,943,000

GIOVANNI ANTINIO GUARDI 1698-1769
Italian, Genre, Portraits, Religious $160,000

1.

2.

MAX GUBLER 1898-1973
Swiss Landscape, Genre, $50,000

RALSTON GUDGEON 1910-1984
British Painter, Landscape $1,000

PIERRE NARCISSE GUERIN 1774-1833
French Genre, Religious $30,000

LOUIS GUGLIELMI 1906-1956
American, Abstract, genre $45,000

NICOLAS GUIBAL 1725-1784
French Painter, Portraits $1,500

1.

2.

RENI GUIDO 1575-1642
Italian Painter, Mythology, Portraits, Religious $2,000,000

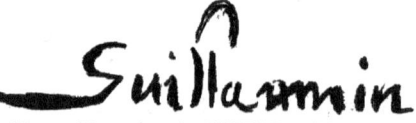

ARMAND (Jean Baptiste) GUILLAUMIN 1841-1927
French Painter, Genre, Landscape $200,000

F'.GUILMANT

FELIX GUILMANT 1800's
French, Painter, Genre $1,000

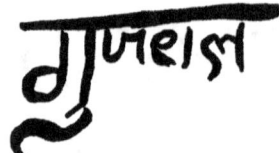

SATISH GUJRAL 1925-
India Architect, Painter, Abstract, Genre $4,000

HERBERT JAMES GUNN 1893-1964
British, Painter, Genre, Landscape $60,000

ROGER VON GUNTEN 1933-
Swiss Landscape $10,000

1.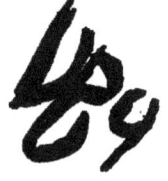

2.

PHILIP GUSTON 1913-1980
American Abstract $1,835,500

ALBERT PARIS GUTERSLOH 1887-1973
Austrian Landscape, Portrait, Still Life, Avant Garde $75,000

1.

2.

RENATO GUTTUSO 1912-1987
Italian Painter, Landscape, Genre $100,000

Artists starting with the letter "H"

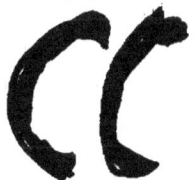

JEAN PAUL HAAG 1800's
French Genre, Portraits $7,000

CARL HAAG 1820-1915
Swedish Landscape, Genre $7,500

CORNELIS CORNELISZ VAN HAARLEM 1562-1638
Dutch Old Master $200,000

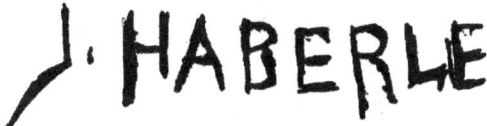

JOHN HABERLE 1856-1933
American, Humorous, Genre $450,000

HUGO VON HABERMANN 1849-1921
German Nudes, Landscape $4,000

1. **I· HACKAERT**

2.

JAN (also Joan) HACKAERT (also Hackert, Hakkert) 1628-1699
Netherlandish Landscapes, Genre, Portraits $25,000

ARTHUR HACKER 1858-1919
British, Landscape, Genre $25,000

JACOB PHILIPP HACKERT 1737-1807
German Seascape, Landscape $200,000

T, HADDON

ARTHUR TREVOR HADDON 1864-1941
British Arabians, Landscape $5,000

K Hagemeister

KARL HAGEMEISTER 1848-1933
German, Painter, Portraits, Landscape $10,000

1. *Hage*

2. *Hagen*

3. *H*

JORIS VAN DER HAGEN 1615-1669
Netherlandish Landscapes Castles $200,000

L. Haghe

LOUIS HAGHE
$4,000

Wm. Hahn

WILLIAM HAHN 1829-1887
American, Painter, Genre, Landscape $8,000

GEORG · HINZ.

GEORG HAINZ-1700
German Still Life, Portraits $40,000

G. H. Hall

GEORGE HENRY HALL 1825-1913
American N.A. Painter, Genre $40,000

HARRY HALL 1814-1882
British Sporting, Landscape $45,000

NOEL HALLE 1711-1781
French Painter, Religious, Allegory, Landscape $20,000

CLAUDE GUY HALLE 1652-1736
French Painter, Religious $5,000

ROBERT HALLOWELL 1886-1939
American, Illustrator, Seascape $2,500

1. 2. 3.

DIRCK HALS (also Dirk) 1591-1656
Netherlandish, Parties, Genre, Portraits, Landscape $175,000

1. 2.

FRANS HALS (elder) 1584-1666
Dutch Genre, Portraits $12,350,000

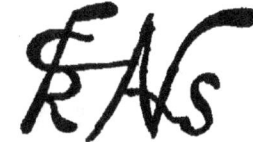

FRANS HALS (younger) 1617-1669
Dutch Genre, Still Life $12,000

ANDRE HAMBOURG 1909-
French Painter, Genre, Portraits $60,000

HAMILTON HAMILTON 1847-1928
American N.A. Landscape, Genre $10,000

JEAN LOUIS HAMON 1821-1874
French Genre $3,000

CHARLOTTE HAMPEL 1863-
German, Painter, Still Life $3,500

JOHANN HAMZA 1850-1927
German Painter $30,000

T. K. HANNA-

THOMAS KING HANNA 1872-1951
American Illustrator, Genre, Landscape $6,500

A.C. Hansen

ARMIN HANSEN 1886-1957
American, Landscape, Genre $30,000

H.W. HANSEN—

HERMAN W. HANSEN 1854-1924
American Cowboys, Genre $60,000

Hansen

KARL HEINZ HANSEN BAHIA 1915-1978
German Genre $1,000

S.H.

SIMON HANTAI 1922-
Hungarian Painter, Seascape $200,000

Harari

HANANIAH HARARI 1912-
American, Illustrator, Genre $1,000

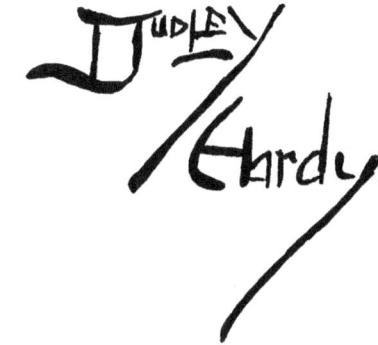

DUDLEY HARDY 1867-1922
British Portraits, Landscape $3,000

THOMAS BUSH HARDY 1842-1897
British Seascapes $7,500

1.

2.

JAMES HARDY JNR. 1832-1889
British Watercolour, Landscape, Genre $30,000

JOE HARGAN 1952-
Scottish Marines $2,000

KEITH HARING 1958-1990
American, Figures, Genre $150,000

ALEXEI HARLAMOFF 1848-1915
Russian Portraits, Landscape, Genre $300,000

LILY HARMON 1913-
American, Painter, Genre, $1,000

WILLIAM MICHAEL HARNETT 1851-1892
American Painter, Still Life, Genre $250,000

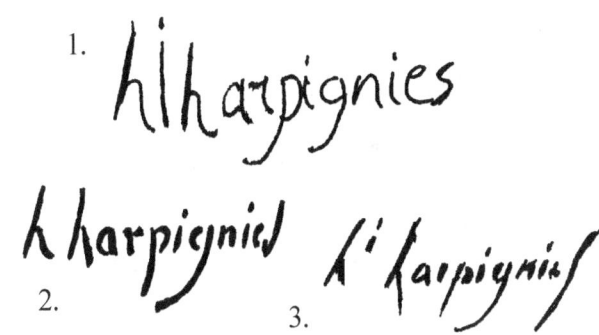

HENRI JOSEPH (also Henry) HARPIGNIES 1819-1916
French Landscape, Portraits $40,000

H. HARRIS

H. HARRIS 1900's
British Dogs $3,000

E Harris

EDWIN HARRIS 1855-1906
British Portraits, Genre $40,000

Birge Harrison.

LOWELL BIRGE HARRISON 1854-1929
American N.A. Landscape $20,000

J.C. Harrison   **J.C. Harrison**

JOHN CYRIL HARRISON 1898-1985
British, Landscape, Animals $10,000

KEVIN PRO HART 1928-
Australian Landscape, Genre $3,000

T. DYKE HART 1900's
British Marines $1,000

WILLIAM HART 1882-1901
British, Painter, Genre, Landscape $10,000

GRACE HARTIGAN 1921-
American Abstract, Genre $10,000

MARSDEN HARTLEY 1878-1943
American Impressionist $1,652,000

RACHEL HARTLEY 1884-
American Illustrator, Genre $7,500

HANS HARTUNG 1904-1989
French, Abstract $1,500,000

KARL HARTUNG 1908-1967
German, Painter, Abstract $3,000

G. Hartwick.

GUNTHER HARTWICK   -1857
American, Landscape $10,000

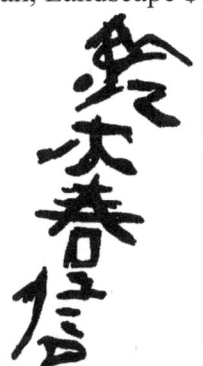

SUZUKI HARUNOBU 1725-1770
Japanese Woodblocks, Portraits $20,000

Harold Harvey

HAROLD HARVEY 1874-1941
British Painter, Genre $30,000

Marion Harvey

MARION RODGER HAMILTON HARVEY 1886-
British, Painter, Dogs $1,000

D. F. Hasbrouck-

DUBOIS FENELON HASBROUCK 1860-1934
American, Landscape, $4,000

Kiyoshi - Hasegawa

KIYOSHI HASEGAWA 1891-1980
Japanese, Painter, Landscape, Woodblocks $100,000

1
2.

Childe Hassam

CHILDE HASSAM 1859-1935
American A.N.A. Impressionist $20,000,000

John Hauser

JOHN HAUSER 1859-1913
American, Indians, Genre $20,000

VH Haudebout Lescot

HORTENSE VICTOIRE HAUDEBOUT-LESCOT 1784-1845
French Genre, Lithographer $25,000

HENRY A. HAWKINS

HENRY A. HAWKINS 1820-1881
British, Portraits, Animals $7,000

CW Hawthorne

CHARLES WEBSTER HAWTHORNE 1872-1930
American N.A. Impressionist $35,000

Hayden

HENRI HAYDEN 1883-1970
Polish Cubist, Genre $400,000

Hayet

LOUIS HAYET 1864-1940
French Landscape $150,000

P Hayden

PALMER COLE HAYDEN 1890-1973
American, Blacks, Harlem Renaissance, Genre $1000

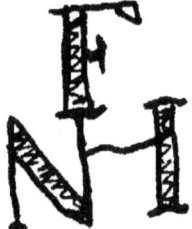

NICCOLO FRANCESCO HAYM 1688-1729
Italian, Painter

1.

2.

STANLEY WILLIAM HAYTER 1901-1989
British, Painter, Abstract $60,000

N. S. Haseltine

WILLIAM S. HAZELTINE 1835-1900
American N.A. Landscape $60,000

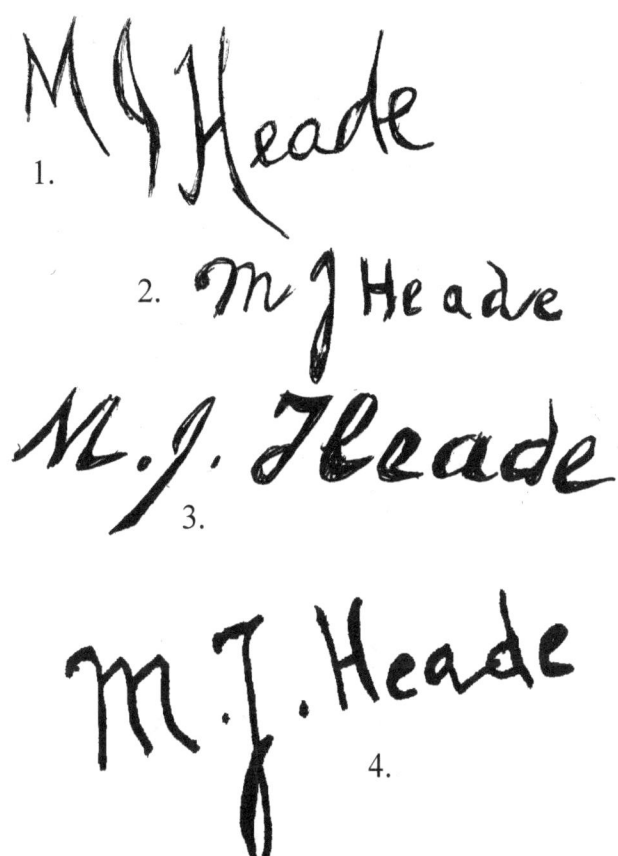

1.

2.

3.

4.

MARTIN JOHNSON HEADE 1819-1904
American, Floral, Landscape $2,000,000

ERNEST HEBERT 1817-1908
French Genre, Landscape, Religious, Portraits $75,000

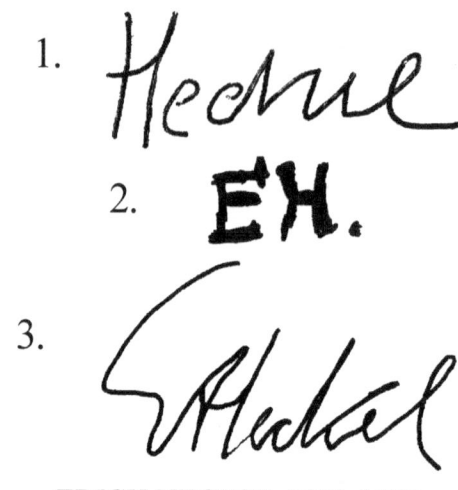

1.

2. **EH.**

3.

ERICH HECKEL 1883-1970
German Painter, Landscape, Portraits, Abstract $1,758,000

FRANZ HECKENDORF 1888-1962
German Landscape $15,000

CORNELIS DE HEEM 1631-1695
Dutch, Still Life, Florals $500,000

1.

2.

3.

4.

5.

JAN DAVIDSZ DE HEEM 1606-1684
Netherlandish Still Life $6,000,000

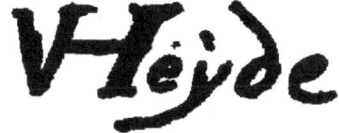

EGBERT VAN HEEMSKERCK 1635-1704
Netherlandish Genre, Portraits $45,000

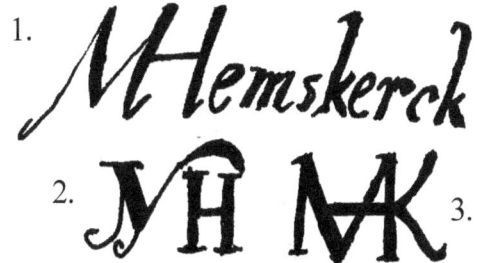

1.

2.   3.

MARTEN VAN HEEMSKERK 1498-1574
Dutch Painter, Allegory, Religious $600,000

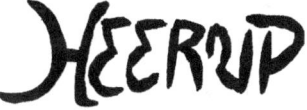

HENRY HEERUP 1907-
Danish Abstract, Allegory $150,000

JAN VAN DER HEIJDEN 1637-1712
Netherlandish Architecture, Old Master, Landscape, Genre

FRANCOIS JOSEPH HEIM 1787-1865
French, Painter, Genre $15,000

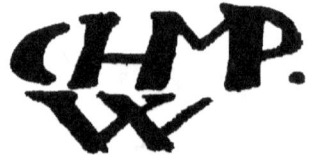

WOLFGANG HEIMBACH 1615-1678
German Genre $100,000

Th. Th Heine

THOMAS THEODOR HEINE 1867-1948
German, Illustrator, Genre $30,000

ĐE

JOSEPH also Josef) HEINZ (also Heintz) 1565-1609
German PainterPortraits, Allegory, Religious $200,000

1.
2. HELIKER

JOHN EDWARD HELIKER 1909-
American Abstract $2,500

JEAN HELION 1904-1987
French Abstract $550,000

Johan van Hell

JOHAN VAN HELL 1889-1952
Dutch, Seascape, Genre $20,000

1. *MVH*

2. *He Hemont*

3. *MVHESSemont*

MATTHEUS VAN HELLEMONT 1623-1674
Flemish Genre, Landscape, Religious $20,000

Helleu

PAUL CESAR HELLEU 1859-1927
French Painter, Portraits, Landfscape $500,000

R.Hellwag

RUDOLF HELLWAG 1866-1942
German Landscape, Genre $4,500

Bartholomeus Van der

1. *Helst* 2. *B.pvander helst*

3. *B.Van der helst*

4. *Van der Helst*

BARTHOLOMEUS VAN DER HELST 1613-1670
Netherlandish Portraits $200,000

HH

JAN VAN (Jan Sanders) HEMISSEN 1500-1566
Flemish Portraits, Genre, Portraits, Religious $300,000

JHenderson

JOSEPH HENDERSON 1832-1908
British Landscape, Genre $10,000

Hennequin

PHILIPPE AUGUSTE HENNEQUIN 1763-1833
French Genre, Mythology $16,000

1. *JJHENNER*

2. *II HENNER*

JEAN JACQUES HENNER 1829-1905
French Painter, Nudes, Landscape, Genre $30,000

E. Martin Hennings

ERNEST MARTIN HENNINGS 1886-1956
American, Landscape, Genre $40,000

ROBERT HENRI

ROBERT HENRI 1865-1929
American N.A. Ashcan $500,000

F. Henri

FLORENCE HENRI 1893-
American Painter $4,000

D.M.HENRY

DAVID MORRISON REID HENRY Circa 1900's
British, Seascape $2,500

E·L·Henry

EDWARD LAMSON HENRY 1841-1919
American Landscape, Genre $50,000

Barbara Hepworth

BARBARA HEPWORTH 1903-1975
British Abstract Sculptor $2,600,000

herbin

AUGUSTE HERBIN 1882-1960
American Cubist $475,000

hèrbt

ADOLF HERBST 1909-1983
Swiss, Painter, Genre $12,000

Herkenrath

PETER HERKENRATH 1900-
German, Painter, Portraits $8,000

HH

HUBERT HERKOMER 1849-1914
German Genre, Landscape, Portraits $15,000

D. Hernandez

DANIEL HERNANDEZ 1856-1932
Peruvian Genre, Portraits $25,000

S. Herran

SATURNINO HERRAN 1887-1918
Mexican, Painter, Genre $10,000

G·V·HERP

GUILLIAM VAN HERP 1614-1677
Flemish Genre, Religious $30,000

f Mevrera

FRANCESCO DE HERRERA (The Younger) 1622-1685
Spanish Painter, Genre $1,500

J.F.Herring

JOHN FREDERICK HERRING JNR. 1815-1907
British Sporting, Landscape, Genre $60,000

J.F.Herring

JOHN FREDERICK HERRING SNR. 1795-1865
British Animals, Landscape $2,250,000

Ch.Herrmann Léon

CHARLES HERRMANN-LEON 1838-1908
French, Genre, Portraits $8,500

L Hersent

LOUIS HERSENT 1777-1860
French Portraits $20,000

Jules R. Herve

JULES HERVE 1887-1981
French, Paris, Streets, Genre $20,000

H

JOHANN MICHAEL HESS 1768-1830
Hungarian Painter $2,000

PHILIPP FRIEDRICH VON HETSCH 1758-1839
German Painter, Allegory, Portraits $5,500

WILLEM DE HEUSCH 1625-1692
Netherlandish Landscapes, Genre $25,000

JACOB DE HEUSCH 1657-1701
Dutch Landscape, Genre $70,000

OTTO HEYDEN 1820-1897
German Painter $30,000

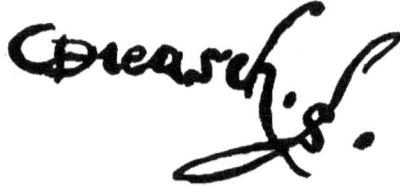

JAN VAN DER HEYDEN (also Heijde) 1637-1712
Dutch Landscape, Architectural, Genre $700,000

1. **HEYER·A**

HEYER A. 2.

ARTHUR HEYER 1872-1931
German Animals, Genre, Landscape $10,000

J Heyerdahl

HANS OLAF HEYERDAHL 1857-1913
Norway Painter, Landscape $75,000

HANS HEYSEN

SIR HANS HEYSEN 1876-1968
Australian Landscape, Genre $150,000

A.T. Hibbard

ALDRO T. HIBBARD 1886-1972
American N.A. Seascape, Landscape $15,000

J. Hickel

JOSEF HICKEL (also Hickl) 1736-1807
German Portraits, Genre $10,000

1. **VICTOR HIGGINS—**

2. **VICTOR HIGGINS—**

VICTOR HIGGINS 1884-1949
American N.A. Painter, Genre, Landscape $25,000

1. 2. 3.

THEODORE HILDEBRANDT 1804-1874
German, Genre, Portraits

THOMAS HILL 1829-1908
American Rocky Mountain School, Landscape $70,000

TRISTRAM HILLIER 1905-1983
British Landscape, Still Life $60,000

LAURA COOMBS HILLS 1859-1952
American Painter, Still Life, Portraits $25,000

ANNA HILLS 1882-1930
American Landscape $4,000

THOMAS HEWES HINCKLEY 1813-1896
German Sporting, Landscape $15,000

1.

Clarence Hinkle

2. **HINKLE**

CLARENCE HINKLE 1880-1960
American, Plein Aire, California, Landscape $20,000

HINSBERGER

ALEXIS HINSBERGER 1907-
French Painter, Genre $10,000

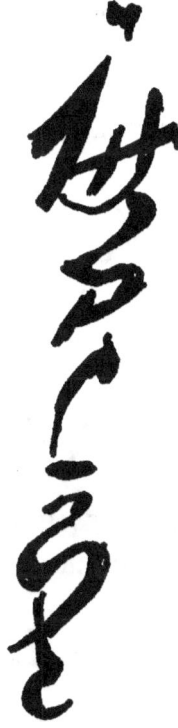

(Ando) I UTAGAWA HIROSHIGE 1797-1858
Japanese Woodblocks, Landscape $450,000

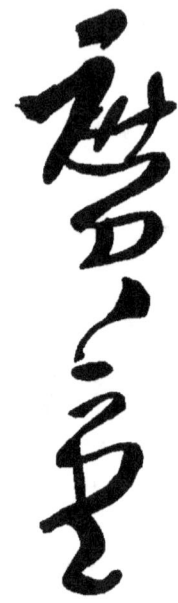

II UTAGAWA HIRONOBU HIROSHIGE 1829-1896
Japanese Woodblocks, Landscape $3,000

JOSEPH HIRSCH 1910-1981
American Realist, Genre $15,000

CLAUDE RAQUET HIRST 1855-1942
American Painter $40,000

GEORGE HITCHCOCK 1850-1913
American, A.N.A., Illustrator, Genre, Landscape $60,000

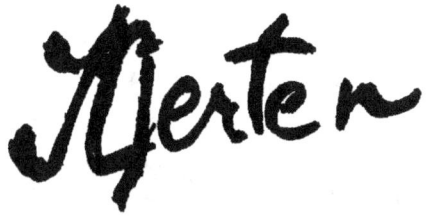

SIGRID HJERTEN 1885-1948
Swedish Painter, Genre, Landscape $100,000

1. 2.

3.

MEINDERT (also Meyndert, MinderHout) HOBBEMA 1638-1709
Netherlandish Landscape, Animals $9,200,000

GEORGE THOMPSON HOBBS 1946-
American, Painter, Landscape, Still Life $5,000

PIERRE HODE 1889-1942
French Cubist, Landscape $100,000

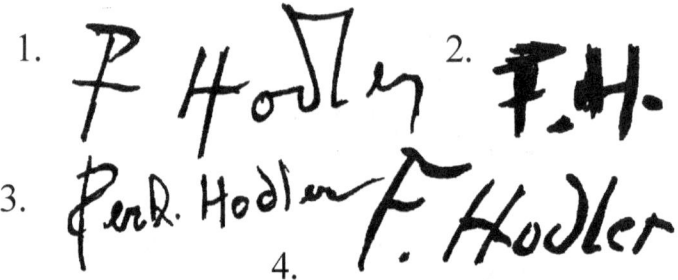

FERDINAND HODLER 1853-1918
Swiss, Landscape, Genre $2,125,000

ARTHUR HOEBER

ARTHUR HOEBER 1854-1915
American, A.N.A., Allegory, Landscape $6,500

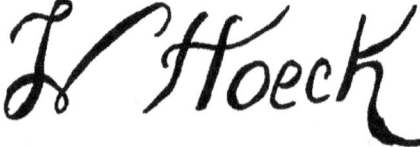

JAN VAN DEN HOECKE 1611-1651
Flemish Portraits, Allegory, Landscape $80,000

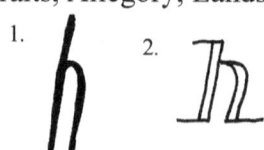

HEINRICH HOERLE 1895-1936
German Painter, Portraits, Still Life $9,500

G. Hoet

GERARD HOET (also Hoedt) 1648-1733
Dutch Painter, Mythology, Genre, Portraits $40,000

1. 2.

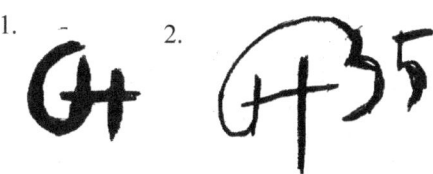

KARL HOFER 1878-1955
German Painter, Genre, Landscape, Expressionist $80,000

Höfer

HEINRICH HOFER 1825-1878
German Landscape $25,000

1.

2.   3.

JOSEF HOFFMAN 1870-1956
Austrian Secessionist, Designer, Abstract $6,000

1.

2.

HANS HOFFMANN 1880-1966
American Abstract $600,000

Hoffnung

GERARD HOFFNUNG 1925-1959
British Illustration $2,000

_W. M._

WILLIAM HOGARTH 1697-1764
British Portraits, Genre, Engraver $600,000

Alexandre Hogue

ALEXANDRE HOGUE 1898-1992
American Painter, Landscape $15,000

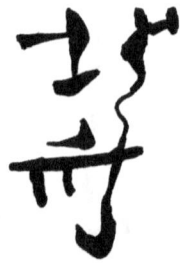

KATSUSHIKA HOKUSAI 1760-1849
Japanese, Woodblocks $150,000

1. *H H*

2. **HH** *ĦĦ*

4. *HANZ HOLB*

5. **H H**

HANS HOLBEIN (Younger) 1497-1543
German Portraits, Allegory, Religious, Genre $2,000,000

AHOLD

ABEL HOLD -1850
British Still Life, Landscape $3,500

R.G. Holdredge

RANSOME G. HOLDREDGE 1836-1899
American Indians $5,000

EDWIN HEADLEY HOLGATE 1892-1977
Canadian Painter, Landscape, Genre $20,000

A. Hollaender

ALFONSO HOLLAENDER 1845-1923
Italian Painter, Genre, Allegory $7,000

289

C Holsöe

CARL WILHELM HOLSOE 1863-1935
Danish Landscape, Genre $100,000

1.   2.

PH PH

CORNELIS HOLSTYN 1618-1658
Dutch, Landscape, Mythology $5,000

Holty

CARL HOLTY 1900-1973
American, Abstract $6,500

A.Holy

ADRIEN HOLY 1898-1978
French, Painter, Landscape, Still Life $4,000

1. *W H*   2. *WH*

3. *W.Homer*   4. *W.H.*

WINSLOW HOMER 1836-1910
American N.A. Impressionist $36,000,000

1. *MDH*

2. *M D Hondecoeter*

3. *M.D. Hundekoeter*

MELCHIOR D. HONDECOETER 1636-1695
Dutch Animal Painter, Still Life $275,000

1. *AEG*

2. *Arakam Hundius*

ABRAHAM HONDIUS 1625-1695
Dutch Animals, Portraits, Mythology $125,000

horst

WILLEM VAN HONTHORST 1594-1666
Netherlandish Portraits, Genre, Mythology $15,000

1. *Honthorst* 2. *GH*

3. *GHonDHorst*

GERARD Van (also Gerrit) HONTHORST 1590-1656
Netherlandish Genre (Candle Light) $350,000

1. *DH* 2. *PDH* 3. *L Hooch*

P.D.HOOGH

PIETER DE HOOCH (also Hoogh) 1629-1684
Netherlandish Genre, Portraits $300,000

HORATIUS DE HOOCH (also Hoogh)-1686
Netherlandish Landscapes, Portraits $10,000

BERNARD DE HOOG 1867-1943
Dutch, Painter, Genre $20,000

1. 2.

SAMUEL VAN HOOGSTRATEN 1627-1678
Dutch Portraits, Religious $200,000

R-HOPE-

OBERT HOPE 1869-1936
British Painter, Landscape, Genre $4,000

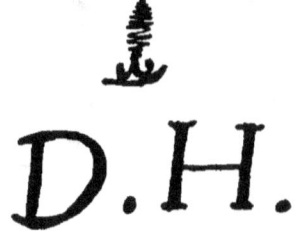

D.H.

DANIEL HOPFER -1537
Dutch Old Master $5,000

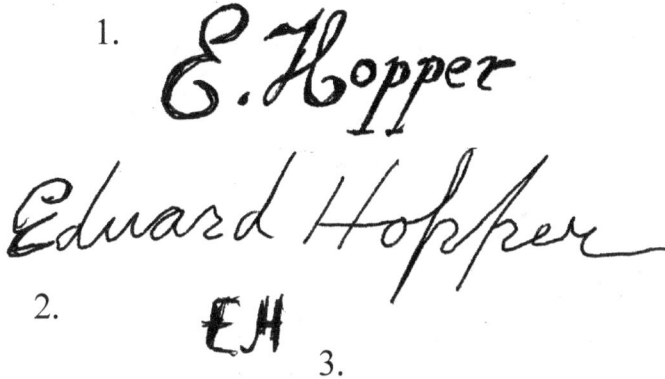

1.

2.

3.

4.

EDWARD HOPPER 1882-1967
American, Illustrator, Landscape, Genre $26,800,000

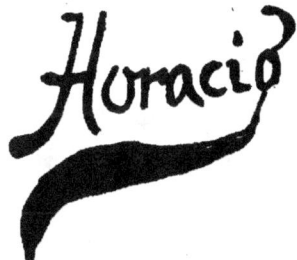

HORACIO 1912-1972
Mexican Painter, Genre $8,000

1.

2.

JAN JOZEF (also Josef) HOREMANS 1682-1759
Flemish Genre, Allegory $200,000

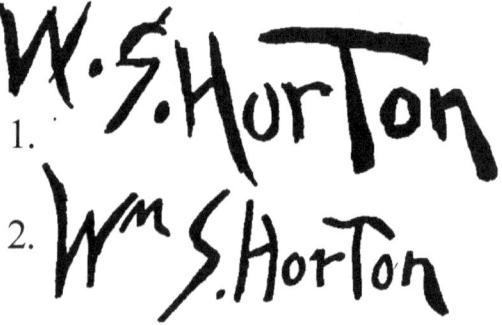

EDWARD ATKINSON HORNEL 1864-1933
Australian Painter, Landscape, Genre $80,000

WILLIAM S. HORTON 1865-1936
American, Landscape$100,000

KARL HOSCH 1900-1972
German Painter, Genre, Landscape $8,000

MICHEL ANGE HOUASSE (also Ouasse) 1680-1730
French Landscape, Portraits, Mythology $30,000

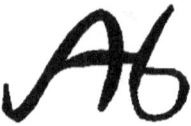

ARNOLD HOUBRAKEN 1660-1719
Dutch Painter, Mythology, Religious, Genre $6,000

1. 2.

GH GH

GERARD HOUCKGEEST 1600-1661
Netherlandish Architectural Interiors $15,000

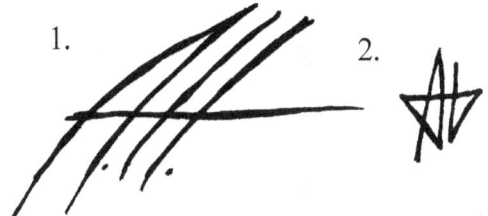

1. 2.

ANDRE HOUDIAKOFF 1900's
European, Stage, Costume Design $4,000

GEORGE HOUSTON

GEORGE HOUSTON 1869-1947
British R.S.A. Watercolour, Landscape $20,000

Ken Howard

KEN HOWARD 1932-
British City Scenes, Portraits, Landscape $6,500

A. C. Howland

ALFRED CORNELIUS HOWLAND 1838-1909
American Landscape, Genre $1,500

J. HRYNKOWSKI

JAN HRYNKOWSKI 1891-1971
Polish Landscape $1,000

H.S.Hubbell—

HENRY SALEM HUBBELL 1870-1949
American A.N.A. Illustrator, Genre $10,000

1.   2.

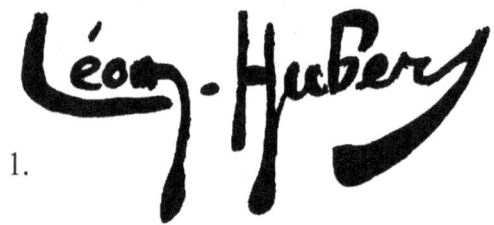

KARL HUBBUCH 1891-1980
German, Painter, Portrait, Genre $15,000

1.

2.

LEON CHARLES HUBER 1858-1928
French Floral, Genre, Still Life $12,000

RUDOLF JOHANN HUBER 1668-1748
Italian Portraits, Landscape, Animals $10,000

1.

2.

3.

JAN VAN HUCHTENBURGH 1647-1733
Netherlandish Genre Street Scenes $25,000

JACOB VAN HUCHTENBURGH 1640-1675
Netherlandish Landscapes, Genre, Portraits $50,000

GRACE CARPENTER HUDSON 1865-1937
American, Illustrator, Landscape, Painter $40,000

THOMAS HUDSON 1701-1779
British Portraits $50,000

1.

2.

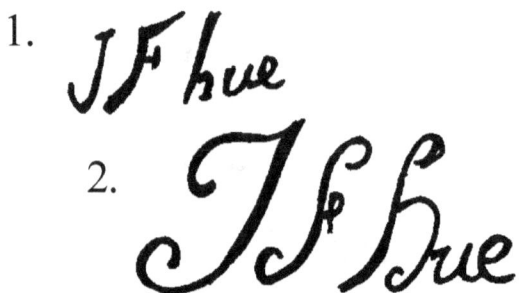

JEAN FRANCOIS HUE 1751-1823
French Seascape, Genre, Landscape $15,000

1.   2.

JEAN BAPTISTE HUET 1745-1811
French Landscape, Animal Painter $200,000

WIILIAM HUGHES 1842-1901
British, Painter, Still Life $12,000

JAN VAN HUGHTENBURGH 1646-1733
Dutch Battle Painter, Genre $15,000

1.

2.

VICTOR HUGO 1802-1885
French Watercolour Abstract, Landscape, Genre $90,000

VICTOR PIERRE HUGUET 1835-1902
French Arabians, Genre $50,000

JAN VAN HUIJSUM 1682-1749
Netherlandish Landscape Still Life, Old Master $6,029,000

ABRAHAM HULK JR. 1850-1922
British Landscape $10,000

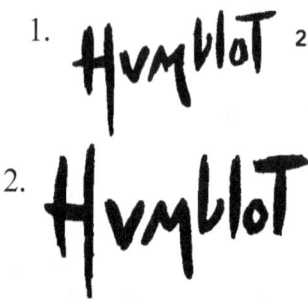

1. 2.

2.

ROBERT HUMBLOT 1907-1962
French Landscape $20,000

THOMAS HUNT 1854-1929
British Watercolour, Landscape $10,000

1. 2.

CHARLES HUNT -1890
British Sporting $5,000

EDGAR HUNT 1876-1953
British Animals $55,000

WALTER HUNT 1861-1941
British, Landscape, Genre $25,000

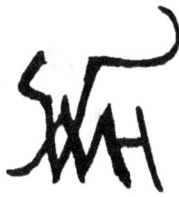

WILLIAM MORRIS HUNT 1824-1879
American Landscape $50,000

EMIL HUNTEN 1827-1902
German, Painter, Genre. Landscape $10,000

COLIN HUNTER 1841-1904
British, Etcher, Painter, Landscape $10,000

CHARLES HUTIN 1715-1776
French, Genre

DANIEL HUNTINGTON 1816-1906
American Landscape, Genre $25,000

PETER HURD 1904-1984
American N.A. Illustrator, Landscape $45,000

Louis B. Hurt

LOUIS BOSWORTH HURT 1856-1929
British, Landscape $125,000

1. 2. 3.

MAQBOOL FIDA HUSAIN 1915-
India Modern, Landscape $35,000

V. HUSZAR

VILMOS HUSZAR 1884-1960
Hungarian, Landscape, Still Life $10,000

- F T HUTCHENS -

FRANK TOWNSEND HUTCHENS 1869-1937
American, landscape, Genre $7,500

1. R G Hutchison

2. Gemmell Hutchison

ROBERT GEMMELL HUTCHISON 1855-1936
British Painter, Genre $40,000

CHARLES F. HUTIN 1715-1776
French Genre $40,000

THOMAS SWIFT HUTTON 1875-1935
British Landscape $2,000

1.

2.

JAN VAN HUYSUM 1682-1749
Dutch Still Life, Landscape, Genre $3,000,000

Artists starting with the letter "I"

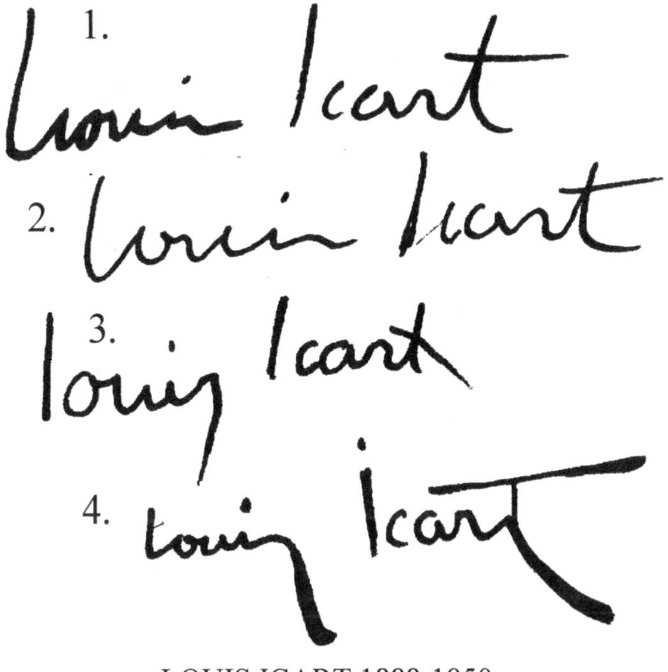

1.

Louis Icart

2.

Louis Icart

3.

louis Icart

4.

Louis Icart

LOUIS ICART 1888-1950
American Allegory $375,000

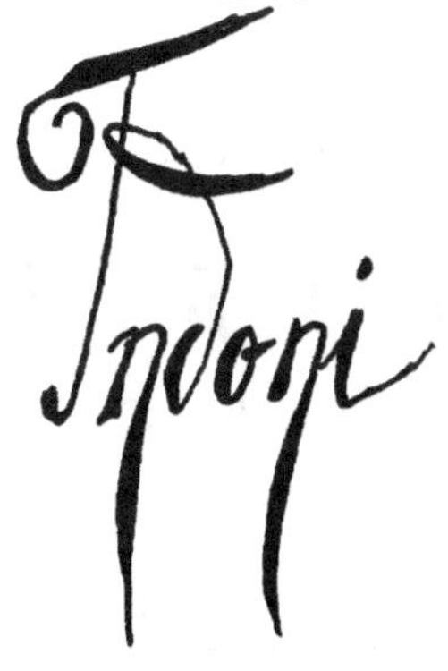

Indoni

FILIPO INDONI 1800's
Italian Painter, Landscape, Genre $15,000

G. Induno

GIROLAMO INDONI 1800's
Italian, Painter, Landscape, Genre $15,000

1. INCRES

2. *Ingres*

3. *J. Ingres*

4. INGRES

5. *Ingres*

JEAN AUGUSTE DOMINIQUE INGRES 1780-1867
French Painter, Portrait $2,000,000

H. INMAN

HENRY INMAN 1801-1846
American, Illustrator, Indians, Landscape $10,000

G. Inness

GEORGE INNESS 1825-1894
American Landscape $150,000

V. Irolli

VINCENZO IROLLI 1860-1949
Italian, Painter, Genre $100,000

I RVINE

WILSON HENRY IRVINE 1869-1934
American, A.N.A.,Genre, Landscape, Lyme Painter $50,000

Isaac Isaacs

ISAAC ISAACSZ 1599-1665
Netherlandish Allegorical $6,000

J. Isabey

JEAN BAPTISTE ISABEY 1767-1855
French Miniature Painter, Religious $60,000

Israel

DANIEL ISRAEL 1858-1901
Austrian Genre $40,000

Isaac Isaacs

ISAAC ISRAELS 1865-1934
Dutch, Painter, Genre $200,000

1. *[signature: Josef Israels]*

2. *[signature: Jos/Israels]*

JOSEF ISRAELS 1824-1911
Dutch Landscape, Genre, Seascape $40,000

[signature: Itaya]

FOUSSA ITAYA 1919-
French, Animals, Genre $3,500

[signature: M. Izquierdo]

MARIA IZQUIERDO 1906-1955
Mexican, Painter, Portraits, Landscape $120,000

Artists starting with the letter "J"

AY JACKSON

ALEXANDER YOUNG JACKSON 1882-1974
Canadian Painter, Landscape $100,000

Max Jacob

MAX CYPRIEN JACOB 1876-1944
French Painter, Genre, Landscape $7,500

A. Jacobs

ADOLPHE JACOBS 1887-1910
German, Landscape, Genre $50,000

J. Jacobs

JURIAEN JACOBSZ 1625-1685
Netherlandish Hunting, Genre $2,500

Paul Jacoulet

PAUL JACOULET 1902-1960
French Watercolour $35,000

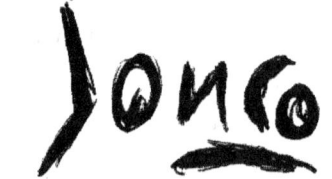

1.

2.

CHARLES EMILE JACQUE 1813-1894
French Landscape, Barbizon, Genre, Animal Painter $30,000

MARCEL JANCO 1895-1984
Rumanian Painter, Genre $40,000

JEAN JANSEM 1920-
Armenian Painter, Genre $100,000

VICTOR HONORE JANSSENS 1664-1739
Flemish Painter, Religious, Landscape, Allegory $5,000

1. K DU.JARDIN

2. K DV. JARDIN

KAREL DU JARDIN 1625-1678
Dutch Animal, Landscape Painter $500,000

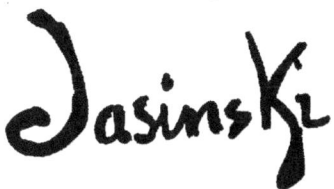

JOSE MARIA JARDINES 1862-
Spaniah, Painter, Landscape, Genre $10,000

Jasinski

ZDZISLAW JASINSKI 1862-1932
Polish Painter, Genre $2,500

1. E Jeaurat

2. E Jeaurat

ETIENNE JEAURAT 1699-1789
French Genre, Religious, Landscape $30,000

ALEXEJ JAWLENSKY 1864-1941
Russian, Painter, Abstract Expressionist $600,000

VLADIMIR IVANOVICH JEDRINSKY 1900's
Russian Stage Costume Design $1,000

JOHANN LAURENTS JENSEN 1800-1856
Danish, Still Life, Portraits $400,000

FLORIS JESPERS 1889-1965
Belgian Painter, Genre, Landscape $160,000

LUIS JIMENEZ Y ARANDA 1845-1928
Spanish Painter, Genre $800,000

L JIRLOW

LENNART JIRLOW 1936-
Swedish Painter, Genre, Landscape, Portraits $45,000

John

AUGUSTUS JOHN 1878-1961
British, R.A. Painter, Genre, Landscape $50,000

Gwen John

GWEN JOHN 1876-1939
British Painter, Genre $300,000

JASPER JOHNS 1930-
American Abstract Contemporary $80,000,000

David Johnson **D.J**

1.

2.

D

DAVID JOHNSON 1827-1908
American N.A. Landscape $200,000

E. Johnson

EASTMAN JOHNSON 1824-1906
American, Painter, Genre $90,000

E.K. Johnson

E. KILLINGWORTH JOHNSON 1825-1896
British R.W.S. Landscape, Genre $15,000

MARSHALL JOHNSON

MARSHALL JOHNSON 1915-
American Seascape $5,000

Robert Johnson

ROBERT JOHNSON 1890-1964
Australian Landscape $15,000

Frans H. Johnston

FRANS H. JOHNSTON 1888-1948
Canadian, Landscape $15,000

J. Johnston

JOHN JOHNSTON 1753-1818
American Painter, Genre $2,000

H BOLTON JONES

HUGH BOLTON JONES 1848-1927
American, N.A., Landscape $30,000

JOE JONES 1909-1963
American Painter, Still Life, Seascape $60,000

f . de . jongh

FRANS DE JONG-1705
Netherlandish Dragons Allegorical $5,000

1.

2.

LUDOLF DE JONGE 1616-1697
Dutch Genre, Portraits, Landscape $17,000

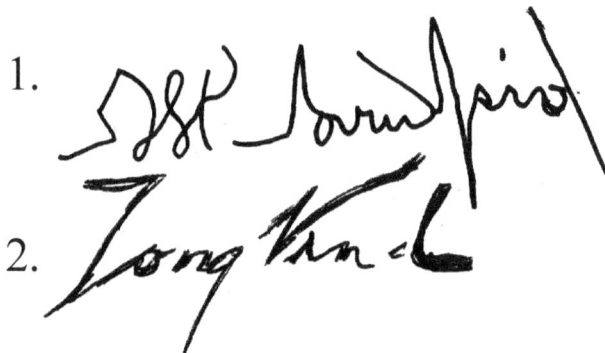

JOHAN BARTOLD JONGKIND 1819-1891
Dutch, Impressionist, Landscape $170,000

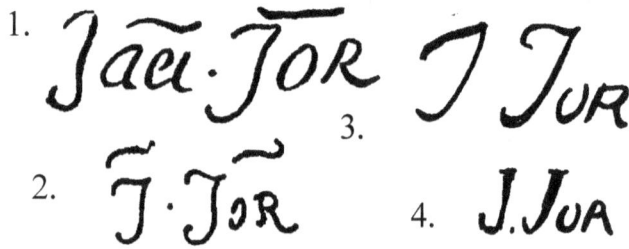

JACOB JORDAENS 1593-1678
Netherlandish Allegorical Religious, Genre $300,000

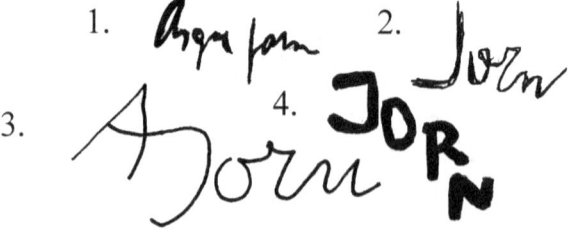

ASGER OLUF JORGENSEN JORN 1914-1973
Danish Abstract, $300,000

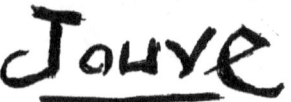

PAUL PIERRE JOUVE 1880-1973
French Illustrator, Animals, Landscape $75,000

1. *Jouvenet*

2. *Jouvenet*

JEAN JOUVENET 1644-1717
French Painter, Genre, Portraits $2,500

Mervin Jules

MERVIN JULES 1912-
American Painter, Genre $1,500

Jul Jungheim

JULIUS JUNGHEIM 1876-1957
German Painter, Genre, Landscape $2,500

*L·H
JVNCNICKEL*

LUDWIG HEINRICH JUNKNICKEL 1881-1965
German Landscape, Portraits, Seascape $15,000

Artists starting with the letter "K"

1. **KÁDÁR BÉLA**
2. **KÁDÁR BELA**

BELA KADAR 1877-1956
Hungarian, Cubism, Genre, Landscape $20,000

F.H KAEMMERER

FREDERIK HENDRIK KAEMMERER 1839-1902
French Landscape, Genre, Portraits $75,000

Carl Kahler

CARL KAHLER 1855-
Austrian Landscape, Genre $15,000

Frida Kahlo

FRIDA KAHLO 1910-1954
Mexican, Painter, Genre, Still Life $5,616,000

W Kahn

WOLF KAHN 1927-
American Landscape $15,000

1. WKALF
2. WKalf   3. W.KALF

WILLEM KALF 1622-1693
Dutch Old Master, Genre, Still Life $40,000

AKallenberg

ANDERS KALLENBERG 1834-1902
Swedish Landscape $5,000

Kamrowski

GEROME KAMROWSKI 1914-
American, Modernist, Abstract $1,000

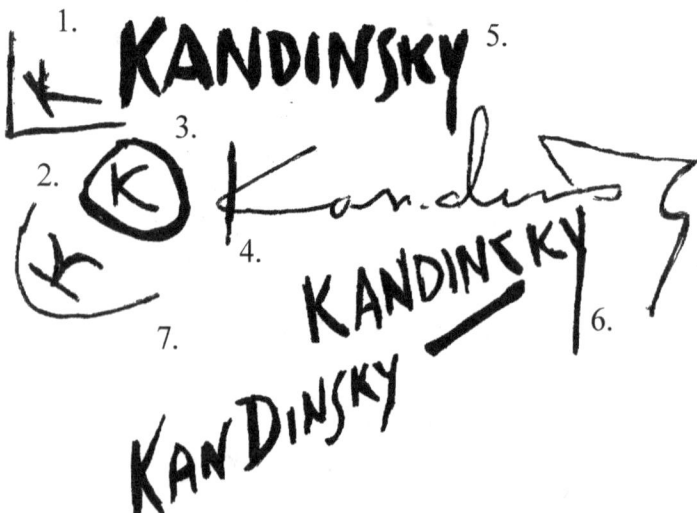

WASSILY KANDINSKY 1866-1944
Russian, Blau Reiter, German Expressionist $40,000,000

JOHN KANE 1860-1934
American, Landscape $15,000

ALEXANDER KANOLDT 1881-1939
German, Painter, Landscape, Still Life $25,000

MORRIS KANTOR 1896-1974
American Abstract, Landscape $5,500

MADHOOR KAPUR 1947-
India Modern $9,000

BERNARD KARFIOL 1886-1952
American, Painter, Landscape, Genre $8,500

LUDWIG KARSTEN 1876-1926
Norway Impressionist, Genre $150,000

MANE-KATZ 1. 2. M.K.

MANE- KATZ 1894-1962
American Painter, Genre $35,000

Hugo Kauffmann

HUGO KAUFFMANN 1844-1915
German Painter, Genre, Portraits $90,000

AK

ANGELLICA KAUFFMANN 1741-1807
Swiss Painter, Mythology, Genre, Portraits $40,000

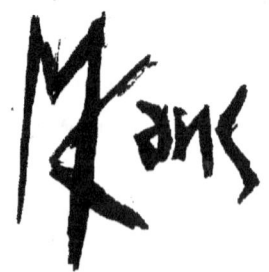

MAX KAUS 1890-1972
German Landscape $30,000

James Kay

JAMES KAY 1858-1942
British, Landscape, Seascape $30,000

OTIS KAYE 1885-1974
American, Genre $35,000

HILDE KAYN 1903-1950
American Painter, Genre, Landscape $3,000

CHARLES KEENE 1823-1891
British Illustrator Cartoonist $1,500

ALEXANDER KEIRINCX 1600-1652
Netherlandish Landscapes, Genre $100,000

WILLIAM KEITH 1839-1911
American Rocky Mountain School, Landscape $25,000

Toon Kelder

TOON KELDER 1894-1973
Dutch, Painter, Genre, Landscape $7,000

FERDINAND KELLER

FERDINAND KELLER 1842-1922
German, Allegory, Landscape, Genre $15,000

Kelly

SIR GERALD KELLY 1879-1972
British, P.R.A., R.H.A., H.R.S.A., Portraits, Landscape $10,000

P. KELPE

PAUL KELPE 1902-1985
American Abstract $35,000

Kemble

EDWARD WINDSOR KEMBLE 1861-1933
British Illustrator, Genre, Blacks $4,500

J.F.K

JOHN FREDERICK KENSETT 1816-1872
American, Hudson River, Landscape $1,248,000

ROCKWELL KENT 1882-1971
American, A.N.A., Illustrator, Genre, Landscape $45,000

JESSIE KEPPIE-1951
British Painter $2,500

IDA KERKOVIUS 1879-1970
German Abstract, Landscape $20,000

FERDINAND VAN KESSEL 1648-1696
Flemish Landscape, Animal, Still Life $30,000

JAN VAN KESSEL 1626-1679
Flemish Still Life, Floral, Animal Painter $500,000

1. 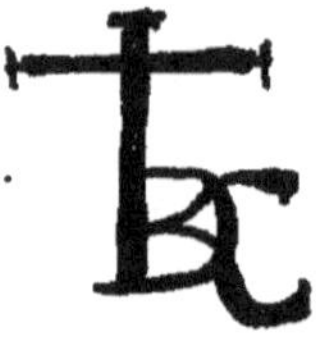

2. 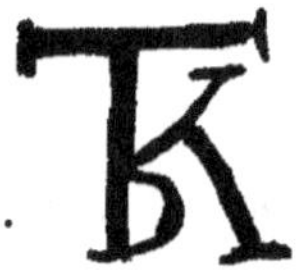

THOMAS DE KEYSER 1596-1679
Dutch Portraits, Genre $20,000

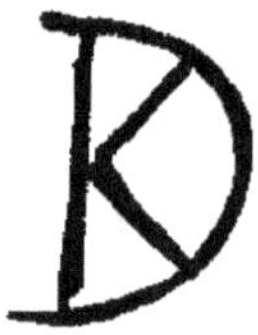

HENDRIL DE KEYSER 1565-1621
Dutch Painter, Portraits $2,500

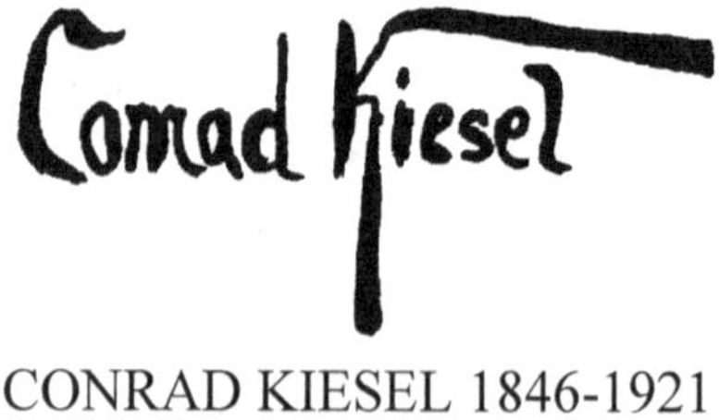

CONRAD KIESEL 1846-1921
German, Painter, Genre $100,000

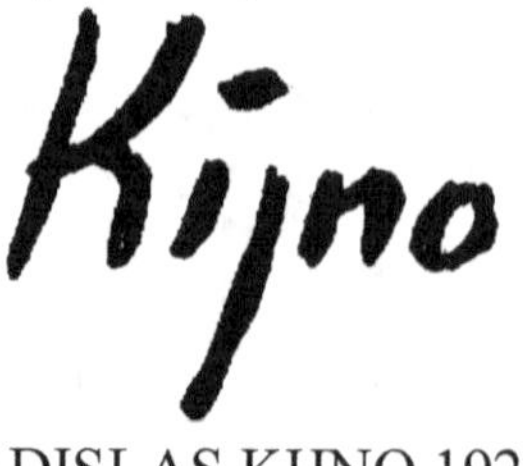

LADISLAS KIJNO 1921-
French Abstract $55,000

Kikoine

MICHEL KIKOINE 1892-1968
Russian Painter, Genre, Landscape $15,000

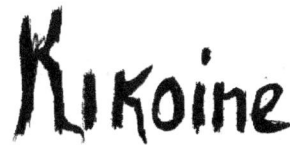

1. G.G.Kilburne

G.G.Kilburne
2.

GEORGE GOODWIN KILBURNE 1834-1924
British Watercolour $15,000

A. Kindler

ALBERT KINDLER 1833-1876
German Landscape, Genre $10,000

Yeend King

JOHN YEEND KING 1855-1924
British Painter $15,000

Paul King 2. Paul King
1.

PAUL KING 1867-1947
American A.N.A Landscape $3,500

Kingman

DONG KINGMAN 1911-1985
American M.N.A. Illustrator, Genre $14,000

Klinkenberg

JOHANNES (also Johan Christiaan) KAREL KLINKENBERG
1852-1924 Dutch Landscape $70,000

Otto Kirberg

1.

2.

Otto Kirberg

OTTO KARL KIRBERG 1850-1926
German Painter, Genre $20,000

ELKirchner

ERNST LUDWIG KIRCHNER 1880-1938
German Expressionist $1,500,000

KIRKMAN

JAY KIRKMAN' 1900's
British Painter $6,000

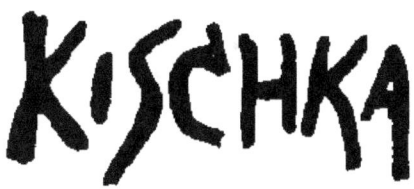

I. KISCHKA 1908-1974
French, Landscape $2,500

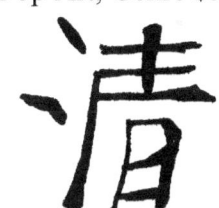

MOISE KISLING 1891-1953
French Painter, Landscape, Genre $300,000

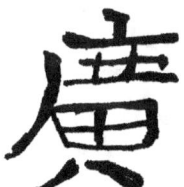

R. B. KITAJ 1932-
American, Pop Art, Genre $3,000,000

清

廣

TORII KIYOHIRO 1737-1765
Japanese Woodblock $4,000

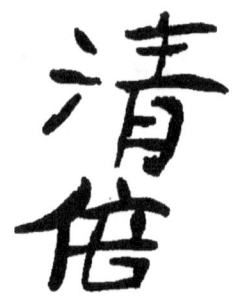

TORII KIYOMASU II 1706-1763
Japanese Woodblock $6,000

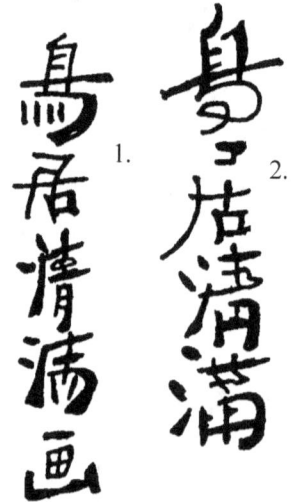

TORII KIYOMITSU 1735-1785
Japanese Woodblock $3,500

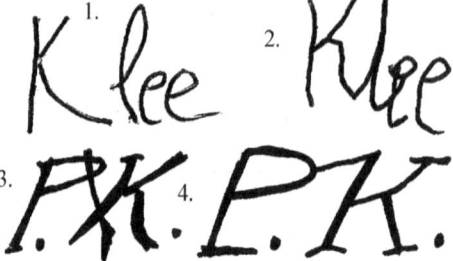

PAUL KLEE 1879-1940
German Abstract, Expressionist $7,000,000

1.

2.

3.

le monochrome

4.

5.

6.

YVES KLEIN 1928-1962
French Paris School, Sponges, Blue, Fire Paintings $4,720,000

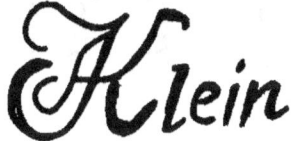

JOHANN ADAM KLEIN 1792-1875
German Landscape, Genre, Animal Painter $30,000

FRANK KLEINHOLZ 1900-
American Painter, Landscape, Genre $1,000

PAUL KLEINSCHMIDT 1883-1949
German, Expressionist, Landscape, Genre $25,000

E. KLEMM 1800's
Austrian, Painter, Genre $2,500

JULIUS SERGIUS VON KLEVER 1850-1924
Russian, Painter, Seascape, Landscape $15,000

GUSTAV KLIMT 1862-1918
Austrian Impressionist $135,000,000

Ernst Klimt

ERNST KLIMT 1864-1892
Austrian Painter, Portraits $30,000

FRANZ KLINE 3. *Franz Kline*

1.

2.

FRANZ KLINE 1910-1962
American Abstract $6,400,000

M. Klinger

MAX KLINGER 1857-1920
German Painter, Landscape, Genre $35,000

A Kloeber

AUGUST VON KLOEBER 1793-1864
German Painter $1,000

2. *a Klomp*

1. *A'klomp* 3. *A Klomp*

ALBERT (also AELBERT) JANSZ KLOMP 1618-1688
Netherlandish Cows Landscapes, Genre $15,000

CONSTANTIN KLUGE 1911-
French Landscape $7,500

KARL KNATHS 1891-1971
American N.A. Abstract $13,000

LUDWIG KNAUS 1829-1910
German Genre, Landscape, Animals, Portraits $40,000

SIR GODFREY KNELLER 1646-1723
Dutch Portraits $25,000

LOUIS ASTON KNIGHT 1873-1949
American, Painter, Genre, Landscape $50,000

DAME LAURA KNIGHT 1877-1970
British, Illustrator, Genre $45,000

Ridgway Knight

DANIEL RIDGWAY KNIGHT 1839-1924
American Sheep $50,000

A. Roland Knight

A. ROLAND KNIGHT 1800's
British Animals, Landscape $3,500

Knight

MERVYN KNIGHT 1956-
British Landscape $1,200

JAMES KNOX

JAMES KNOX 1866-
American Landscape $5,000

W.K.NOX

WILFRID KNOX 1889-1966
British Marines, Landscape $2,000

1. *Knüpfer*

2.

Knüpfer

NICOLAUS KNUPFER 1603-1660
German Allegorical, Portraits $4,000

GRAHAM KNUTTEL 1900's
Irish Illustration, Still Life $7,000

WILHELM VON KOBELL 1766-1855
German Genre, Animals $90,000

PYKE KOCH 1901-1991
Dutch Painter, Sporting $130,000

JOHN KOCH 1909-1978
American, Painter, Genre $300,000

2.   3.

BAREND CORNELIS KOEKKOEK 1803-1862
Dutch Landscape, Genre $150,000

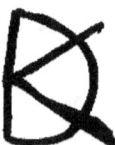

JOHAN DANIEL KOELMAN 1831-1857
Dutch Painter, Landscape $7,500

WILLIAM HENRY DETHLEF KOERNER 1878-1938
American, N.A., Illustrator, Cowboys, Genre

ALEXANDER MAX KOESTER 1864-1932
American Landscape $200,000

OSKAR KOKOSHKA 1886-1980
German Expressionist $2,700,000

GEORGE KOLBE 1877-1947
German Painter, Portraits $20,000

RUDOLF KOLLER 1828-1905
Swiss Landscape, Portraits, Animals $40,000

KARL IVANOVICH KOLLMAN 1788-1846
Russian, Painter, Landscape, Genre $3,000

KATHE KOLLWITZ 1867-1945
German Expressionist, Lithos, Genre $299,000

1.

2.

PHILIPS DE KONINCK (also Koningh) 1619-1688
Netherlandish Landscapes Genre (like Rembrandt) $175,000

SALOMON KONINCK (also Koningh) 1609-1663
Dutch Genre, Portraits, Mythology $25,000

DANIEL DE KONINK 1668-1720
Netherlandish Portraits $20,000

SEIKI KORODA 1866-1924
Japanese Impressionist Plein AireYoga Style $300,000

FRANZ KORWAN 1865-
German, Painter, Landscape $2,000

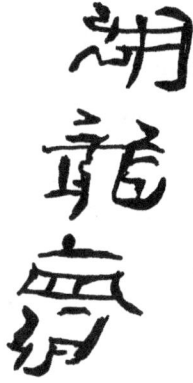

ISODA KORYUSAI 1764-1788
Japanese Woodblocks $5,000

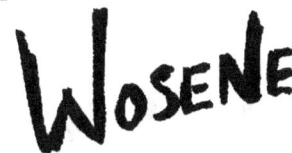

WOSENE KOSROF 1950-
Ethiopia Abstract $1,000

A.L. KOSTER

ANTOINIE LUIS LODEWIJK KOSTER 1859-1937
Dutch, Landscape $5,000

L. KOWALSKY

LEOPOLD FRANZ KOWALSKY 1856-1931
French Painter, Genre, Landscape $75,000

JACOB KRAMER 1892-1962
British Portraits, Genre $25,000

LK

LEE KRASNER 1908-1984
American Abstract Expressionist $3,170,000

BRUNO KRAUSKOPF 1892-1960
German, Landscape, Genre $12,000

PINCHUS KREMEGNE 1890-1981
Russian Painter, Landscape $30,000

1. **KROHA**

2.

JIRI KROHA

PER KROHG 1889-1949
Norwegian, Painter, Landscape, Genre $30,000

LEON KROLL 1884-1974
American, N.A. Realiist, Landscape $60,000

JULIUS KRONBERG 1850-1921
Swedish, Genre, Mythology, Portrai$ts, $28,000

1. L. ✡ K.

2. Louis KRONBERG.

LOUIS KRONEBERG 1872-1965
American, N.A. Painter, Genre $4,000

1. SK.

2. S. Kroyn

PEDER SEVERIN KROYER 1851-1909
Danish Painter Marines Beaches $400,000

1.

2.

ALFRED KUBIN 1877-1959
German Expressionist, Genre, Landscape $45,000

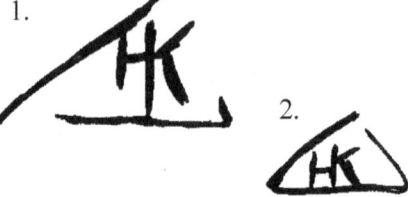

NICOLAI (also Nikolai) KULBIN 1868-1917
Russian, Portraits $1,000

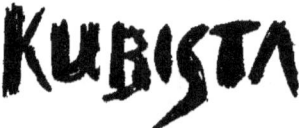

BOHUMIL KUBISTA 1884-1918
Czechoslavakian Landscape, Portraits $10,000

Kuehne

MAX KUEHNE 1880-1968
American Landscape, Genre $15,000

1.   2.

ABRAHAM WOLFGANG KUFPNER 1760-1817
German, Painter

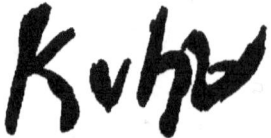

PETER KUHFELD 1952-
British Architectural Landscape, Genre $10,000

OTTO AUGUST C. KUHLER 1894-1977
American, Painter, Landscape, $1,000

WALT KUHN 1880-1949
American Clowns $275,000

1.

2.

3.

WILHELM KUHNERT 1865-1926
German Animals, Landscape $100,000

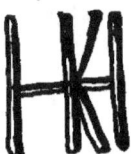

HANS VON KULMBACH 1476-1522
German Painter,Genre, Religious $65,000

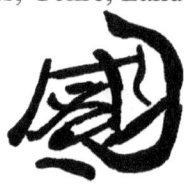

REINHOLD KUNDIG 1888-1984
Swiss, Portraits, Genre, Landscape $10,000

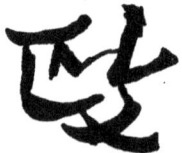

UTAGAWA KUNIMASA 1773-1810
Japanese Woodblocks $10,000

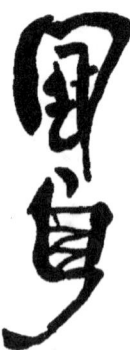

UTAGAWA KUNISADA 1786-1864
Japanese Woodblocks $130,000

YASUO KUNIYOSHI 1893-1953
American Realist, Genre $500,000

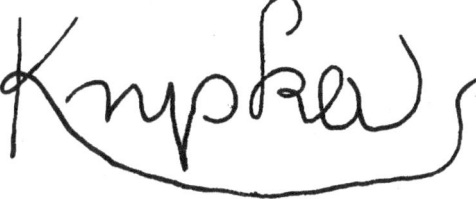

MORTON KUNSTLER 1930-
American Cowboy $5,000

JOHANN KUPETZKY 1667-1740
German Portraits, Landscape $25,000

FRANTISEK (also Franz, Franck) KUPKA 1871-1957
Czech Futurist, Expressionist $1,000,000

CHARLES EUPHRASIE KUWASSEG Jr. 1838-1904
French, Seascape, Landscape $20,000

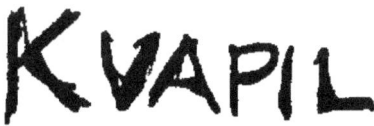

CHARLES KVAPIL 1884-1957
Belgian, Painter, Landscape $20,000

Artists starting with the letter "L"

C. L'Eplattenier

CHARLES L'EPLATTENIER 1874-1964
Swiss Landscape $4,000

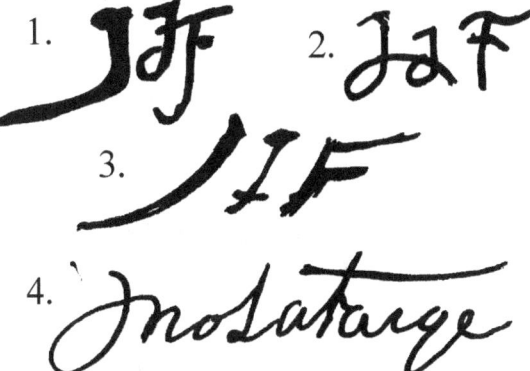

1. 2. 3.

4.

JOHN LA FARGE 1835-1910
American N.A. Watercolour, Still Life, Landscape $90,000

PV Laar

PIETER VAN LAAR 1600-1658
Dutch Genre, Landscape, Animals $35,000

ALEXANDER LABAS 1900-1983
Russian Painter

_L_ ABISSE

FELIX LABISSE 1905-1982
French Painter, Landscape, Genre $30,000

Lacasse

JOSEPH LACASSE 1894-1975
Belgian Landscape, Genre $40,000

lacaze

GERMAINE LACAZE 1907-
French Genre, Landscape, Still Life $10,000

L. Lagrenee

LOUIS LAGRENEE 1724-1805
French Painter, Religious, Allegory $60,000

1. *Lagrenee*

2. *Lagrenee*

JEAN JACQUES LAGRENEE 1740-1821
French Painter, Religious, Mythology, Portraits $150,000

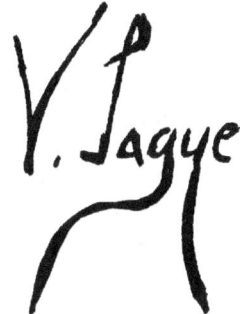

VICTOR LAGYE 1829-1896
Belgian, Illustrator, Landscape, Genre $5,000

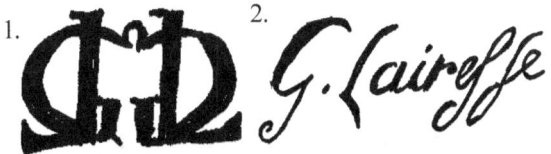

GERARD DE LAIRESSE 1640-1711
Dutch Allegory, Genre, Portraits, Mythology $200,000

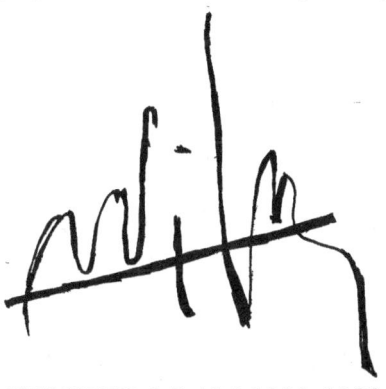

WILFREDO LAM 1902-1982
Cuban, Abstract $1,322,500

N.C. LAMBERT

CAMILLE NICOLAS LAMBERT 1876-
Belgian, Painter, Genre, Landscape $10,000

JEAN LAMBERT-RUCKI 1888-1967
French Painter, Genre $20,000

CHARLES ZACHARIE LANDELLE 1812-1908
French, Painter, Genre, Landscape $35,000

RICARDO VERDUGO LANDI 1871-1930
Italian Painter, Landscape $6,000

ANDREA LANDINI 1847-
Italian Painter, Genre $50,000

SIR EDWIN HENRY LANDSEER 1802-1873
British, Sporting, Genre, Landscape $500,000

OTTO LANGE 1879-1944
German Expressionist $4,500

RUTGER VAN LANGEVELT 1635-1695
Netherlandish Architecture Interiors $2,500

1. 2.

CHARLES LAPICQUE 1898-1988
French Landscape, Seascape $50,000

NICOLAS LARGILLIERE 1656-1746
French Portraits $400,000

1.

2.

3.

3.

MIKHAIL FEDEROVICH (also Michel) LARIONOFF 1881-1964
Russian Rayonist, Genre, Landscape, Birds $100,000

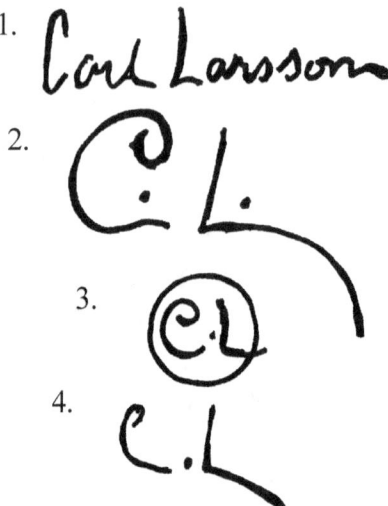

1.
2.
3.
4.

CARL OLAF LARSSON 1853-1919
Swedish Painter, Landscape, Genre $450,000

1. 2.

PIETER LASTMAN 1562-1633
Netherlandish Allegorical, Landscape, Genre, Religious

PHILIPP DE LASZLO 1869-1937
British Painter, Genre $30,000

GER LATASTER 1920-
Dutch, Abstract, Landscape, Still Life $40,000

1. $\int_{de} L$ **2.** G. LATOIX

GASPARD LATOIX-1904
American Cowboys $8,000

A. Laugé

ACHILLE LAUGE 1861-1944
French Landscape, Genre $25,000

D. Laugée

DESIRE FRANCOIS LAUGEE 1823-1896
French, Portraits, Genre $5,000

Georges Laugee

GEORGES LAUGEE 1853-
French Genre, Portraits $9,000

Sydney Laurence

SIDNEY LAURENCE 1865-1940
American Landscape $35,000

M.L.

Marie Laurencin

MARIE LAURENCIN 1885-1956
French Painter, Genre $1,300,000

1.
H.LAURENS 2. ⊔

HENRI LAURENS 1885-1954
French Cubist $1,472,000

Jean Paul Laurens

JEAN PAUL LAURENS 1838-1921
French Painter, Genre, Religious $20,000

1.
Lautrec

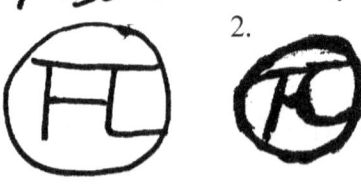

3. 2.

HENRI DE TOULOUSE LAUTREC 1864-1901
French Impressionist $3,000,000

A. Laux

AUGUST LAUX 1853-1921
American Animals, Landscape $7,500

SIR JOHN LAVERY 1856-1941
British Painter, Genre $1,983,240

JACOB LAWRENCE 1917-
American WPA Illustrator, Genre, $35,000

1.

2.

ERNEST LAWSON 1873-1939
American, N.A., Impressionist $450,000

HIPPOLYTE LAZERGES 1817-1887
French Religious Painter, Arabs $60,000

AUGUSTIN LAZO 1901-1971
Mexican, Costume Stage Design, Genre $1,000

Blanche Lazzell

BLANCHE LAZZELL 1878-1956
American Abstract $25,000

1. *Lebarbier*

2. *Le Barbier*

JEAN JACQUE LE BARBIER 1738-1826
French Painter, Portraits, Allegory $9,000

1. *B*

2. *CLB*

3. *Le Brun*

CHARLES LE BRUN 1619-1690
French Portraits, Religious, Mythology $150,000

Jules LeFebvre

JULES JOSEPH LE FEBVRE 1836-1911
French Landscapes, Nudes $14,000

Aug. LEGRAS.

AUGUST LE GRAS 1864-1915
Dutch Painter, Landscape $2,000

F. lemoyne

1.

2. *F le mo yne*

FRANCOIS LE MOYNE (also Lemoine) 1688-1737
French Genre, Portraits, Allegory, Religious $450,000

a X

Lepunce

A. X. LE PRINCE 1799-1826
French Genre, Landscape $20,000

1.

JB. Le Punce

2.

Le Lrince

JEAN BAPTISTE LE PRINCE 1733-1781
French Genre, Portraits, Landscape $800,000

1. *B.W.LEADER* 3.

2. *BW LEADER* *B.W.LEADER*

BENJAMIN WILLIAMS LEADER 1831-1923
British, R.A. Landscape, Genre $35,000

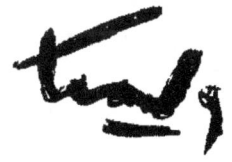

FERNANDO LEAL

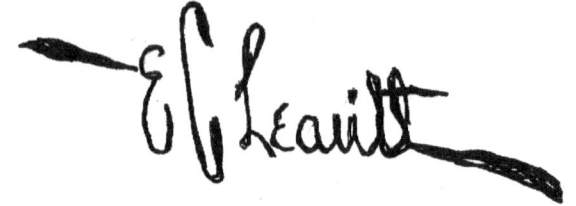

EDWARD CHALMERS LEAVITT 1842-1904
American, Painter, Still Life $9,000

1.   2.

HENRI LEBASQUE 1865-1937
French Painter, Genre, Landscape $400,000

LAWRENCE LEBDUSKA 1894-1966-
American, Allegory, Landscape $2,000

ALBERT LEBOURG 1849-1928
French Paris Streets, Impressionist $1,000,000

FRANZ LEBRET 1820-1909
Dutch Landscape $4,500

Rico Lebrun

RICO LEBRUN 1900-1964
American N.A. Painter, Landscape, Genre $4,500

Mme *Le Brun* 1.

2. *L. E Vigee Le Brun*

MARIE LE LEBRUN 1735-1842
French Landscape, Portraits

SFL

GABRIEL FERNANDEZ LEDESMA 1900-1983
Mexican Still Life, Genre $30,000

JLedger

JANET LEDGER 1900's
British Landscape $1,000

Doris Lee

DORIS LEE 1905-
American, Illustrator, Blacks, Genre $25,000

Leech

JOHN LEECH 1817-1864
British, Illustrator, Genre, Landscape $4,500

Leech

WILLIAM JOHN LEECH 1881-1968
Irish Painter, Genre, Landscape $70,000

Robert Lefevre

ROBERT LEFEVRE 1756-1830
French Portraits, Genre $70,000

H. LEFLER

HEINRICH LEFLER
$2,000

1. F.L   2. F. LEGER
3. Leger   4. F.L
5. HLEGEF

FERNAND LEGER 1881-1955
French Cubist Abstract $22,407,500

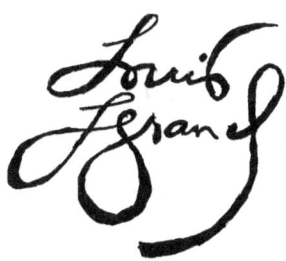

LOUIS LEGRAND 1863-1951
French Painter, Genre $25,000

ALPHONSE LEGROS 1837-1911
French Watercolour, Genre $15,000

WILLIAM ROBINSON LEIGH 1866-1955
American N.A. Illustrator, Indians, Genre $150,000

FREDERICK WILLIAM LEIST 1878-1946
Australian, Seascape, Genre, Landscaper $20,000

HARRY LEITH-ROSS 1886-1973
American Genre, Landscape $10,000

CORNELIS LELIENBERGH 1626-1676
Dutch Still Life, Birds $12,000

ALEXANDER LOUIS LELIOR 1843-1884
French Genre, Religious, Portraits $15,000

MAURICE LELOIR 1853-1940
French Painter, Genre $15,000

PETER LELY (also Van Der Faes) 1617-1680
Dutch Portraits $100,000

MADELEINE LEMAIRE 1845-1928
French Painter, Landscape, Genre $75,000

MARIE THERESE LEMAIRE 1861-
French Florals, Still Life $8,000

F. LEMATTE

JACQUES F. LEMATTE 1850-
French Genre, Portraits $1,500

Lenain

ANTOINE L. LENAIN 1598-1648
French Genre, Portraits $3,500

FL

HEINRICH LENGERICH 1790-1865
German Painter, Religious $8,000

C.A. Lenoir

CHARLES AMABLE LENOIR 1861-
French Genre, Landscape $80,000

1. *A.C. Lens*

2. *A. Lens*

ANDRIES C. LENS 1739-1822
Dutch Portraits, Mythology, Religious $15,000

[signature: Lenthe]

GASTON LENTHE 1805-1860
German Genre

[signature: J Leonardo]

JOSE LEONARDO 1616-1656
Spanish Painter, Religious, Portraits $95,000

[signature: Jns lepape]

GEORGES LEPAPE 1885-1971
French Stage Costume Design, Genre $12,000

[signature: Charles LEPEC]

CHARLES LEPEC 1830-
French Genre $6,000

[signatures: 1. A Lepere 2. A LEPERE]

AUGUSTE LEPERE 1849-1918
French, Etcher, Genre, Landscape $4,000

[signatures: 1. Lepicie 2. Lepicie]

NICOLA BERNARD LEPICIE 1735-1784
French Genre, Portraits, Allegory $90,000

J. Lepine

JOSEPH LEPINE 1900's
French Painter, Genre $4,000

LEPRIN

MARCEL LEPRIN 1891-1933
French Landscape, Genre $150,000

-AUGUSTE LEROUX-

JULES MARIE AUGUSTE LEROUX 1871-1954
French Painter, Genre $20,000

Jesus Leuus

JESUS MARIANO LEUUS 1948-
Mexican Painter, Genre, Religious $7,000

Hayley Lever

RICHARD HAYLEY LEVER 1876-1958
American, Water Scenes, Landscape, Genre $20,000

1.   2.

Levier   Levier

CHARLES LEVIER 1920-
American Paris Streets, Genre $5,000

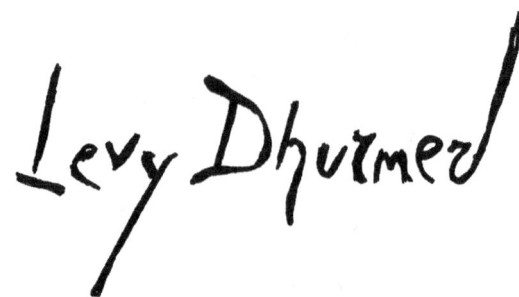

LUCIEN LEVY-DHURMER 1865-1953
French Painter, Genre, Landscape $60,000

1.

3.

2.

PERCY WYNDHAM LEWIS 1882-1957
British Portraits, Compositions, Abstract $30,000

MARTIN LEWIS 1883-1962
American, Etcher, Painter, Genre $8,000

1.

2.

3.

4.

5.

6.

LUCAS VAN LEYDEN 1494-1533
Dutch Old Master, Genre, Religious, Portraits $20,000

HENDRIK LEYS 1815-1869
Belgian Genre, Religious,Portraits $25,000

1.
2.
LEON AUGUSTIN LHERMITTE 1844-1925
French, Painter, Genre, Landscape $500,000

1.
2.
ANDRE LHOTE 1885-1962
French Cubism, landscape, Portraits $90,000

JONAS LIE 1880-1940
American N.A. Seascape, Landscape $80,000

1.
2.
3.
MAX LIEBERMANN 1847-1935
German Expressionist $1,576,000

N de Liemackere

NICOLAAS DE LIEMAEKER (also Liemaker) 1575-1646
Dutch Painter, Religious $10,000

1.
Joseph Lies

2.
Joseph Lies

JOSEPH LIES 1821-1865
Belgian Landscape,Genre $4,500

Camille Lieucy

CAMILLE LIEUCY
Painter

I L

JAN LIEVENS 1607-1674
Netherlandish Portraits, Landscape $2,800,000

HVLimborcht

HENDRIK VAN LIMBORCH (also Limborck) 1680-1758
Dutch Landscape, Religious, Allegory $6,000

R. LINDNER

RICHARD LINDNER 1901-1978
American Painter, Abstract $375,000

1. *LINER*

2. *Liner*

CARL LINER 1914-
Swiss Abstract $25,000

O. LINET

OCTAVE LINET 1870-1962
French, Painter, Still Life $1,000

1. *J. Lingel Bach*

2. *Lingelbach*

JOHANNES LINGELBACH 1622-1674
Dutch Landscape, Genre $185,000

L intott

BERNARD LINTOTT 1875-1951
American, Watercolour, Portraits $5,000

Lipchitz

JACQUES LIPCHITZ 1891-1973
American Cubist, Genre $1,300,000

·PHILIPPINVS··

·DEFLOREN

TIA·

FILIPPINO LIPPI 1457-1504
Italian Allegorical, Portraits $400,000

Wm·H·Lippincott

WILLIAM HENRY LIPPINCOTT 1849-1920
American, Illustrator, Genre, Landscape $20,000

A. Lismer

ARTHUR LISMER 1885-1969
Canadian Landscape $20,000

DIRCK VAN DER LISSE-1669
Netherlandish Nymphs Allegorical, Landscape $75,000

Nat. Little

NATHANIEL STANTON LITTLE 1893-
American, Illustrator, Landscape, Seascape $2,500

Stuart Lloyd

W. STUART LLOYD 1875-1929
British City Scenes, Landscape $4,500

GEORGE EDWARD LODGE 1860-1954
British Painter, Landscape $20,000

AUGUST LOHR 1843-1919
German, Painter, Landscape $45,000

CARL LOHSE 1900's
German Genre, Portraits $2,500

1. LOIR-LUIGI

2. LOIR LUIGI

LUIGI LOIR, (also Loir Luigi) 1845-1916
French Landscape, Paris Streets, Genre $90,000

GUSTAVE LOISEAU 1865-1935
French Painter, Landscape $250,000

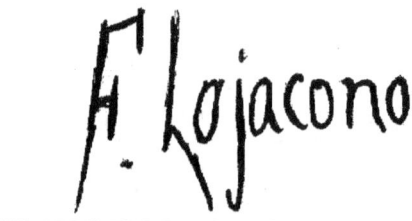

FRANCESCO LOJACONO 1841-1915
Italian Painter, Genre, Landscape $50,000

JOHN ARTHUR LOMAX 1857-1923
British Painter, Genre $10,000

GIOVANNI P. LOMAZZO 1538-1600
Italian Painter, Portraits $2,000

PAUL DE LONGPRE 1855-1911
American Floral, Still Life $7,500

LOUIS MICHEL VAN LOO 1707-1771
French Portraits, Genre $200,000

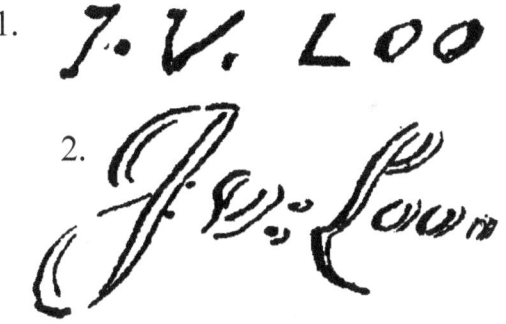

JACOB VAN LOO 1614-1670
Netherlandish Genre Allegorical $90,000

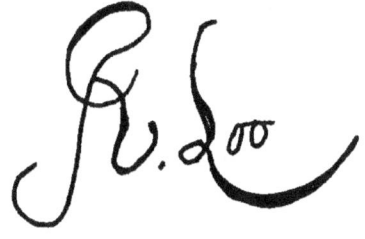

JACOB VAN LOO 1614-1670
Dutch Portraits, Genre, Allegory $90,000

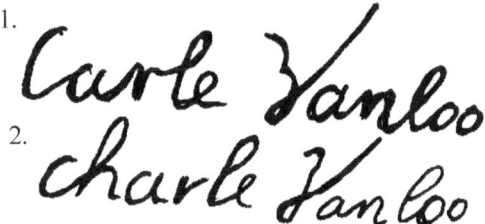

CHARLES A. VAN LOO 1705-1765
French Painter, Portraits, Religious, Allegory $15,000

JEAN BAPTISTE VAN LOO 1684-1745
French Portraits, Religious $100,000

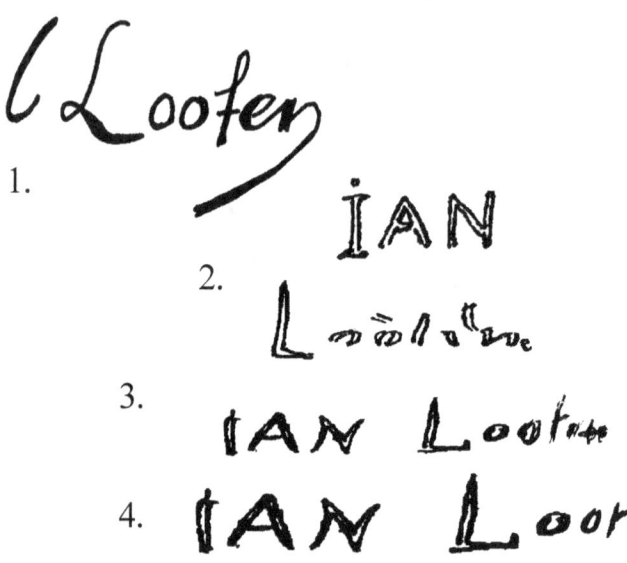

1.

2.

3.

4.

JAN LOOTEN 1618-1681
Netherlandish Mountain Landscapes, Genre $200,000

RICHARD LORENZ 1858-1915
American, Illustrator, Genre, Cowboys, Landscape $15,000

1.

2.

BERNARD LORJOU 1908-1986
French, Abstract, Genre, Landscape $45,000

ANTON DE LORME 1610-1673
Dutch Painter, Genre $20,000

SFL

GABRIEL LUDWIG LORY 1763-1840
Swiss Landscape $9,000

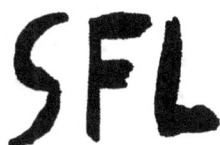

ROBERT LOTIRON 1886-1966
$5896

1. **L LOTUS**

2. **L.Loto**

LORENZO LOTTO 1480-1554
Italian Painter, Religious, Landscape, Mythology $175,000

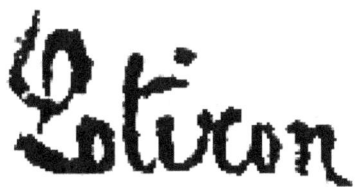

MORRIS LOUIS 1912-1962
American, Painter, Genre $1,808,000

C. LOVERIDGE

CLINTON LOVERIDGE 1824-1902
British Landscape $15,000

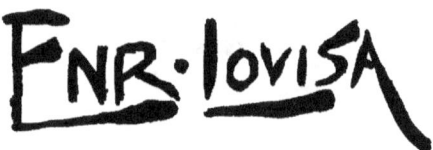

ENRICO LOVISA 1900's
Spanish Portraits $6,000

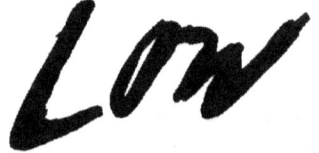

SIR DAVID LOW 1891-1963
British Cartoonist, Genre $1,500

C. F. Lowcock

CHARLES FREDERICK LOWCOCK -1921
British, Genre $3,000

ORSON LOWELL

ORSON LOWELL 1871-1956
American, Illustrator, Genre $5,000

I, E, LOWRY

LAURENCE STEPHEN LOWRY 1887-1976
British Genre $3,000,000

RodRiguez LOZANO

MANUEL RODRIGUEZ LOZANO 1896-
Mexican, Painter, genre $15,000

1.

2.

LOUIS LOZOWICK

LOUIS LOZOWICK 1892-1973
American Illustrator, Genre, WPA Artist $200,000

OSSIP LUBITCH 1869-1986
French, painter, Landscape, Genre $5,000

BOGDAN THEODOR LUBIENIECKI 1600's
Polish, Painter

1.   2.

3.

MAXIMILIEN LUCE 1858-1941
French, Landscape, Genre $400,000

LUIGI LUCIONI 1900-1989
American, A.N.A. Painter, Landscape $60,000

HAL LUDLOW

HENRY (HAL) STEPHEN LUDLOW 1861-
British Painter, Genre $1,500

J. LUKE

JOHN LUKE 1906-1975
Irish Painter, Genre $290,000

George Luks –

GEORGE BENJAMIN LUKS 1867-1933
American Ash Can School, Genre $500,000

Luminais

EVARISTE VITAL LUMINAIS 1822-1896
French Genre, Portraits $2,500

Aage Lund

AAGE LUND 1900'S
Swedish Painter, Genre $5,000

Lurcat

JEAN LURCAT 1892-1966
French Surrealist, Landscape, Genre $75,000

Dan Lutz

DAN LUTZ 1906-1978
American Watercolour $1,000

MARIETTE R. LYDIS 1890-1970
Austrian Genre, Portraits $6,000

ALBERT LYNCH 1851-
Peruvian, Illustrator, Genre $30,000

MICHAEL LYNE 1912-1989
British Painter, Genre, Landscape $10,000

1.

2.   3.

JAN VAN DER LYS (also Dirk Liss) 1600-1657
Dutch Landscape, Genre, Portraits $1,000

NICOLAS LYTRAS 1883-1927
Greek Landscape $50,000

Artists starting with the letter "M"

DIRK MAAS (Maes) 1656-1717
Dutch Landscape, Animal Painter $17,000

MANABU MABE 1910-
Latin American Abstract, Compositions $20,000

JAN VAN MABUSE 1470-1541
Dutch Painter

ROBERT RUSSELL MAC NEE 1880-1952
British, Landscape, Genre $9,000

MINO MACCARI 1898-1989
Italian Painter, Genre, Landscape $25,000

1.

2.

ROMULO MACCIO 1931-
Argentinian Painter, Genre $25,000

1.

2.

3.

STANTON MACDONALD WRIGHT 1890-1974
American Synchromist, Landscape, Abstract $485,000

WILLIAM DARLING MACKAY 1844-1924
British Painter, Genre, Landscape $7,500

THOMAS MACKAY-1913
British Genre $3,000

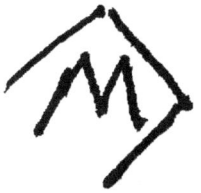

AUGUST MACKE 1887-1914
German Expressionist, Genre, Landscape $3,810,000

JEAN MACLANE

JEAN MACLANE 1878-1964
American N.A. Impressionist, Portraits, Landscape $15,000

ALEXANDER MACLEAN 1867-1940
British Landscape, Genre $7,000

ELISEE MACLET 1881-1962
French Painter, Landscape $55,000

PAUL MADELINE 1864-1921
French Landscape. Genre $70,000

RAIMUNDO DE MADRAZO Y GARRETA 1841-1920
Spanish Painter, Genre $100,000

EUGENE REMY MAES 1849-1931
Belgian Florals, Still Life $20,000

1.

2.

3.

4.

5.

NICOLAES MAES (also Nicolaas, Maas) 1632-1693
Netherlandish Portraits, Portraits,Religious,Old Master $500,000

GODFRIED MAES (also Maas) 1649-1700
Dutch Painter, Allegory,Religious $1,500

EMIL MAETZEL 1877-1955
German Landscape, Nudes $3,000

J.C. MAGGS 1819-1895
British Painter, Animals $90,000

ALBERTO MAGNELLI 1888-1971
Italian Landscape, Portraits, Compositions $600,000

1. 2. 3.

RENE MAGRITTE 1898-1967
Belgian Surrealist, Genre $12,700,000

LEO MAILLET 1902-
French Gravure, Paris Streets $3,000

ARISTIDE MAILLOL 1861-1944
French Painter Sculptor, Landscape $2,800,000

ZVI MAIROVITCH 1911-1973
Israeli Painter, Portraits, Landscapes, Seascapes $8,500

KONSTANTIN YEGOROVICH MAKOVSKY 1839-1951
Russian Painter, Genre, Nudes $100,000

CEES MAKS 1876-1965
Dutch Painter $10,000

KARL WILHELM C. (also Carl) MALCHIN 1838-1923
German Landscape $3,500

FEDERICO MALDARELLI 1826-1893
Italian Genre $45,000

LEO MALEMPRE -1901
French Painter, Portraits, Genre, Landscape $5,000

KASIMIR MALEVITCH 1878-1935
Russian Suprematist, Cubist $17,000,000

CHRISTIAN FRIEDRICH MALI 1832-1906
German Landscape, Genre $45,000

PHILIPPE ANDREEVICH MALIAVINE 1869-1939
Russian Landscape, Genre $25,000

1.

2.

(EMMANUEL RADINSKI) MAN RAY 1890-1976
American Photo,Abstract, Portraits $1,504,440

1.

2.

3.

4.

KAREL VAN MANDER 1548-1606
Dutch Painter, Genre, Religious $20,000

ALFRED MANESSIER 1911-1993
French Painter, Landscape, Genre $185,000

1.

2.

3.

EDOUARD MANET 1832-1883
French Impressionist $24,000,000

PEPPINO MANGRAVITE 1896-1978
Latin American Painter, WPA, Genre $8,500

HENRI MANGUIN 1874-1949
French Painter, Portraits, Landscapes $400,000

JAN MANKES 1889-1920
Dutch Painter, Landscape $50,000

HARRINGTON MANN

HARRINGTON MANN 1864-1937
British Painter, Genre $90,000

A. Mann

ALEXANDER MANN 1853-1908
British Painter, Genre $60,000

1. *MANN* 2. *MANN*

CYRIL MANN 1911-1980
British Painter $10,000

Manoury

ARMAND MANOURY-1893
French Landscape, Genre $1,000

1. *π. Mansuroff*

2. *P. Mansouroffn*

PAUL MANSOUROFF 1896-1983
Russian Painter $10,000

ϕANDREAS MANTINIAϕ

ANDREA MANTEGNA 1431-1506
Italian Religious Allegory, Portraits $28,600,000

N MANVEL

NICOLAUS MANVEL 1484-1530
German Painter

Manzur

DAVID MANZUR 1929-
Latin American Abstract, Genre $15,000

1. *Carlo Maratt*

2. *Carlo Maratti*

CARLO MARATTI (also Maratta) 1625-1713
Italian Painter, Portraits, Religious, Mythology $1,100,000

1. *Fr Marc*   3. *F.M.*

2. *Marc*   4. *M.*

FRANZ MARC 1880-1916
German Blau Reiter $5,061,000

1. *E. March*

2. *M March*

ESTEBAN MARCH 1590-1660
Spanish Battle, Religious Painter $10,000

MAREVNA

MARIA VOROBIEFF MAREVNA 1892-1984
French Painter, Genre, Landscape $25,000

L.L. Margolies

SAMUEL L. MARGOLIES 1897-1974
American Painter, Landscape $2,500

Mariani

POMPEO MARIANI 1857-1927
Italian Painter, Genre, Landscape $20,000

1. *Marin*

2. *marin*

JOHN MARIN 1870-1953
American Modernist, Landscape $175,000

FILIPPO TOMMASO MARINETTI 1876-1944
Italian Abstract, Futurist $15,000

1.

2.

MARINO MARINI 1901-1980
Italian Painter Sculptor $2,687,000

VAN ROIJMERSWAELE MARINUS 1493-1567
Netherlandish Genre $25,000

WILLEM MARIS 1844-1910
Dutch Painter, Landscape $15,000

KYRA GAITHER MARKHAM 1891-1967
American Genre, Landscape $25,000

GEORGE MARKS 1876-1922
British Landscape, Genre $2,500

HENRY STACY MARKS 1829-1898
British Genre, Portraits $9,000

GEORGES PHILIBERT CHARLES MARONIEZ 1865-1934
French Marines Seascapes, Landscape $15,000

ALBERT MARQUET 1875-1947
American Painter, Still Life $1,000,000

1. *J. MARREL*

2. *Jacob. Marrell*

JACOB MARREL 1614-1681
German Still Life $400,000

Otho Marseus van Schuck : fecit

OTTO VAN SCHRIECK MARSEUS 1620-1678
Netherlandish Forest Scenes, Landscape $30,000

Reginald Marsh

REGINALD MARSH 1898-1954
American N.A. Illustrator, Genre $350,000

John S. de Martelly

JOHN S. DE MARTELLY 1903-
American Painter, Landscape $2,000

Willy Martens

WILLY MARTENS 1856-1927
Dutch Landscape, Genre $4,500

DAVID STONE MARTIN 1913-
American Illustrator $1,000

FLETCHER MARTIN 1904-1979
American A.N.A. Illustrator $2,000

BENITO QUINQUELA MARTIN 1890-1977
Argentinian Painter, Seascape, Genre $15,000

FRANCOIS MARTIN KAVEL 1861-1931
French Genre, Landscape, Portraits, Still Life $15,000

1.

2.

JACQUE MARTIN-FERRIERE 1893-1975
French Painter, Genre, Landscape $20,000

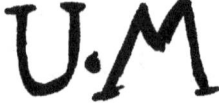

ULRICH MARTINELLI 1911-1989
Swiss Genre, Landscape $2,500

SEBASTIAN MARTINEZ 1602-1667
Spanish Religous Painter $15,000

EDOUARDO MARTINO 1838-1912
Italian Painter, Seascape $10,000

ALFRED MARXER 1876-1945
Swiss Seascape, Portraits, Landscape $5,500

PINCHUS MARYAN 1927-1977
American Painter, Expressionist $15,000

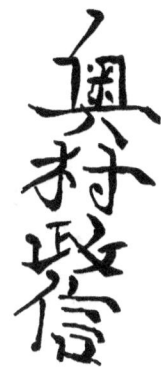

OKUMURA MASANOBU 1686-1764
Japanese Woodblocks $25,000

FM

FRANS MASEREEL 1888-1972
Belgian Expressionist, Genre $8,000

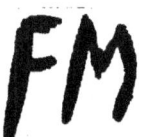

1.   2.

FRANCISCO MASRIERA Y MANOVENS 1842-1900
Spanish Painter, Genre $40,000

P Massani

POMPEO MASSANI 1850-1920
Italian Landscape, Genre $10,000

7CANES MASSijs

JAN MASSIJS 1505-1575
Netherlandish Genre, Portraits $10,000

1.

2.

ANDRE MASSON 1896-1987
French Cubist $250,000

JOANNES MASSiis

JAN MASSYS (also Metsys) 1509-1574
Dutch Genre, Religious $30,000

A. F. Mathews

ARTHUR F. MATHEWS 1860-1945
American Plein Aire, California, Landscape $50,000

GEORGES MATHIEU 1921-
French Abstract $100,000

THOMAS MATHISEN Circa 1600's
Netherlandish Genre $5,000

1.
Henri Matisse

2.
H Matisse 4. *H. Matisse*

3.
Henri. matiss

HENRI MATISSE 1869-1954
French Fauvist $18,496,000

ROBERTO ECHAURREN MATTA 1912-
Chillian Painter $2,400,000

Henry Mattson

HENRY MATTSON 1887-1971
American Painter, WPA, Portraits $2,500

maufra

MAXIME MAUFRA 1862-1918
French Seascapes $40,000

ALFRED H. MAURER 1868-1932
American Abstract, Landscape $150,000

ANTON MAUVE 1838-1888
Dutch Painter, Genre, Landscape $30,000

E.T. MAXWELL 1900's
British Landscapes $3,500

PHILIP WILLIAM MAY 1864-1903
British Illustrator, Cartoonist, Genre $1,000

JEAN LE MAYEUR 1880-1958
British Painter, Landscape $50,000

PAUL MAZE 1887-1979
French Landscape, Genre $10,000

JOHN MCAULIFFE 1848-1921
American Painter, Genre $30,000

JAMES MCBEY 1883-1959
British Landscape, Portrait $12,000

JERVIS MCENTEE 1828-1891
American N.A. Landscape, Genre $25,000

TOM MCEWAN R.S.W. 1861-1914
British Watercolour, Genre $8,000

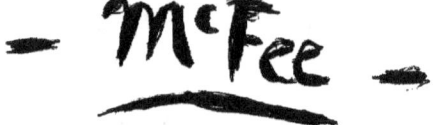

HENRY LEE MCFEE 1886-1953
American Landscape, Still Life $20,000

JOHN MCGHIE 1867-1941
British Painter, Genre, Landscape $15,000

THOMAS H. MCKAY 1875-1941
American Painter, Landscape $2,000

WILLIAM MCTAGGART 1903-1981
British Painter, Landscape $15,000

FRANK MECHAU 1903-1946
American A.N.A. Illustrator, Genre, WPA $15,000

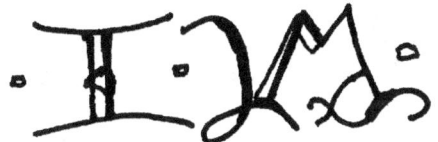

ISRAEL VAN MECKENEM 1450-1517
German Genre $55,000

JOSEPH R. MEEKER 1827-1889
American Landscape $20,000

JAN VAN DER MEER 1656-1705
Dutch Landscape, Sheep $3,500

BAREND VAN DER MEER 1659-1702
Dutch Still Life $35,000

LUDWIG MEIDNER 1884-1966
German Expressionist $50,000

JEAN LOUIS-ERNEST MEISSONIER 1815-1891
French Painter, Genre $125,000

Anton Melbye

ANTON D. H. MELBYE 1818-1875
Danish Seascape, Landscape $15,000

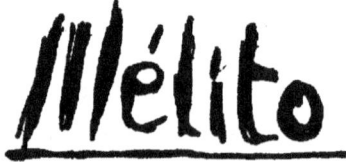

1.

2.

JULIUS GARI MELCHERS 1860-1932
American N.A. Painter, Genre $90,000

Mélito

MAURICE MELITO 1920-
French Painter, Portraits $2,500

Mendz

LEOPOLDO MENDEZ 1903-1969
Mexican Genre $1,000

Menkes

SIGMUND MENKES 1896-
American N.A. Painter, Genre, Landscape $40,000

ANJOLIE ELA MENON 1940-
India Modern, Portraits $7,500

FRANS MENTON 1550-1615
Dutch, Religious $2,000

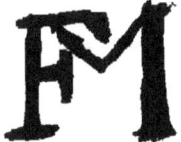

ADOLPH VON MENZEL 1815-1905
German Illustrator, Genre, Landscape $1,570,000

CARLOS
MERIDA
CARLOS MERIDA 1891-1984
Mexican Abstract, Genre $70,000

DANIEL MERLIN 1861-1933
French Painter, Genre $7,500

W. W. Mesdag

HENRIK WILLEM MESDAG 1831-1915
German Landscape, Seascape, Portraits $75,000

W.L. METCALF

1.

2.

W. L. METCALF

WILLARD L. METCALF 1858-1925
American Impressionist, Landscape $1,584,000

CM 1.

2. *G Metsu*

GABRIEL METSU 1629-1667
Netherlandish Genre Portraits $300,000

M. Meucci

MICHELANGELO MEUCCI 1800's
Italian Landscape Still Life $4,000

E'dm. vander Meulen

EDMOND VAN DER MEULEN 1841-1905
Belgian Illustrator, Genre $6,000

W. Meyerheim

WILHELM ALEXANDER MEYERHEIM 1815-1882
German Painter, Genre $15,000

米友仁

MI YU JEN 1090-1170
Chinese Watercolour $1,000

T. M.

THEOBALD MICHAU 1676-1765
Flemish Old Master, Genre, Landscape $100,000

G.C. Michelet

G.C. MICHELET 1900's
French Painter $15,000

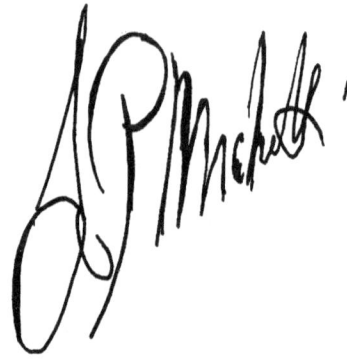

FRANCESCO PAOLO MICHETTI 1851-1929
Italian Painter, Landscape, Allegory, Genre $40,000

1.

2.

3.

4.

MICHIEL JANSZOON VAN MIEREVELT 1567-1641
Netherlandish Portraits $45,000

1.

2.

3.

4.

5.

6.

FRANS VAN (the elder) MIERIS 1635-1681
Netherlandish Portraits Genre $600,000

WILLEM VAN MIERIS 1662-1747
Dutch Genre, Portraits, Allegory, Mythological $100,000

1.

2.

FRANS VAN I Elder MIERIS 1635-1681
Dutch Genre, Portraits $650,000

FRANS VAN II Younger MIERIS 1689-1763
Dutch Genre, Portraits, Allegory $70,000

1.

2.

PIERRE (also La Romain) MIGNARD 1612-1695
French Allegory, Portraits, Mythology $25,000

1.

2.

GIUSEPPE MIGNECO 1908-
Italian Painter, Genre, Landscape $60,000

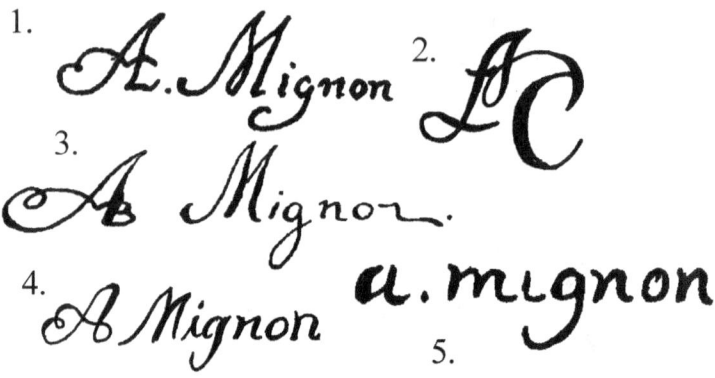

1. 2. 3. 4. 5.

ABRAHAM MIGNON 1640-1679
German Still Life $300,000

MIGNOT

LOUIS REMY MIGNOT 1831-1870
American N.A. Landscape $2,092,500

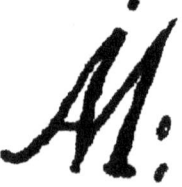

DANIEL (the elder) MIJTENS 1590-1647
Netherlandish Portraits $5,000

J MILDER

JAY MILDER 1934-
American Painter, Genre $6,000

Milich

ABRAM ADOLPHE MILICH 1885-1964
Polish Landscape $6,000

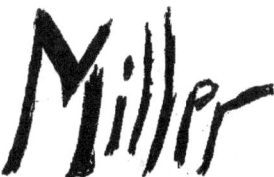

KENNETH HAYES MILLER 1876-1952
American Etcher, Genre $70,000

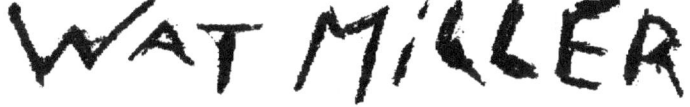

RICHARD EDWARD MILLER 1900's
American Impressionist, Genre $200,000

WAT MILLER 1900's
British Painter, Genre $3,500

RICHARD EMIL MILLER 1875-1943
American N.A. Landscape, Genre $600,000

WILLIAM RICKARBY MILLER 1850-1923
American Illustrator, Genre, Landscape $20,000

1. *JF Millet*

2. *J.F.M.*

3. *F. Millet*

4. *J. F. Millet*

JEAN FRANCOIS MILLET 1814-1875
French Barbizon, Landscape, Genre $2,145,000

R. W. Milliken

ROBERT W. MILLIKEN 1900's
British Painter, Landscape $1,000

Jos Milne

JOSEPH MILNE 1861-1911
British Painter, Genre, Landscape $4,000

W. W. Milne

WILLIAM WATT MILNE 1800'S
British Landscape, Genre $10,000

H. V. Minderhout

HENDRIK VAN MINDERHOUT 1632-1696
Dutch Seascape, Genre, Landscape $100,000

A Mintchine

ABRAHAM MINTCHINE 1898-1931
Russian Painter, Genre, Landscape $20,000

F. Miralles

FRANCISCO MIRALLES 1850-1901
Spanish Paris Streets, Genre $150,000

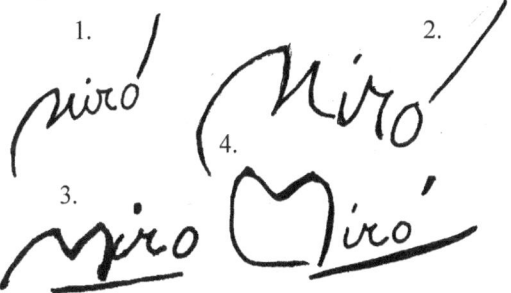

JOAN (also Juan) MIRO 1893-1983
Spanish Abstract $12,600,000

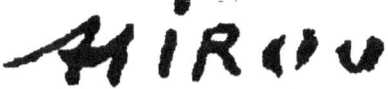

ANTON MIROU 1585-1662
German Landscapes Villages, Portraits $100,000

Alfred R. Mitchell

ALFRED R. MITCHELL 1888-1972
American Plein Aire, Landscapes, California $15,000

O. Modersohn

OTTO MODERSOHN 1865-1943
German Painter, Genre, Landscape $35,000

1. *Modigliani*

2. *modigliani*

AMEDEO MODIGLIANI 1884-1920
Italian Painter, Nudes $31,300,000

Wally Moes

WALLY MOES 1856-1918
Dutch Painter, Genre $12,000

PP^L

PIETER VAN MOL 1599-1650
Dutch Portraits, Religious, Allegory $10,000

S.R.

PIER FRANCESCO MOLA 1612-1666
Italian Old Master, Landscape, Genre $3,000,000

1. *Molenaer*

2. *Molcnacr*

3. **MOLENÆR**

4. *M. Molenaar*

JAN MIENSE MOLENAER 1610-1668
Netherlandish Genre Peasants $275,000

CM

CORNELIS MOLENAER 1540-1591
Dutch Landscape, Religious, Mythology $5,000

N. Molenaar

NICOLAAS (also Klaes) MOLENAER 1630-1676
Dutch Landscape, Genre $30,000

Molyn

PIETER MOLIJN 1595-1661
Dutch Old Master, Landscape $35,000

Oskar Moll

OSKAR MOLL 1875-1947
German Painter, Genre, Landscape $50,000

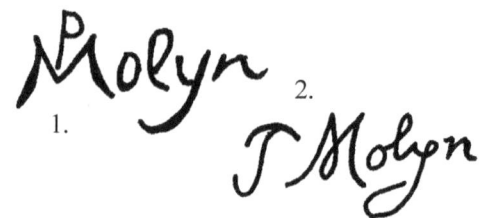

PIETER MOLYN 1637-1701
Dutch Seascape, Animals

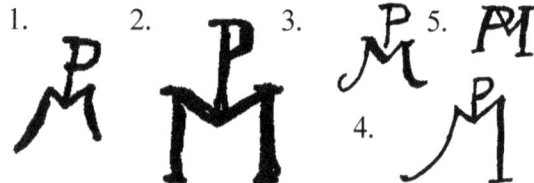

PIETER DE MOLYN 1599-1661
Dutch Landscape, Genre $35,000

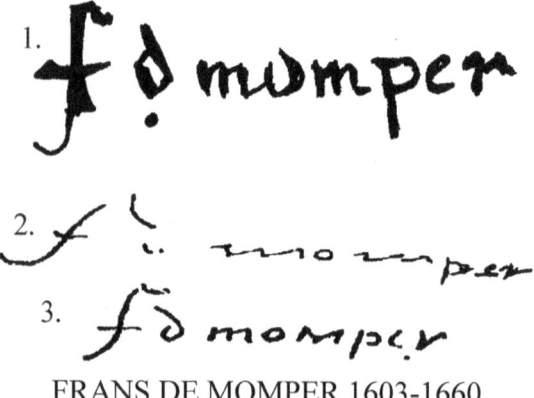

HENDRIK MOMMERS 1623-1697
Dutch Animals, Landscape, Genre $40,000

FRANS DE MOMPER 1603-1660
Netherlandish Landscapes $90,000

1. MONDRIAN 2. PM

3. *Piet Mondriaan*

4. *Piet Mondrian*

5. **PM**

6. ℝ

7. P. MONDRIAAN

8. PM 9. PM 10. PM

11. ℝ

12. PM

13. P. MONDRIAAN

14. ℝ. 16. *5iel Mondriaan*

15. PM 17.

18. PIET MONDRIAN

19. P. M. 20. P. MONDRIAAN

PIET (also Pieter Corelis) MONDRIAN 1872-1944
Dutch Destijl, Flowers, Landscapes, Block Art $40,000,000

1.

2.

3.

4.

5.

6.

7.

8.

9.

10.

11.

12.

13.

CLAUDE MONET 1840-1926
French Landscapes, Still, Portraits, Impressionist $80,000,000

GEORGE DANIEL DE MONFRIED 1865-1929
French Painter, Still Life, Portraits $15,000

LOUIS DE MONI 1698-1771
Dutch Portraits, Genre $25,000

1.

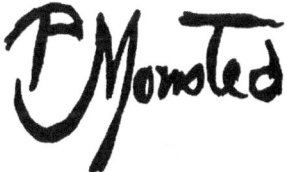

2.

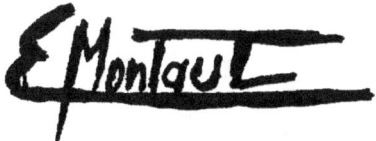

JEAN BAPTISTE MONNOYER 1634-1699
Dutch Still Life, Portraits $200,000

PEDER MORK MONSTED 1859-1941
Danish Landscape, Still Life $75,000

E. MONTAUT 1889-1909
French Painter, Genre $10,000

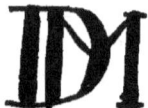

DIETRICH MONTEN 1799-1843
German Genre, Military $2,500

1.

2.

PIERRE-EUGENE MONTEZIN 1874-1946
French Painter, Genre, Landscape $75,000

1.

2.

DOLPHE JOSEPH THOMAS MONTICELLI 1824-1886
French Landscape, Genre $70,000

RAYMOND A. MONVOISIN 1794-1870
French Miniature Painter, Mythology $35,000

1.

2.

KAREL DE MOOR 1656-1738
Netherlandish Portraits, Genre $75,000

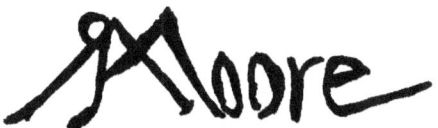

RUBENS ARTHUR MOORE-1920
British Cities Streets, Landscape $3,000

HENRY MOORE, O.M., C.H. 1898-1986
British Sculpture $6,167,500

MAX VON MOOS 1903-1979
Swiss Painter $30,000

ARMANDO MORALES 1927-
Latin American Abstract $160,000

EDWARD MORAN 1829-1895
American Seascapes, Landscape $30,000

PETER MORAN 1841-1914
American Indians, Landscape, Genre $10,000

1.

2.

THOMAS MORAN 1837-1926
American N.A. Landscape, Genre $2,752,500

PAT MORAN 1900's
British Still Life $5,000

GIORGIO MORANDI 1890-1964
Italian Landscape, Painter $1,300,000

ANGELO MORBELLI 1853-1919
Italian Painter, Genre, Landscape $2,202,000

GUSTAVE MOREAU 1826-1898
French Painter, Allegory $2,500,000

1.

2.

[signature: Rco r. moreelse]

[signature: Moreelse] 3.

PAULUS MOREELSE 1571-1638
Dutch Portraits, Genre, Allegory $200,000

[signature: W. F, A L VAARZON MOREL]

WILLEM VAARZON MOREL 1868-
Dutch Genre, Portraits $5,000

[signature: Henry Moret]

HENRI MORET 1856-1913
French Painter, Landscapes $100,000

[signature: Lucien Philippe Moretti]

LUCIEN PHILIPPE MORETTI 1922-
French Painter, Genre $15,000

[signature: Fred Morgan.]

FREDERICK MORGAN 1856-1927
British Genre, Portraits $75,000

[signature: E.M]

ERNST MORGENTHALER 1887-1962
Swiss Genre, Landscapes, Still Life $10,000

Berthe Morisot

BERTHE MORISOT 1841-1895
French Impressionist, Genre, Portraits, Landscape $3,850,000

L. Morland

GEORGE MORLAND 1763-1804
British (Check Nation) Animal Painter, Genre $65,000

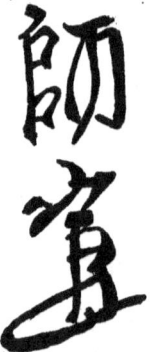

HISHIKAWA MORONOBU 1618-1703
Japanese Woodblock $3,500

1. *George L.K. Morris*

2. **MORRIS**

GEORGE L.K. MORRIS 1905-1975
American Abstract $40,000

Morocco.

ALBERTO MORROCCO 1917-
British Painter, Genre, Landscape $5,000

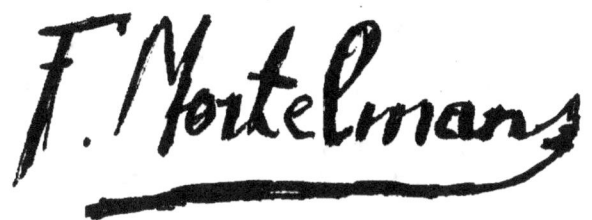

FRANZ MORTELMANS 1865-1936
Belgian Florals $25,000

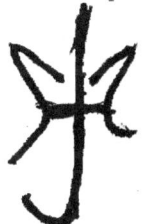

JOSEPH MORVILLER 1800-1870
American Landscape, Genre $7,500

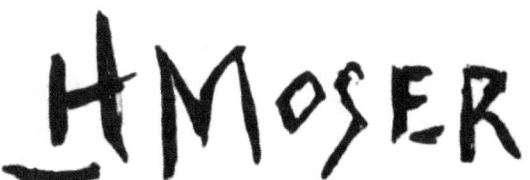

JACOB VAN MOSCHER Circa 1600's
Netherlandish Landscapes $30,000

JAMES HENRY MOSER 1854-1913
American Watercolour, Landscape $2,000

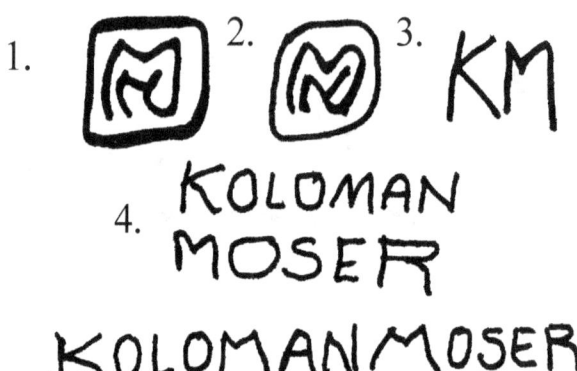

1. 2. 3. KM

4. KOLOMAN MOSER

5. KOLOMAN MOSER

KOLOMAN MOSER 1868-1918
Austrian Secessionist, Portraits, Landscapes, Designer

Henry Mosler

HENRY MOSLER 1840-1920
American Indians, Genre, Landscape $18,000

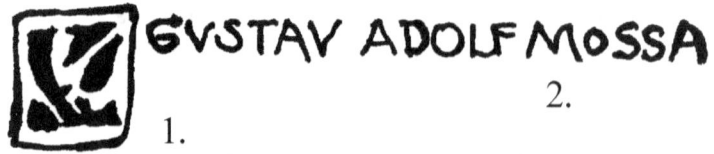

GVSTAV ADOLF MOSSA
2.
1.

GUSTAV ADOLF MOSSA 1883-1971
French Watercolour, Genre $40,000

G · MOSTART · F

GILLIS MOSTAERT 1533-1598
Netherlandish Religious Allegory, Genre, Landscape $60,000

1.

2.

ROBERT MOTHERWELL 1915-1991
American Abstract $7,922,500

1.

2.

ISAAC DE MOUCHERON 1667-1744
Netherlandish Marines, Landscapes, Portraits $30,000

1.

2.

3.

4.

5.

FREDERIK DE MOUCHERON 1633-1686
Netherlandish Landscape, Genre $40,000

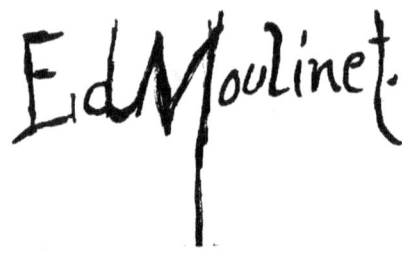

ANTOINE EDOUARD JOSEPH MOULINET 1833-1891
French Still Life, Genre $15,000

WILLIAM MOUNCEY 1852-1902
British Painter, Genre, Landscape $6,000

WILLIAM SYDNEY MOUNT 1807-1869
American N.A. Landscape, Genre $70,000

PIERRE MOURGUE
French Stage Costume Design $1,000

NICOLAAS (also Claes) MOYAERT 1600-1659
Dutch Portraits, Landscape, Allegory, Religious $12,000

Ch. Mozin

CHARLES LOUIS MOZIN 1806-1862
French Genre, Seascape, Landscape $12,000

HMücke

HEINRICH (also Karl Anton) MUCKE 1806-1891
German Painter, Genre $5,000

1. *Otto Mühuller*

2. *Otto Mueller*

3. *Otto Mueller*

OTTO MUELLER 1874-1930
German Expressionist $300,000

Hugo Mühlig

HUGO MUHLIG 1854-1929
German Genre, Landscape $50,000

W. Muller

WILLIAM JAMES MULLER 1812-1845
British Watercolour, Genre, Landscape $25,000

C.L. muller

CHARLES LOUIS LUCIEN MULLER 1815-1892
French Painter, Genre $20,000

W.Mulready

WILLIAM MULREADY 1786-1863
British Painter, Genre, Landscape $40,000

1. *E. Munch*

2. *E. Münch*

EDVARD MUNCH 1862-1944
German Expressionist $7,000,000

MUNIER

EMILE MUNIER 1810-1895
French Painter, Genre $80,000

Munkacsy

MICHEL LIEB MUNKACSY 1844-1900
Hungarian Painter, Genre, Landscape $35,000

Hugh Monro

HUGH MUNRO 1873-1928
British Watercolour, Genre, Landscape $7,500

1.

Münter 2.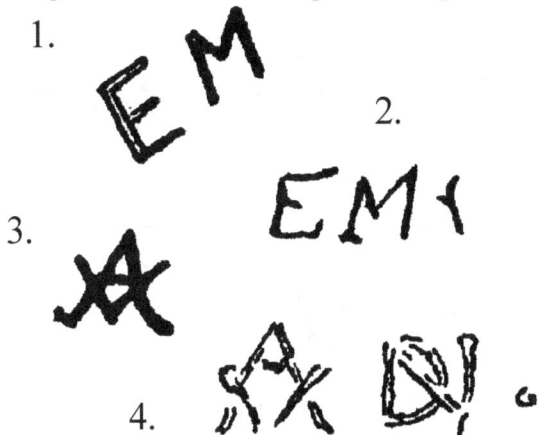

GABRIELE MUNTER 1877-1962
German Abstract, Expressionist $200,000

GERHARD MUNTHE 1849-1929
Norwegian Painter, Landscape, Seascapes $10,000

1.

2.

3.

4.

EMANUEL MURANT 1622-1700
Netherlandish Villages Scenes, Landscape, Genre $10,000

BARTOLOME ESTEBAN MURILLO 1618-1682
Spanish Painter, Genre, Religious, Portraits $4,230,000

J FRANCIS MURPHY.

JOHN FRANCIS MURPHY 1853-1921
American N.A. Landscape $10,000

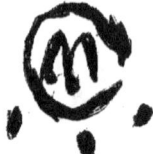

HERMAN D. MURPHY 1867-1945
American N.A. Illustrator, Landscape $10,000

MUSIC

ANTONIO ZORAN MUSIC 1909-1952
Italian Painter, Landscape, Genre $250,000

MICHIEL VAN MUSSCHER 1645-1705
Dutch Portraits, Landscape $35,000

JEROME MYERS

JEROME MYERS 1867-1940
American N.A. Etcher, Genre, Painter $20,000

DAVID MYNETT 1942-
British Landscape $1,000

JOHANNES MYTENS 1614-1671
Dutch Portraits, Landscape $40,000

Artists starting with the letter "N"

2.

1.

ELIE NADELMAN 1882-1946
American Painter, Sculpture, Genre $40,000

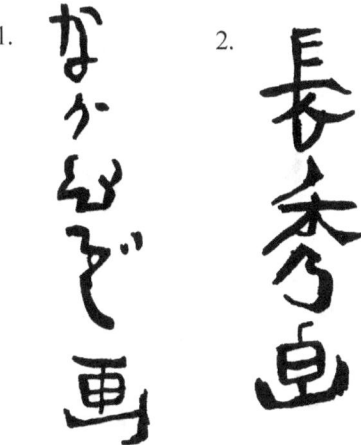

1.   2.

YURAKUSAI NAGAHIDE 1805-1842
Japanese Woodblocks, Actors $3,000

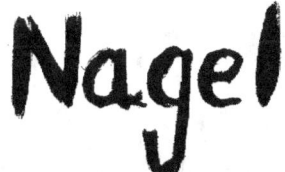

OTTO NAGEL 1894-1967
German Painter, Landscape $15,000

CHARLES CHRISTIAN NAHL 1818-1878
American Genre, Landscape $20,000

Naigeon

JEAN G. NAIGEON 1797-1867
French Genre, Portraits $7,000

NAKIAN

REUBEN NAKIAN 1897-1986
American Painter $35,000

B. Naldini

BATTISTA GIOVANNI NALDINI 1537-1584
Italian Painter, Genre, Religious, Portraits $40,000

E. Narjot

ERNEST NARJOT 1826-1898
American Landscape, Genre $7,000

NARVAEZ

FRANCISCO NARVAEZ 1908-1928
Venezualan Sculptor, Portraits $20,000

1.
2.
Nason   Nason

PIETER NASON 1612-1690
Netherlandish Still Life, Portraits $40,000

R NATALI

RENATO NATALI 1873-1979
Italian Painter, Genre, Landscape $5,000

1.

2.

ROBERT NATKIN 1930-
American Abstract $10,000

C Natoire

CHARLES JOSEPH NATOIRE 1700-1777
French Painter, Genre, Religious, Mythology $500,000

1.

2.

JEAN MARC NATTIER 1685-1766
French Portraits $500,000

BRUCE NAUMAN 1941-
American Contemporary $9,906,000

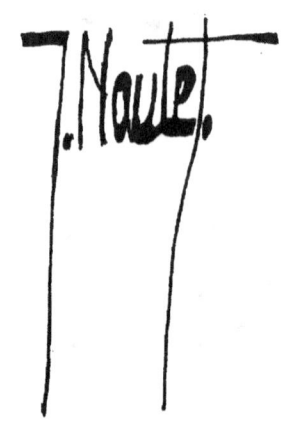

JEAN NAUTET 1900's
French Painter, Genre $1,000

JOSEPH FRANCOIS NAVEZ 1787-1869
Belgian Genre, Portraits, Religious, Landscape $10,000

OTTO WILHELM ERNST NEBEL 1892-1973
German Abstract $15,000

1.

2.

JAN VAN NECK 1635-1714
Netherlandish Genre Portraits $15,000

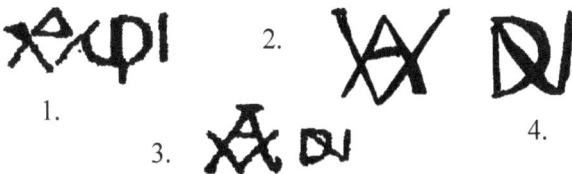

PEETER NEEFFS 1580-1656
Belgian Churches $40,000

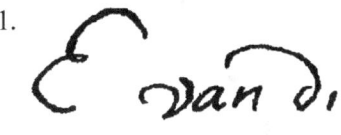

AERT VAN DER NEER 1603-1677
Netherlandish Moonlight Fires and Winter Scenes $800,000

EGLON HENDRIK VAN DER NEER 1634-1703
Netherlandish Genre Court Painter $1,000,000

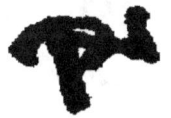

MICHAEL NEHER 1798-1876
German Architectural $30,000

PIETER DE NEIJN 1597-1639
Netherlandish Landscapes, Genre $45,000

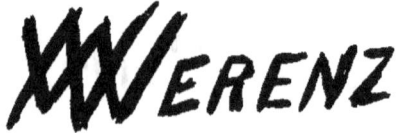

WILHELM NERENZ 1804-1871
German Genre $1,500

Nerly

FEDERIGO NERLY 1807-1878
German Landscape, Portraits $15,000

Nessi

MARIE-LUCIE NESSI 1910-
French Landscape $5,000

T. Netscher

THEDORUS NETCHER 1661-1732
Dutch Genre, Portraits

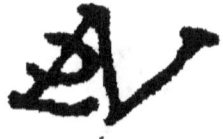

LAURENTIUS DE NETER 1600-
German Genre, Nymphs $10,000

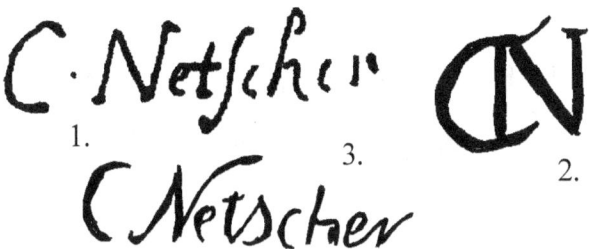

1. 3. 2.

CASPAR (also Gaspard) NETSCHER 1639-1684
German Portraits, Genre, Landscapes $90,000

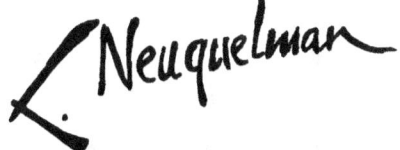

LUCIEN NEUQUELMAN 1909-1989
French Landscape, Marine, Genre $25,000

ALPHONSE DE NEUVILLE 1836-1885
French Genre, Animals, Portraits $6,000

LOUISE (Berliowsky) NEVELSON 1904-1988
American Sculptor $634,000

CHRISTOPHER R. W. NEVINSON 1889-1946
British Landscape, Portraits, Still Life $55,000

Hugh Newell

HUGH NEWELL 1830-1915
American Landscape $3,500

G. Glen Newell

G. GLENN NEWELL 1870-1942
American A.N.A. Landscape $1,000

1.

Barnett Newman

2.

BBNewman

BARNETT NEWMAN 1905-1970
American Minimalist $3,500,000

Dale Nichols

DALE NICHOLS 1904-
American Illustrator, Genre, Landscape $15,000

Nicholson

SIR WILLIAM NICHOLSON 1872-1949
British Landscapes $100,000

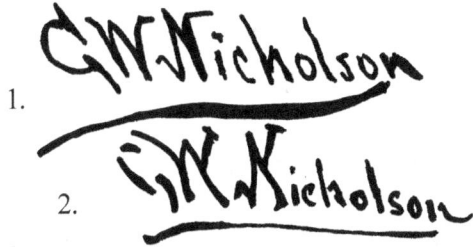

1.

2.

GEORGE WASHINGTON NICHOLSON 1832-1912
American Seascape, Genre, Landscape $3,500

1.

2.

3.

ISAAC (also Isaak) VAN NICKELEN 1660-1703
Netherlandish Architecture Interiors, Genre, Portraits $40,000

ERSKINE NICOL 1825-1904
British Painter, Genre $15,000

KASPER NIEHAUS 1889-1974
Dutch Painter, Genre, Landscape $3,500

JAIS NIELSEN 1885-1961
Danish Painter, Genre, Landscape $10,000

RUDOLFO NIETO 1937-1988
Mexican Painter, Modern $15,000

ADRIAEN VAN NIEULANDT 1587-1658
Netherlandish Allegorical, Portraits $25,000

WILLEM VAN NIEULANT 1584-1635
Flemish, Landscape, Religious, Painter, Engraver $40,000

LEA NIKEL 1918-
Israeli Abstract $10,000

GOSTA ADRIAN NILSSON 1884-1965
Swedish Abstract, Compositions $15,000

GIUSEPPE DE NITTIS 1846-1884
Italian Landscape, Portraits $650,000

JULES NOËL

JULES ACHILLE NOEL 1815-1881
French Paris Streets, Landscape, Genre $30,000

Nolde

EMIL NOLDE 1867-1956
German Expressionist $1,500,000

1.

Nölken 2.

FRANZ NOLKEN 1884-1918
German Painter, Expressionist $65,000

1.

2.

PIETER NOLPE 1601-1670
Dutch Landscape, Genre $24,000

1. *Zeeman*

2. *R· Zeemen*

REINIER (Zeeman) NOOMS 1623-1668
Netherlandish Boats Marines, Portraits, Landscapes $40,000

JAN VAN NOORT 1620-1676
Dutch Old Master, Landscapes, Genre $30,000

FEDERICO NORDALM 1949-
Latin American Landscape, Still Life $15,000

B.J.O. NORDFELDT 1878-1955
American Cowboys, Landscapes $20,000

ADELSTEEN NORMANN 1848-1918
Norwegian Landscape $10,000

STEFANO NOVO 1862-
Italian Painter, Genre $50,000

GEORGE L. NOYES 1864-1951
American Landscape, Genre $20,000

CARLO FRANCESCO NUVOLONE 1608-1651
Italian Portraits, Genre, Mythology, Religious $12,000

GIUSEPPE NUVOLONE 1619-1703
Italian Painter, Religious, Allegory, Portraits $50,000

JENNY NYSTROM 1854-1946
Swedish Painter, Genre, Landscape $85,000

Artists starting with the letter "O"

Oberfeuffer

GEORGE OBERTEUFFER 1878-1940
American Landscape, Genre $12,000

J. Ochtervelt

JACOB OCHTERVELT 1634-1710
Netherlandish Genre, Portraits $450,000

LEONARD OCHTMAN

LEONARD OCHTMAN 1854-1934
American Painter, Landscape $20,000

H. Oehmichen

HUGO OEHMICHEN 1843-1933
German Painter, Genre $20,000

Clara Oenicke

CLARA OENICKE 1818-1889
German Painter, Genre, Religious $4,500

TAKANARI OGUISS 1901-1986
Japanese Painter, Portraits, Still Life $550,000

1. 2. 3.

CLAES OLDENBURG 1929-
American Sculpture, Contemporary, Painter $2,210,000

ISAAC OLIVER 1556-1617
British Miniature, Religious, Allegory, Portraits $22,000

PETER OLIVER 1601-1660
British Miniature Painter, Portraits, Landscape $9,000

FRANCISCO OLLER Y CESTERO 1833-1917
Spain Still Life $100,000

BALTHAZAR P. OMMEGANCK 1755-1826
Belgian Landscape, Animals, Genre $10,000

MARIA VAN OOSTERWYCK
1.
2.
MARIA VAN OOSTERWIJCK 1630-1693
Netherlandish Still Life $60,000

JOHN OPIE 1761-1807
British Portraits, Genre $30,000

MERET OPPENHEIM 1913-1986
Swiss Abstract, Landscape, Genre $10,000

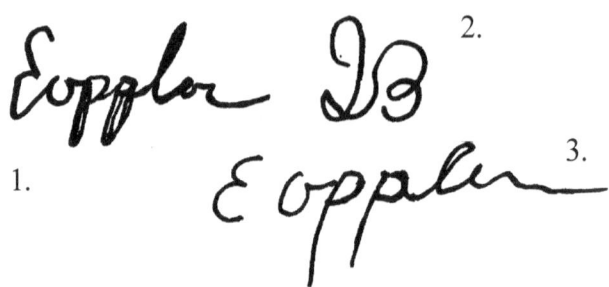

2.

1.

3.

ERNST OPPLER 1867-1929
German Stage Costume Design, Landscape, Genre $50,000

Joseph Ord

JOSEPH BAYAS ORD 1805-1865
American Portraits, Still Life $4,000

Sylvia Ordóñez

SYLVIA ORDONEZ 1956-
Mexican Landscape $20,000

Barnardi van Orley

1.

1422

2.

BARENT VAN ORLEY 1493-1542
Flemish Old Master, Landscape $60,000

1. *Orlik* 2. *Orlik*

EMIL ORLIK 1870-1932
Czech Painter, Landscape, Genre $30,000

ORLOWSKI

HANS ORLOWSKI (also Orlovsky) 1894-
German Painter, Genre, Portraits $7,500

1. *J.C. Orozco*

2. *J.C. Orozco*

JOSE CLEMENTE OROZCO 1883-1849
Mexican Painter, Genre, Landscape $200,000

1. *+P.OP.*

2. *+P.O.*

PEDRO ORRENTE 1570-1644
Spanish Landscape, Animals, Mythology, Religious $100,000

MOsorio

FRANCISCO MENESES OSORIO 1630-1705
Spanish Painter

1. *N Ostade*

2. *Nostade*

3. *N. Ostade*

4. *A∉*

5. *N.oftade*

ADRIAEN VAN OSTADE 1610-1685
Dutch Old Master, Portraits $3,720,000

1. *JsacK. Ostad*

2. *Isak van Ostadg*

3. *Jsack van Ostade*

ISACK VAN OSTADE 1621-1649
Netherlandish Landscapes Winter, Genre $200,000

Edm.H.Osthaus

EDMUND HENRY OSTHAUS 1858-1928
American Sporting, Landscape, Still Life $30,000

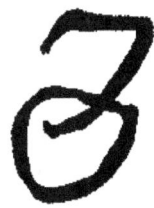

JOHANN NEPOMUK OTT 1804-1875 CK
German Landscape, Genre, Animals $7,500

ROLAND OUDOT 1897-1981
French Painter, Landscape $10,000

JEAN BAPTISTE OUDRY 1686-1755
French Animals Portraits, Still Life $1,033,000

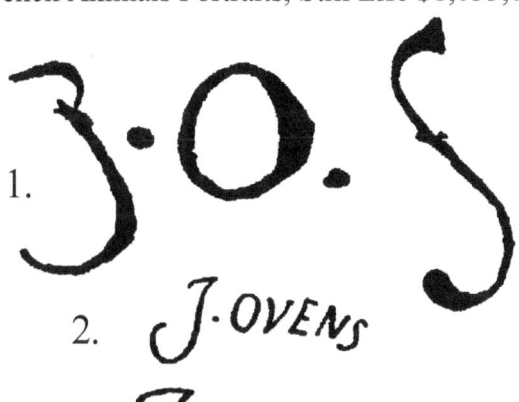

JURGEN OVENS 1623-1678
Dutch Portrait Allegorical, Genre $100,000

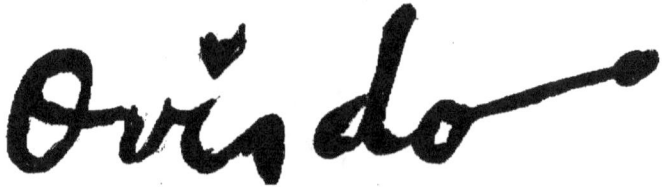

RAMON OVIEDO 1927-
Latin American Composition $7,500

ROBERT EMMETT OWEN 1878-1957
American Painter, Genre, Landscape $10,000

AMEDEE OZENFANT 1886-1967
French Painter, Abstract $150,000

Artists starting with the letter "P"

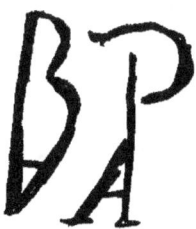

WALTER GILMAN PAGE 1862-1934
American Landscape, Genre $10,000

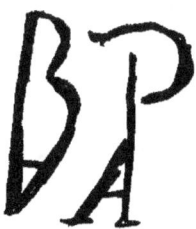

GIOVANNI BATTISTA PAGGI 1554-1627
Italian Churches, Genre, Mythology $20,000

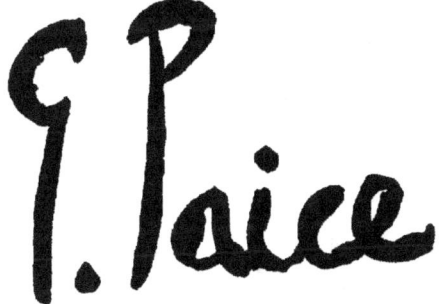

GEORGE PAICE 1854-1925
British Animals, Genre, Landscape $4,000

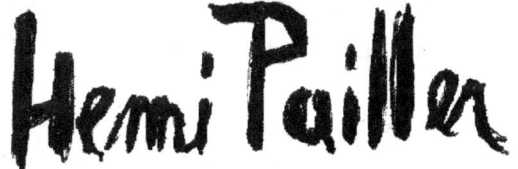

HENRI PAILLER 1876-1954
French Landscape $8,000

KEN PAINE 1900's
British Painter $3,000

2.

1.

3.

AMELIA PALAEZ 1897-1968
French Composition, Portraits $45,000

1.

2.

ANTHONIE (also Antonis, Stevers) PALAMEDESZ
(also Palmedes) Netherlandish Genre, Portrait $125,000

PALMEDESZ PALAMEDESZ (also Palmedes) 1607-1638
Dutch Battle Painter, Landscape $40,000

GIACOMO (also Jacopo Negretti) PALMA 1480-1528
Italian Painter, Genre, Mythology $50,000

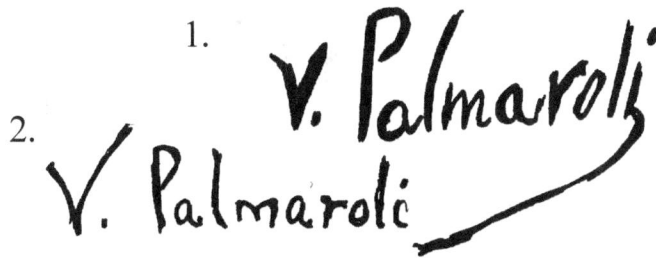

1.
2.

VINCENTE PALMAROLI Y GONZALEZ 1834-1896
Spanish Painter, Genre $90,000

WILLIAM C. PALMER 1906-1987
American Etcher, Genre, Landscape $5,000

IVO PANNAGI 1901-
Italian Compositions $20,000

GIOVANNI PAOLO PANNINI 1695-1768
Italian Architectural Painter $1,256,000

SILVIO D. PAOLETTI 1864-1921
Italian Painter, Genre $15,000

1.   2.

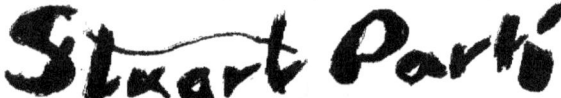

VINCENTA DE PAREDES 1845-1900
Spanish Painter, Genre, Portraits $20,000

JOHN STUART PARK 1862-1933
American Painter, Portraits, Still Life $10,000

1.

2.

JOHN ANTHONY PARK 1880-1962
British Seascape, Genre, Landscape $10,000

LAWTON PARKER 1868-1954
American A.N.A. Landscape $150,000

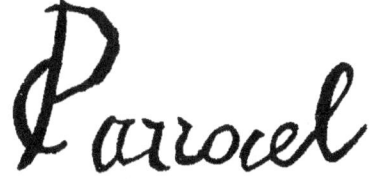

HENRY H. PARKER 1858-1930
British Landscape $25,000

Parrocel

CHARLES PARROCEL 1688-1752
French Battles, Genre, Portraits $12,000

Josephe parrocel

JOSEPH I. FRANCOIS PARROCEL 1704-1781
French Genre, Mythology $3,000

Beatrice Parsons

BEATRICE PARSONS 1870-1955
British Landscape, Still Life $10,000

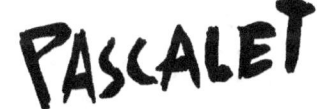

PIERRE PASCALET 1900's
French Landscape $1,000

Pascin

JULES PASCIN 1885-1930
American Painter, Genre $450,000

1. *A. Pasini*

2 *A. Pasini*

ALBERTO PASINI 1826-1899
Italian Painter, Genre $200,000

Passere

GIUSEPPE PASSERE 1654-1714
Italian Old Master, Genre, Allegory $8,000

B. Passig

B. PASSIG 1857-1915
German Painter, Genre $20,000

P Patel

PIERRE PATEL 1605-1676
French Landscape, Religious, Genre $300,000

1. *Pater* 2. *J B. Pater*

3. *B Pater*

JEAN BAPTISTE J. PATER 1695-1736
French Genre, Portraits $375,000

Viola Paterson

MARY VIOLA PATERSON 1898-1982
American Illustrator, Genre, Horses $7,500

FRANK PATON

FRANK PATON 1856-1909
British Watercolour, Genre, Landscape $45,000

McINTOSH
PATRICK

JAMES MCINTOSH PATRICK 1907-
British Landscapes $40,000

Christoff Pauditz

CHRISTOFFER PAUDITZ (also Paudiss) 1618-1666
German Portraits, Genre $20,000

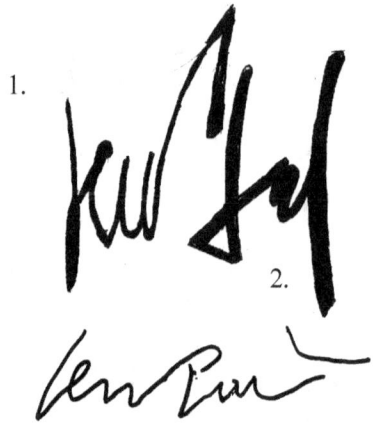

1.

2.

GEN PAUL 1895-1975
French Painter $30,000

1.

2.

FRITZ PAULSEN 1838-1898
German Genre, Portraits $5,000

PIERRE PAULUS 1881-1959
Belgian Landscape $14,000

PHILIPPE PAVY -1887
French Painter, Genre $35,000

JOHN PAWLE 1915-
British Still Life $2,000

EDGAR SAMUEL PAXSON 1852-1915
American Illustrator, Cowboys, Indians $45,000

WILLIAM MCGREGOR PAXTON 1869-1941
American N.A. Painter, Genre, Landscape $150,000

1.

2.

EDGAR PAYNE 1882-1947
American Seascape, Landscape $70,000

CHARLES JOHNSON PAYNE 1884-1967
British Illustrator, Genre $10,000

Rembrandt-Peale

REMBRANDT PEALE 1778-1860
American Portrait, Genre $3,000,000

A. P.

ANNA CLAY POOLE PEALE 1791-1878
American Painter $2,500

MARGUERITE S. PEARSON

MARGUERITE S. PEARSON 1898-1978
American Allegory, Genre $20,000

1. *HMP*   2. *MP*

HERMANN MAX PECHSTEIN 1881-1955
German Expressionist $1,400,000

Fr. Pecht

AUGUST FRIEDRICH PECHT 1814-1903
German Genre, Portraits, Allegory $4,000

1. *C. Pecrus*   2. *Pecrus*

CHARLES FRANCOIS PECRUS 1826-1907
French Painter, Genre, Seascape $20,000

PAUL PEEL

PAUL PEEL 1860-1892
Canadian Painter, Genre, Landscape $300,000

JAN PEETERS 1624-1677
Flemish Seascape, Religious, Genre $20,000

WALDO PEIRCE 1884-1970
American Painter, Genre $8,000

1.

3. APELAEZ-

2.

AMELIA PELAEZ 1897-1968
Latin American Abstract $30,000

1. AHP

2. AH.P. 3. AHP

ALFRED HEINRICH PELLEGRINI 1881-1958
Swiss Painter, Landscape, Genre $10,000

LEON GERMAINE PELOUSE 1838-1891
French Landscape, Genre $30,000

FRANCESCO PELUSO 1863-
Italian Painter, Landscape, Genre $3,500

A. R. PENCK 1939-
German Abstract $140,000

LUCA PENNI 1500-1560
Italian Painter, Mythology, Religious $30,000

EDWIN PENNY 1930-
British Birds Watercolour, Landscape $5,000

J. Peoli

JUAN JORGE PEOLI 1800's
Spanish Genre $6,000

1. 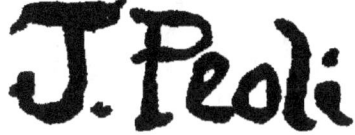   2.

SAMUEL JOHN PEPLOE 1871-1935
British Painter, Still Life, Landscape $150,000

MARTEN PEPYN 1575-1642
Flemish Painter, Genre, Mythology, Religious $7,000

PAUL EMMANUEL PERAIRE 1829-1893
French Landscape, Genre $14,000

FRANCISCO PERALTA DEL CAMPO 1836-1897
Spanish Painter, Genre $25,000

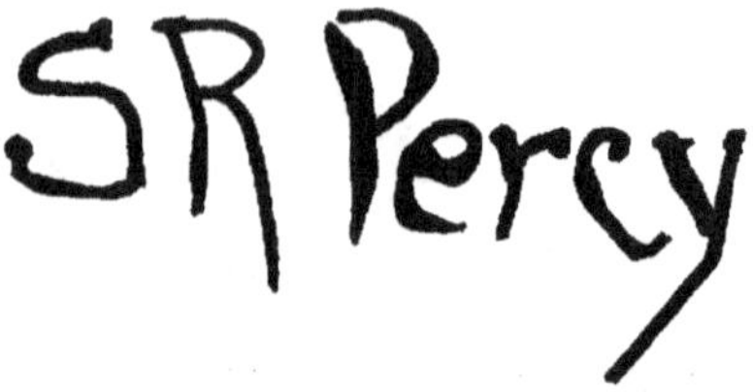

SR Percy

SIDNEY RICHARD PERCY 1821-1886
British Landscape $50,000

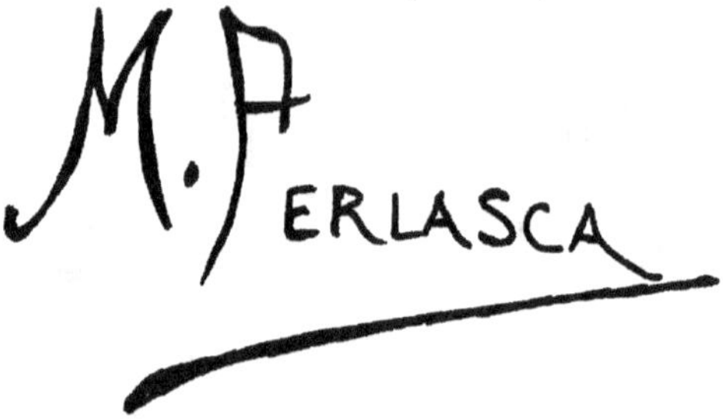

M.PERLASCA

MARTINO PERLASKA 1860-1899
Swiss Still Life $10,000

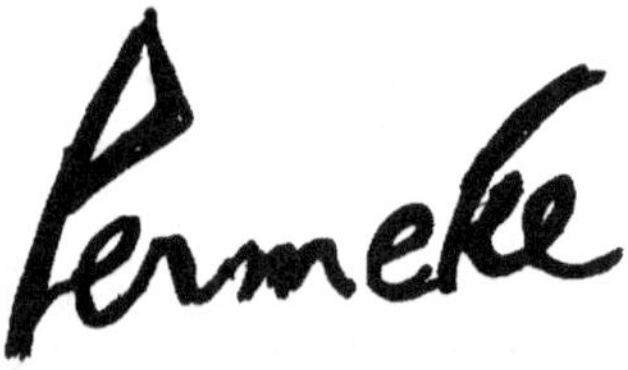

Permeke

CONSTANT PERMEKE 1886-1952
Belgian Landscape $140,000

1. -L-Perrault-

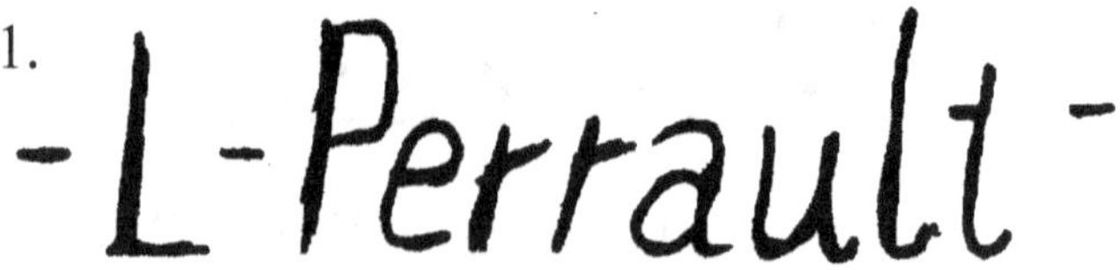

2. L Perrault

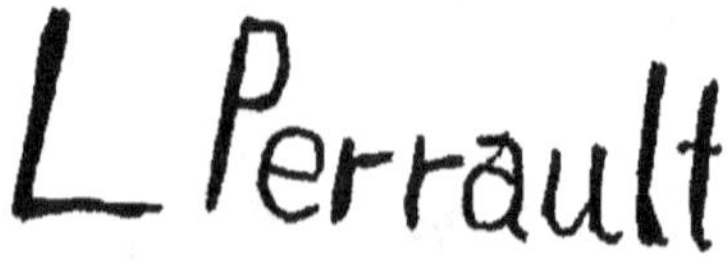

LEON JEAN BASILE PERRAULT 1832-1908
French Painter, Portraits, Genre $100,000

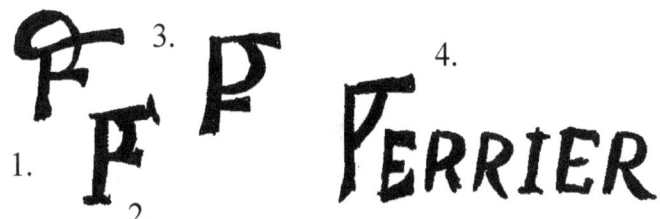

FRANCOIS PERRIER 1590-1656
French Genre, Mythology, Religious $150,000

JEAN BAPTISTE PERRONNEAU 1715-1783
French Portraits $75,000

LILLA CABOT PERRY 1848-1933
American Landscape, Portraits $25,000

PIETRO PERUGINO 1446-1523
Italian Painter, Portraits, Religious $45,000

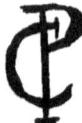

KARL GOTTLIEB PESCHEL 1798-1879
German Painter, Landscape, Religious $1,000

1.

Atonius Pesne

2.

A. Pesne

ANTOINE PESNE 1683-1757
French Portraits $100,000

Storm P

ROBERT STORM PETERSEN 1882-1949
Danish Landscape, Genre $5,000

1.

E. Petitjean

2.

E. Petitjean

EDMOND PETITJEAN 1844-1925
French Landscape, Genre $20,000

J.F. Peto

JOHN FREDERICK PETO 1854-1907
American Still Life $500,000

Pettoruci

EMILIO PETTORUTI 1892-1971
Argentinian Genre, Compositions, Still Life $250,000

Pevsner

ANTOINE PEVSNER 1886-1962
Russian Composition, Painter, Sculpture $100,000

P Peyron

JEAN F, PIERRE PEYRON 1744-1814
French Genre, Allegory, Portraits $20,000

Robert C Lii

ROBERT PHILIPP 1895-1981
American N.A. Painter, Genre $15,000

J. Philippoteaux

PAUL DOMINIQUE PHILIPPOTEAUX 1845-1923
French Painter, Genre, Landscapes, Portraits $40,000

BERT GREER PHILLIPS 1868-1956
American Illustrator, Genre, Landscapes $40,000

GIOVANNI BATTISTA PIAZZETTA 1682-1754
Italian Painter, Portraits, Landscape, Religious $500,000

1. 2.

FRANCIS PICABIA 1878-1953
Spanish Abstract $4,780,880

BERARD PICART 1673-1733
French Old Master, Allegory $20,000

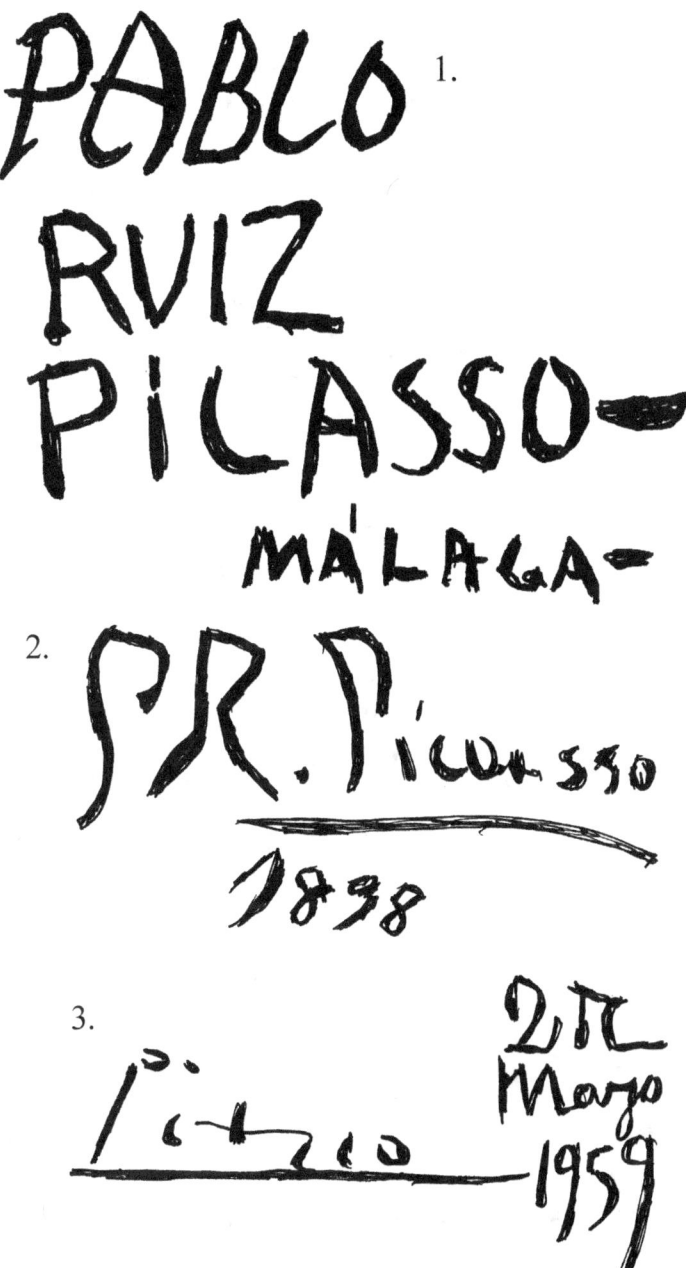

PABLO PICASSO 1881-1974
Spanish Cubist $106,500,000

4.

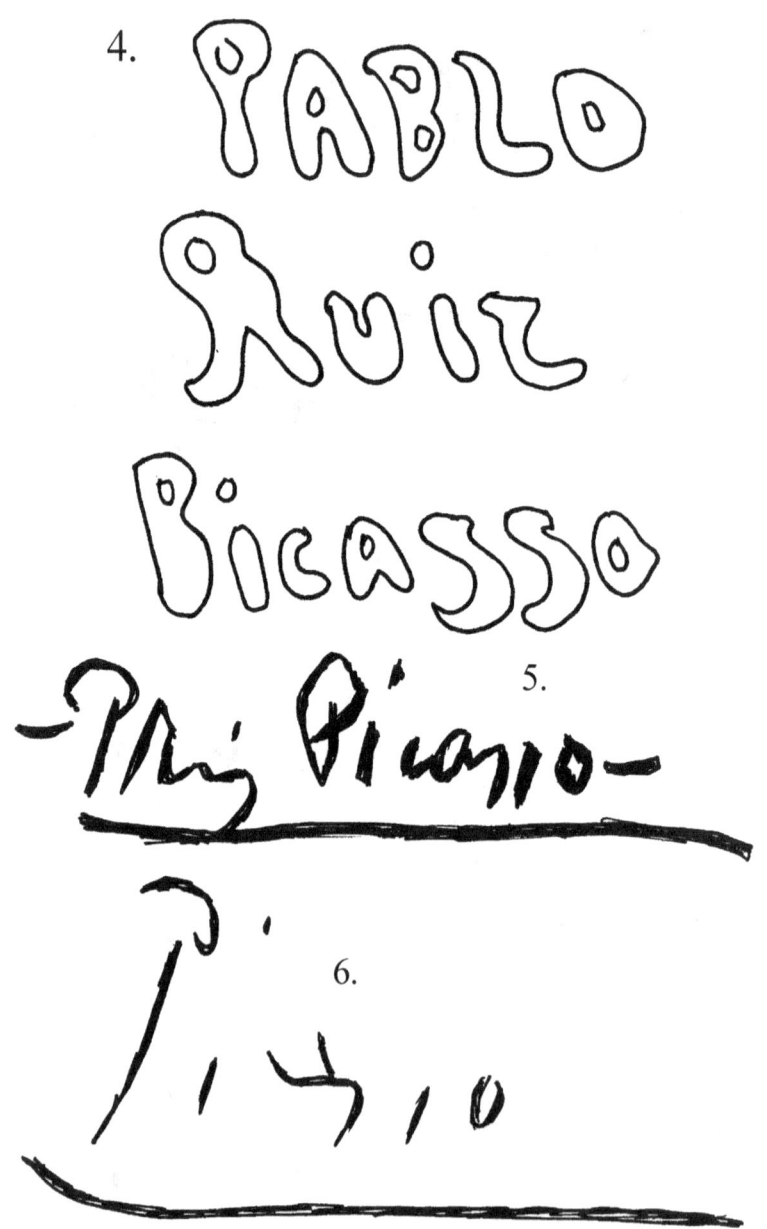

5.

6.

PABLO PICASSO 1881-1974
Spanish Cubist $106,500,000

7.

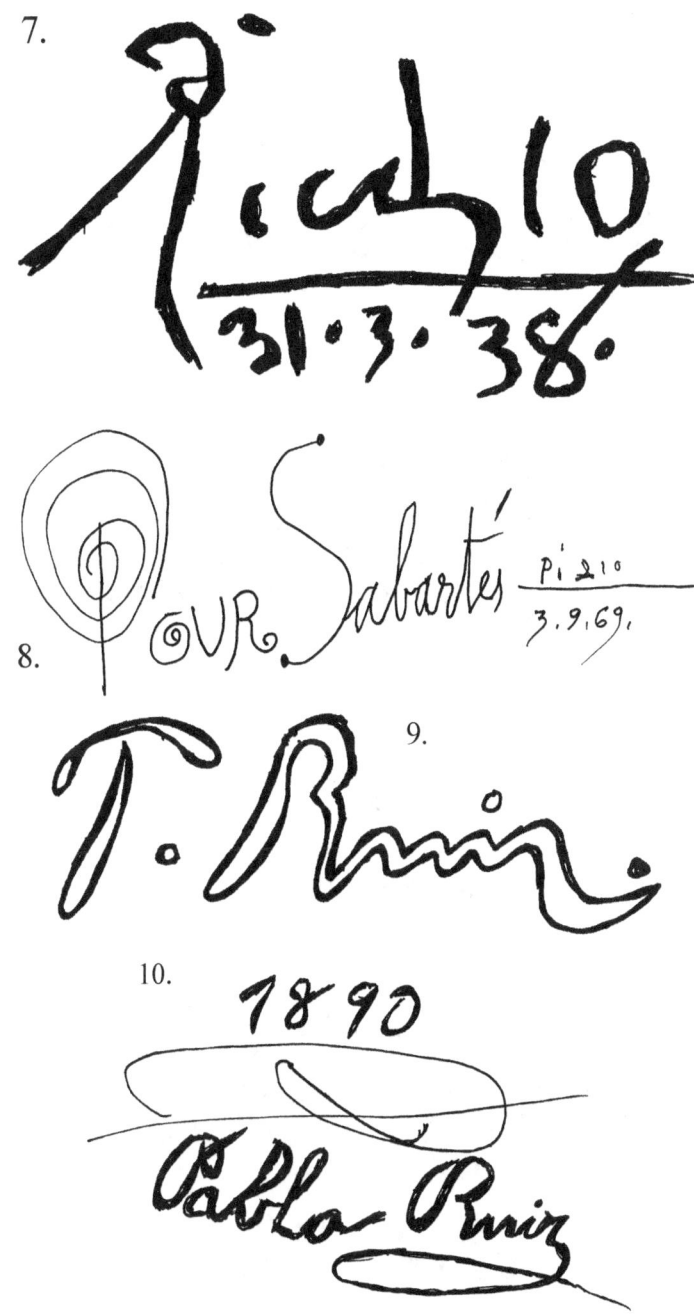

8.

9.

10.

PABLO PICASSO 1881-1974
Spanish Cubist $106,500,000

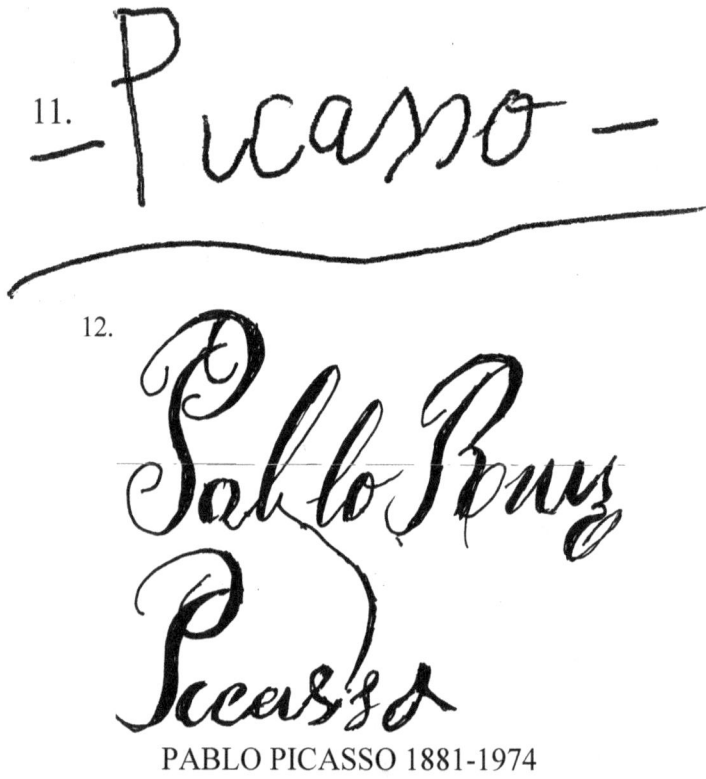

11.

12.

PABLO PICASSO 1881-1974
Spanish Cubist $106,500,000

WILLIAM LAMB PICKNELL 1854-1897
American Landscapes, Genre $30,000

FRANZ XAVIER PIELER 1897-1952
Austrian Still Life $12,000

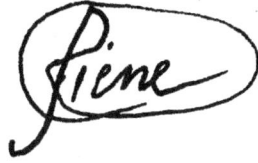

OTTO PIENE 1928-
German Painter, Genre $20,000

1. 2.

JEAN BAPTISTE PIERRE 1713-1789
French Painter, landscape, Portraits, Allegory $80,000

1. 2.

3. 4.

EVERT PIETERS 1856-1932
Dutch Landscape, Genre $25,000

AERT PIETERSZ 1550-1612
Netherlandish Portraits $20,000

EDOUARD PIGNON 1905-1993
French Abstract $55,000

Rodolphe Piguet

RODOLPHE PIGUET 1840-1915
Swiss Genre, Landscapes, Portraits $25,000

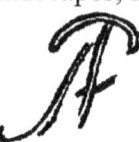

ADAM PIJNACKER 1622-1673
Netherlandish Landscapes $500,000

O. Piltz

OTTO PILTZ 1846-1910
German Animals, Genre $40,000

1. *Robert A Pinchon*

2. *Robert Pinchon*

ROBERT ANTOINE PINCHON 1886-1943
French Landscape, Still Life $100,000

PINELLI

BARTOLOMEO PINELLI 1781-1835
Italian Watercolour, Landscape, Genre $5,000

a. Pinot

ALBERT PINOT 1875-1962
Belgian Painter, Landscape, Genre $5,000

D Piola

DOMENICO PIOLA 1628-1703
Italian Painter, Religious, Portraits, Mythology $125,000

Adolphe Piot

ADOLPHE PIOT 1850-1910
French Painter, Genre $20,000

H Pippin

HORACE PIPPIN 1888-1946
American Sculpture, Landscapes, Blacks, Genre $350,000

*Paul Emile _ Pissarro_*

PAUL EMILE PISSARRO 1884-1972
French Painter, Landscape $10,000

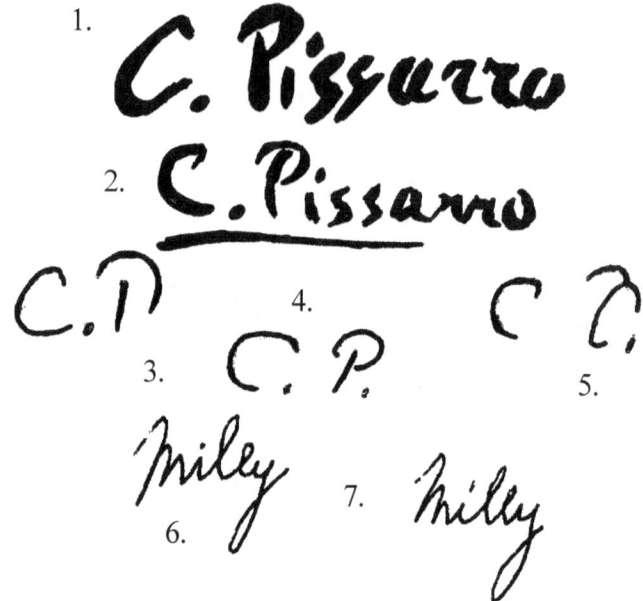

1. C. Pissarro
2. C. Pissarro
3. C. P
4. C. P.
5. C. P.
6. Milly
7. Milly

CAMILLE (MELBY) PISSARRO 1830-1903
French Painter, Landscape, Genre, Impressionist $14,601,000

EP

EDUARD PISTORIUS 1796-1862
German Genre, Animals $3,500

Hobson P. Hman

HOBSON PITTMAN 1900-1972
American Painter, Landscape $10,000

N. Pizzolo

NICCOLO PIZZOLO -1645
Dutch Still Life

JUAN BATLLE PLANAS 1911-1966
Argentinian Composition, Genre $6,000

JOHAN GEORG PLATZER 1702-1760
Swiss Genre, Allegory, Religious $350,000

OGDEN PLEISSNER 1905-1983
American Painter, Landscape $45,000

EGBERT VAN DER POEL 1621-1664
Netherlandish Night Night Landscapes, Portraits, Genre $35,000

1.

2.

3.

4.

CORNELIS VAN POELENBURG 1586-1667
Dutch Landscape, Mythology, Genre $80,000

1.

2.

GEORGES DE POGEDAIEFF 1896-1950
Russian Stage Costume Design $5,000

HECTOR POLEO 1919-
Venezualan Genre $140,000

SERGE POLIAKOFF 1900-1969
Russian Abstract $500,000

JAMES POLLARD 1792-1867
British Sporting, Genre $100,000

ALFRED POLLENTINE 1836-1890
British Water Scenes $9,000

1.

2.

3.

JACKSON POLLOCK 1912-1956
American Abstract $140,000,000

FIDELIO PONCE DE LEON 1895-1949
Cuban Seascapes, Genre $100,000

1.

3.

2.

WILLEM DE POORTER 1608-1648
Netherlandish Allegory, Genre, Portraits $50,000

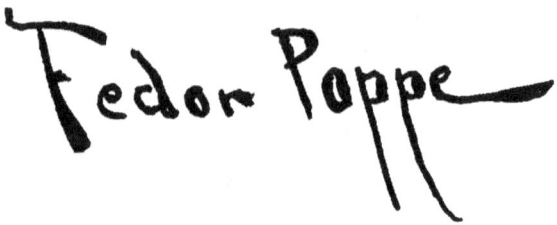

FEDOR POPPE 1850-
German Landscape, Genre $4,000

FAIRFIELD PORTER 1907-1975
American Landscape, Genre $100,000

EDWARD PORTIEL JE 1861-1949
Belgian Portrait, Genre $15,000

CANDIDO PORTINARI 1903-1962
Brazilian Painter, Genre $90,000

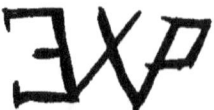

WILHELM E. POSE 1812-1878
German Landscape $6,000

FRANZ JANSZ POST 1612-1680
Dutch Old Master, Genre $4,512,000

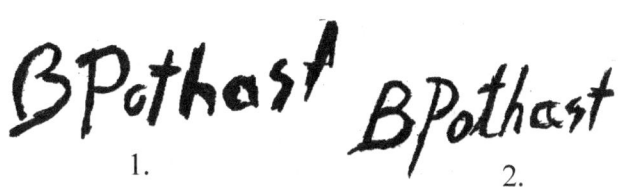

1.   2.

BERNARD POTHAST 1882-1966
Dutch Children, Genre $30,000

LASLETT JOHN POTT 1837-1898
British Painter, Genre $10,000

PIETER SIJMONSZ POTTER 1597-1652
Netherlandish Landscape, Genre, Still Life $25,000

2.

1.   3.

PAULUS POTTER 1625-1654
Dutch Animal, Landscape, Genre $1,000,000

1.

2.

EDWARD HENRY POTTHAST 1857-1927
American N.A. Beach Scenes, Landscape, Genre $150,000

MICHEL MARIE POULAN 1906-
French Painter, Genre $1,000

1.　　　　　　2.

FRANS Elder POURBUS 1545-1581
Flemish Portraits, Religious $20,000

1.　　　　　2.

NICOLAS POUSSIN 1591-1665
French Landscape, Mythology, Genre $21,050,000

ASAHEL POWERS 1813-1843
American Primitive, Portraits $15,000

PRAMPOLINI

1.

2.　E.P.　E. PRAMPOLINI

3.
ENRICO PRAMPOLINI 1894-1956
Italian Portraits, Compositions, Landscape, Genre $85,000

A. Pratella

ATTILIO PRATELLA 1856-1949
Italian Landscapes, Genre $30,000

V. Prax

VALENTINE HERRIETTE PRAX 1899-1981
French Cubist, Landscape, Genre $20,000

P

FRIEDRICH JOHANN PRELLER 1804-1878
German Landscape, Genre, Allegory, Portraits $5,000

Prendergast

MAURICE PRENDERGAST 1859-1924
American Ash Can, Landscape $3,256,000

LW Prentice

LEVI WELLS PRENTICE 1851-1935
American Landscape $50,000

J. Pressmane

JOSEPH PRESSMANE 1904-1967
Russian Painter, Landscape, Genre $15,000

Previati

GAETANO PREVIATI 1852-1920
Italian Genre, Portraits, Allegory $100,000

1.

Emilie Preyer.

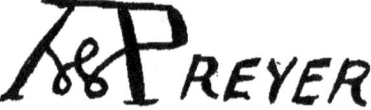

Emilie Preyer. 2.

EMILIE PREYER 1849-1930
German Still Life $50,000

REYER

JOHANN WILHELM PREYER 1803-1889
German Still Life $50,000

**Julius
M
Price**

JULIUS MENDES PRICE 1857-1924
British Genre $10,000

CESAR PRIETO

CESAR PRIETO 1882-1976
Venezualan Painter $3,500

1. 2.

Priking Priking

FRANZ PRIKING 1927-1979
French Landscape $60,000

Prina

ANDRE-JULIEN PRINA 1886-1941
French Landscape, Still Life $10,000

I.C.Pᵣₒˢ.F

GIULIO CESARE PROCACCINI 1548-1626
Italian Painter, Religious, Mythology, Portraits $225,000

A·PHIMISTER PROCTOR

ALEXANDER PHIMISTER PROCTOR 1862-1950
American N.A. Animals $150,000

PAlex Protais

PAUL ALEXANDRE PROTAIS 1826-1890
French Battle Painter $3,000

P.F. Prudhon

PIERRE P. PRUDHON 1758-1823
French Portraits, Genre, Religious, Allegory $260,000

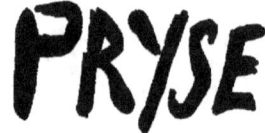

TESSA SPENCER PRYSE 1939-
British Landscape $1,000

FERDINAND LOYEN DU PUIGAUDEAU 1864-1930
French Landscape $90,000

HANS PURRMANN 1880-1966
German Painter, Landscape, Still Life $90,000

ALFONS PURTSCHER 1885-1962
Austria Landscape, Animals $3,000

1.

2.

LEO PUTZ 1869-1940
German Genre, Landscape $120,000

T. Puvis de Chavannes

PIERRE PUVIS DE CHAVANNES 1824-1898
French Impressionist, Landscape, Allegory, Genre $350,000

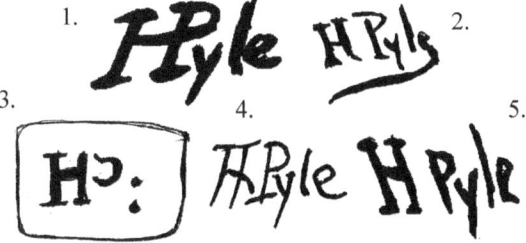

1. HPyle 2. HPyle
3. Hᵒ: 4. HPyle 5. H Pyle

HOWARD PYLE 1853-1911
American N.A. Illustrator, Genre, Landscape $60,000

1. *Pynacker* 2. *Pynaker*

ADAM PYNACKER 1621-1673
Dutch Landscape, Seascape, Animals $550,000

Artists starting with the letter "Q"

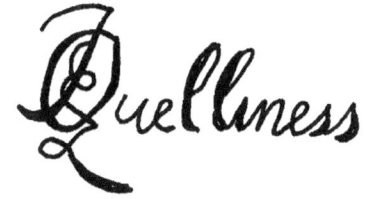

PIETER JANSZ QUAST 1606-1647
Dutch Old Master, Genre $20,000

JAN ERASMUS QUELLINUS 1634-1715
Flemish Painter, Genre, Mythology, Religious $9,000

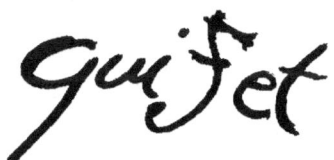

AUGUST QUERFURTH 1697-1761
German Military, Hunt Painter, Genre, Landscape $25,000

ALPHONSE LEON QUIZET 1885-1955
French Landscape, Seascape $40,000

Artists starting with the letter "R"

CORNELIS RAAPHORST 1875-1954
Dutch Painter $8,500

EDMUND RABE 1815-1902
German Landscape $7,500

OSKAR IAKOVLEVICH RABIN 1928-
Russian Genre $7,500

ARTHUR RACKHAM 1867-1939
British Illustrator, Genre, Landscape $100,000

ZYGNUNT RADNICKI 1900's
Polish Landscape $1,000

Fr.

FRANZ RADZIWILL 1895-1983
German Woodcut, Genre, Landscape $125,000

1. *JF RAFFAËLLI*   2. *JFR*
3. *JF RAFFAËLLI*

JEAN FRANCOIS RAFFAELLI 1850-1924
French Landscape Villages, Genre $100,000

Raffele

AMBROGIO RAFFELE 1845-1928
Italian Painter $1,000

1. *Milne Ramsey*

2. *Milne-Ramsey*

MILNE RAMSEY 1847-1915
American Landscape, Genre $10,000

R   A   N   S   O   N

PAUL RANSON 1864-1909
American Stage Costume Design, Nabis School, Landscape

J. Raoux

JEAN RAOUX 1677-1734
French Genre $20,000

Raphael *Raphaels*
1.   2.

Raphaello
3.

(Raphael Sanzio), (Raffaello) RAPHAEL 1483-1520
Italian Religious $7,920,000

H. Raschen

HENRY RASCHEN 1854-1937
American Indians, Landscape, Genre $20,000

Rattner
1.   2.
Rattner

ABRAHAM RATTNER 1895-1978
American Painter $10,000

E. Rau

EMIL RAU 1858-1937
German Landscape, Genre $15,000

J. N. Rauch

JOHANN NEPOMUK RAUCH 1804-1847
Austrian Painter, Landscape $5,000

RAUSCHENBERG

ROBERT RAUSCHENBERG 1925-
American Contemporary $7,260,000

Ravisteijn

ARNOLDUS VAN RAVESTEIJN 1605-1690
Netherlandish Portraits Allegory $5,000

1.
AR
2.
J. Ravestein

ANTHONY VAN RAVESTEIJN 1580-1669
Netherlandish Portraits $6,000

1.
Ravesteyn

J. Ravestein
2.

JAN ANTHONISZ VAN RAVESTEIJN
(also Ravesteyn) 1570-1657
Netherlandish Portraits, Old Master, Genre $75,000

G.P. Ream

CARDUCIUS PLANTAGENET REAM 1837-1917
American Still Life $6,500

1. *Recco*

2. *gias Recco*

GIUSEPPE RECCO 1634-1695
Italian Still Life $20,000

1. **E.W. REDFIELD**

2. **E.W. REDFIELD**

EDWARD WILLIS REDFIELD 1869-1965
American Landscape $100,000

1. *Od . R .*

2. **OD. R**

ODILON REDON 1840-1916
French Landscape $3,815,000

P. J. Redoute

PIERRE-JOSEPH REDOUTE 1759-1840
French Painter, Still Life, Portraits $1,300,000

[signature: Anne Redpath]

ANNE REDPATH 1895-1965
British Landscape $25,000

[signature: A.C. Redwood]

ALLEN C. REDWOOD 1844-1922
American Illustrator, War $7,000

[signature: Russell Reeve]

RUSSELL SYDNEY REEVE 1895-1970
British Genre Horses $2,500

[signature: Anton Ref Refregier]

ANTON REFREGIER 1905-1979
American Painter, Genre $1,000

[signature: V Reggianini]

VITTORIO (also Victorio) REGGIANINI 1858-1938
Italian Genre, Portraits $80,000

Regnault

JEAN BAPTISTE REGNAULT 1754-1829
French Genre $80,000

Regoyos

DARIO DE REGOYOS 1845-1913
Spanish Genre $75,000

John R. Reid

JOHN ROBERTSON REID 1851-1926
British Painter, Landscape, Genre $6,500

WINOLD REISS

FRITZ WINOLD REISS 1886-1953
American Illustrator, Indians $2,500

1. *Remband*

2. *Rembrandt*

3. *Rembrandt*

4. *RL* 5. *RL*

6. *Rembrandt*

RL·van Rijn 7.

HARMENSZ VAN RIJN REMBRANDT 1606-1669
Netherlandish Portraits Allegorical $28,690,000

1. *Frederic Remington*

2. *REMINGTON-*

FREDERIC REMINGTON 1861-1909
American A.N.A. Cowboys $5,172,000

P Renard

PAUL RENARD 1871-1920
French Paris Streets, Genre $3,000

1. 2.

3. 4.

PIERRE AUGUSTE RENOIR 1841-1919
French Impressionist $78,100,000

ARNOLD RENTICK 1712-1774
Dutch, Painter

ILYA EFIMOVICH REPIN 1844-1930
Russian Etcher, Portraits, Genre $2,100,000

JEAN RESTOUT 1692-1768
French Portraits, Monks $25,000

ETIENNE RET 1900-
American Portraits, Genre $1,000

A.REVERON

ARMANDO REVERON 1889-1956
Venezualan Painter, Genre, Landscape $160,000

1. *Ravueltas* 2. *FR*

3. *REVUELTAS*

FERMIN REVUELTAS 1903-1935
Mexican Genre $6,500

A.Reyna

ANTONIO REYNA 1860-1937
Spanish Painter, Genre $45,000

Rhana

LISA RHANA 1900's
American Costume Stage Design $1,000

L' Rheiner

LOUIS RHEINER 1863-1924
Swiss Painter, Landscape, Genre $15,000

MANLIO RHO

MANLIO RHO 1901-1957
Italian Painter $40,000

JOSEF ANTON RHOMBERG 1786-1853
German Religious $3,500

1.

2.   3.

JUSEPE DE RIBERA 1590-1652
Spanish Portraits Allegorical, Old Master $4,500,000

THEODULE AUGUSTIN RIBOT 1823-1891
French Painter, Genre, Still Life $90,000

SEBASTIANO RICCI 1659-1734
Italian Genre $280,000

CAMILLO RICCI 1580-1618
Italian Religious $4,000

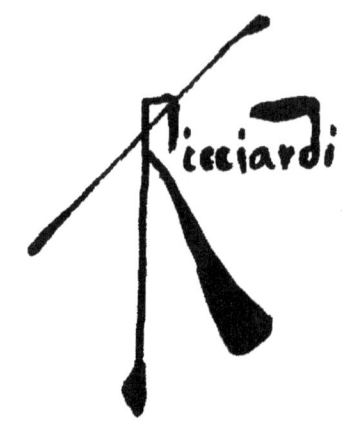

OSCAR RICCIARDI 1864-1935
Italian Seascapes, Genre $15,000

1.   2.

FLEURY FRANCOIS RICHARD 1777-1852
French Genre $8,500

WILLIAM TROST RICHARDS 1833-1905
American N.A. Landscape $90,000

FREDERICK DE BOURG RICHARDS 1822-1903
American Landscape $10,000

F. Richardt

FERDINAND J. RICHARDT 1819-1895
American Landscape $25,000

Léon Richet

LEON RICHET 1847-1907
French Painter, Genre, Landscape $15,000

Herman Richir

HERMAN JEAN JOSEPH RICHIR 1866-1942
Belgian Painter, Genre $15,000

L. Richmond

LEONARD RICHMOND-1965
British Landscape $5,000

Richomme

JULES RICHOMME 1818-1903
French Painter, Genre $1,500

2.

F. Richter   E. Richter

1.

EDOUARD FREDERIC WILHELM RICHTER 1844-1913
French Landscape, Genre $25,000

PHILIP RICKMAN 1891-1982
British Landscapes, Watercolour $8,500

MARTIN RICO Y ORTEGA 1833-1908
Spanish Landscape, Genre $100,000

VIRGINIA RIDLEY 1900'S
British Still Life $1,000

JOHANN ANTON RIEDEL 1736-1816
German Painter

AUGUST (also Heinrich) RIEDEL 1802-1883
German Genre $40,000

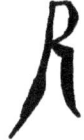

JOHANN E. RIEDINGER 1698-1767
German Portraits $20,000

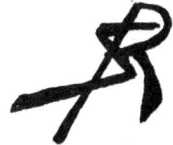

HYACINTHE RIGAUD 1659-1743
French Portraits $500,000

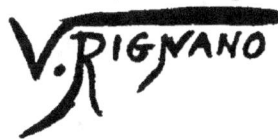

SIGISMUND RIGHINI 1870-1937
German Painter, Landscape $10,000

VITTORIO RIGNANO 1860-1916
Italian Painter, Genre $6,500

ALBERT RIGOLOT 1862-1932
Italian Landscape, Genre $20,000

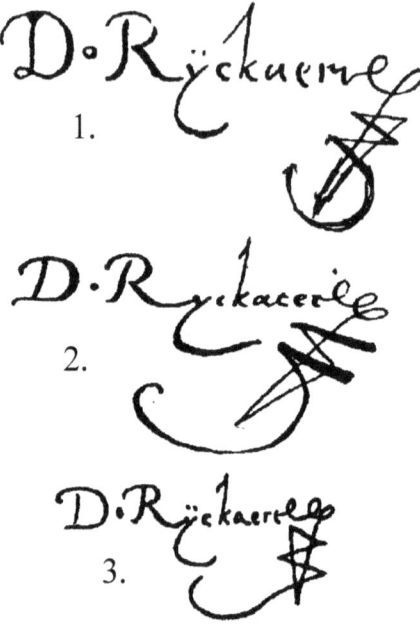

1.

2.

3.

DAVID (the younger) RIJCKAERT 1612-1661
Netherlandish Genre, Old Master $20,000

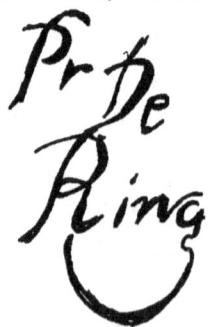

PIETER DE RING 1615-1660
Dutch Still Life $250,000

THIJS RINSEMA 1877-1947
Dutch Still Life $5,000

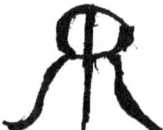

JOZSEF RIPPL-RONAI 1861-1927
Hungarian Painter, Landscape, Genre $25,000

JOHN RITCHIE 1809-1850
British Genre, Landscape $25,000

LOUIS RITMAN 1889-1963
American Landscape, Still Life $90,000

WILLIAM RITSCHEL 1864-1949
American N.A. Plein Aire, Landscape, Impressionist $50,000

1.

2.

3.

DIEGO RIVERA 1886-1957
Mexican Murals, Landscape, Genre $3,082,000

1.

2.

LARRY RIVERS 1923-
American Contemporary $450,000

F'Rizi

FRANCISCO RIZI 1608-1685
Spanish Landscape $10,000

Ellen Robbins

ELLEN ROBBINS 1828-1905
American Watercolour, Still Life $3,500

L. Robert

LEOPOLD ROBERT 1794-1835
French Landscape $7,500

1.
H Robert

H ROBERT
2.

HUBERT ROBERT 1733-1808
French Genre $500,000

JAMES ROBERTS

JAMES ROBERTS 1776-1809
British Sporting, Genre $15,000

William Roberts

WILLIAM ROBERTS
Painter

MOSES.

ANNA MARY ROBERTSON ("GRANDMA") 1860-1961
American Farms $70,000

1. *J. Robie*   2. *J. Robie*

JEAN BAPTISTE ROBIE 1821-1910
Belgian Landscape $55,000

Th. Robinson

THEODORE ROBINSON 1852-1896
American Landscapes, Genre $1,102,500

*W. HEATH
ROBINSON*

WILLIAM HEATH ROBINSON 1872-1944
British Illustration, Genre $30,000

Richard Robjent

RICHARD ROBJENT 1936-
British Landscape $3,500

G Rochegrosse

GEORGES ANTOINE ROCHEGROSSE 1859-1938
French Painter, Genre, Landscape $60,000

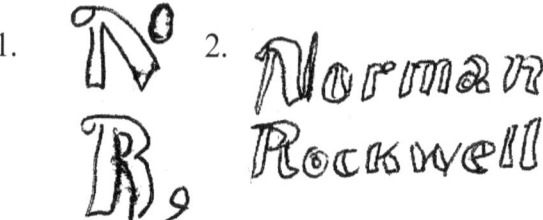

1.　2.

NORMAN ROCKWELL 1894-1978
American Illustrator, Genre $15,400,000

CLEVELAND ROCKWELL 1836-1907
American Landscape, Genre $50,000

1.

2.

ALEXANDER RODCHENKO 1891-1956
Russian Painter $450,000

AUGUSTE RODIN 1840-1917
French Impressionist, Sculptor $4,800,000

KOENRAAD ROEPEL 1678-1748
Dutch Still Life $80,000

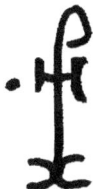

NICHOLAS ROERICH 1875-1947
Russian Stage Costume Design, Landscape $2,200,500

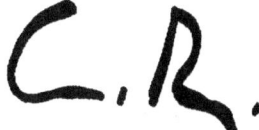

CARL ROESCH 1884-1979
German Genre, Landscape, Portraits $2,500

1.

2.

SEVERIN ROESEN 1815-1871
American Still Life $200,000

2.   3.

1.

CHRISTIAN ROHLFS 1849-1938
German Expressionist, Landscape $100,000

GEORGES ROHNER 1913-
French Landscapes, Portraits, Still Life $15,000

1.

2.

ALEXANDER F. ROLFE -1871
British Watercolour, Landscape, Genre $40,000

WARREN E. ROLLINS 1861-1962
American Cowboys, Landscape $20,000

ANTON ROMAKO 1832-1889
Austrian Allegory, Genre $25,000

UMBERTO ROMANO 1905-1984
American Genre $8,000

1.

2.

THEODOOR ROMBOUTS 1597-1637
Dutch Landscape $30,000

2.

1.

WILLEM ROMEIJN (also Romeyn) 1624-1693
Netherlandish Landscapes, Animals $10,000

FRANCESCO MARIA RONDANI 1450-1548
Italian Painter, Religious, Portraits $225,000

1.   2.

3.

JOHANN HEINRICK (also Hendrich) ROOS 1631-1685
German Landscapes, Portraits $20,000

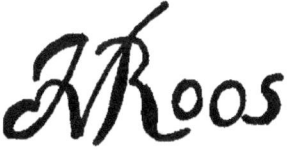

JOHANN MELCHIOR ROOS 1650-1731
German Landscape $10,000

CH. VAN (also Charles) ROOSE 1883-1960
Dutch Floral, Still Life, Portraits $5,000

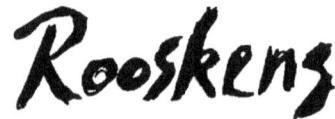

ANTON ROOSKENS 1906-1976
Dutch Abstract $45,000

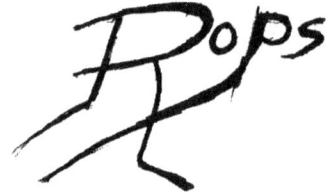

FELICIEN ROPS 1833-1898
Belgian Watercolour, Genre, Landscape $25,000

Roqueplan

JOSEPH CAMILLE ROQUEPLAN 1800-1855
French Landscape $4,000

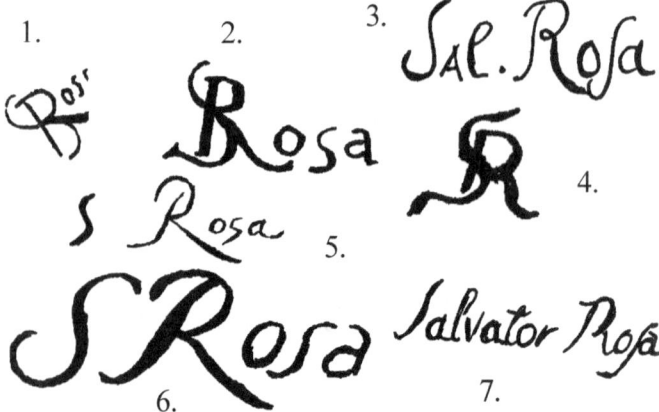

SALVATOR ROSA 1615-1673
Italian Allegorical, Landscapes, Seascapes, Religious $200,000

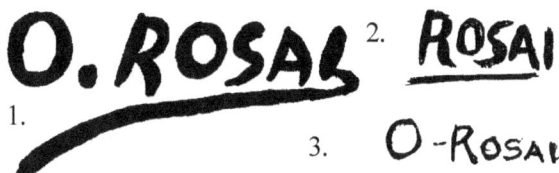

OTTONE ROSAI 1895-1957
Italian Painter, Genre, Landscape $170,000

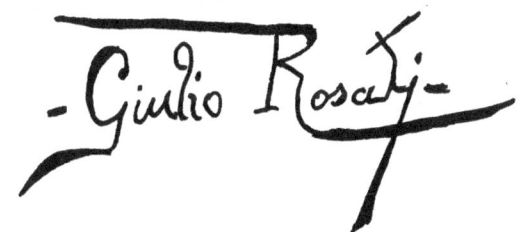

OLGA (also Vladimirona, Rozanova) ROSANOVA 1886-1918
Russian Compositions, Futurist $250,000

GUILIO ROSATI 1835-1917
Italian Painter, Genre $30,000

GUY ROSE 1867-1925
American Impressionist, California, Plein Aire $75,000

FRANZ ROSEL VON ROSENHOF 1626-1700
German Allegorical Animals $10,000

HARRY-ROSELAND

HARRY HERMAN ROSELAND 1868-1950
American Painter, Genre $250,000

H. Roseley

H. ROSELY 1900's
European Painter, Genre, Portraits $1,000

1.

CHARLES ROSEN

2. **CHARLES ROSEN**

CHARLES ROSEN 1878-1950
American N.A. Landscape $35,000

Samuel Rosenberg

SAMUEL ROSENBERG 1896-1972
American Etcher, Genre, Portraits $1,000

Doris Rosenthal

DORIS ROSENTHAL 1895-1971
American Illustrator, Genre, Landscape $1,500

M. Rosentalis

MOSHE ROSENTHALIS 1922-
CzechPainter, Portraits, Still Life $5,500

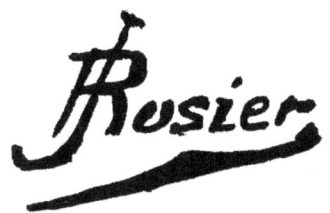

JEAN ROSIER 1858-1931
Belgian Painter, Genre $4,000

1. 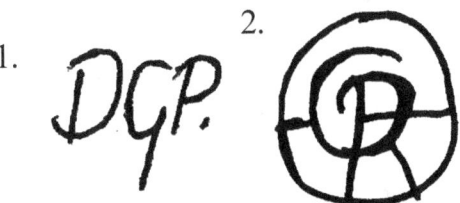 2.

DANTE GABRIEL ROSSETTI 1828-1882
British Genre, Allegory $2,000,000

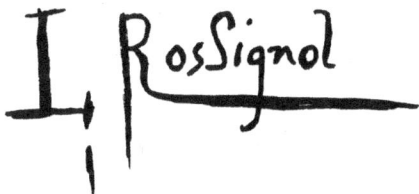

LILY ROSSIGNOL 1900's
French Painter $8,500

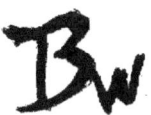

VLADIMIR BARANOFF ROSSINE 1888-1944
Russian Genre, Portraits, landscape $500,000

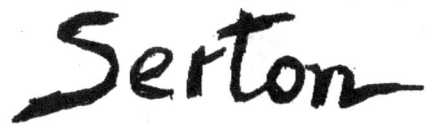

PIET SERTON VAN ROSWEYDE
Painter

SUSAN ROTHENBERG 1945-
American Contemporary $500,000

GEORGE FREDERIC ROTIG 1873-1961
French Landscape $8,500

1. 2.

HANS (JOHANN) ROTTENHAMMER 1564-1625
German Old Master, Genre $200,000

1.

2.

3.

KARL SCHMIDT- ROTTLUFF 1884-1976
German Expressionist $400,000

1. 2.

KARL ROTTMAN 1797-1850
German Landscape $100,000

GEORGES ROUAULT 1871-1958
French Religious, Genre $1,760,000

HENRI ROUSSEAU 1875-1933
French Painter, Genre, Landscape $4,040,000

THEODORE ROUSSEAU 1812-1867
French Landscape $130,000

PHILIPPE ROUSSEAU 1816-1887
French Painter, Genre, Landscape $25,000

ERNEST ARTHUR ROWE 1863-1922
British Landscape $6,500

THOMAS ROWLANDSON 1756-1827
British Watercolour, Genre, Landscape $100,000

P. Roy

PIERRE ROY 1880-1950
French Painter, Landscape, Still Life $125,000

যামিনী রায়

JAMINI ROY 1887-1972
India Painter, Portraits $5,000

1. *F. Roybet*

2. *F. Roybet*

FERDINAND ROYBET 1841-1920
French Painter, Genre $8,500

1. *Rubens*   *PE PA RVBENS* 2.

PETER PAUL RUBENS 1577-1640
Dutch Genre $76,600,000

1. *rubin* 2. *Rubin*

REUVEN RUBIN 1893-1974
Israeli Landscape, Genre $90,000

Olaf Rude

OLAF RUDE 1886-1957
Danish Painter, Landscape $30,000

Rüegg

ERNST GEORG RUEGG 1883-1948
Swiss Painter, Genre, Landscape $2,500

Andrée Ruellan

ANDRE RUELLAN 1905-
American Painter, Genre, Landscape $3,500

C.P.Rug

GEORG PHILIPP RUGENDAS (Elder) 1666-1742
German Landscape $8,000

1.

2.

3.

4.

5.

6.

7.

8.

9.

10.

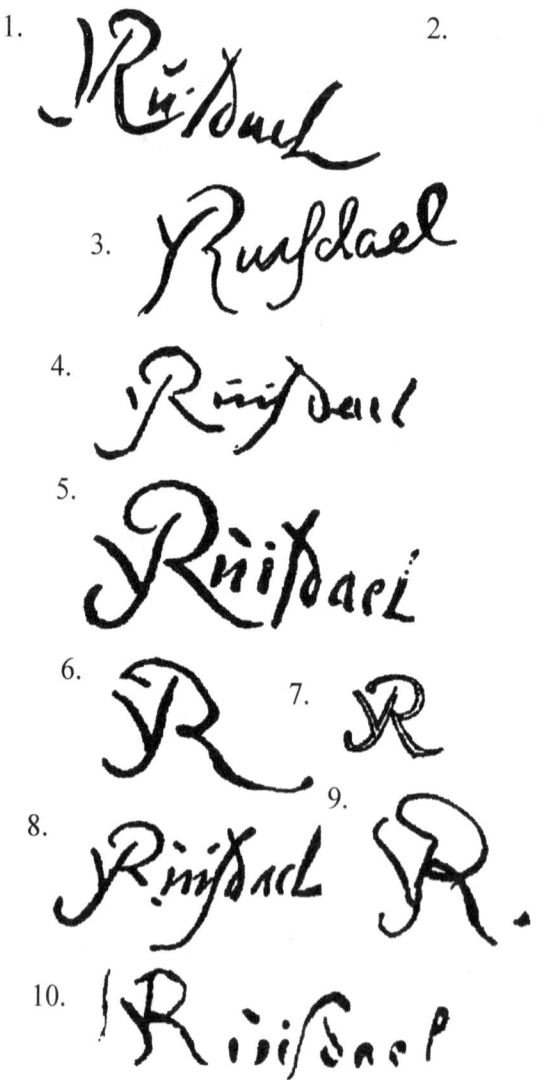

JACOB ISAACKSZ VAN RUISDAEL 1628-1682
Netherlandish Landscape $200,000

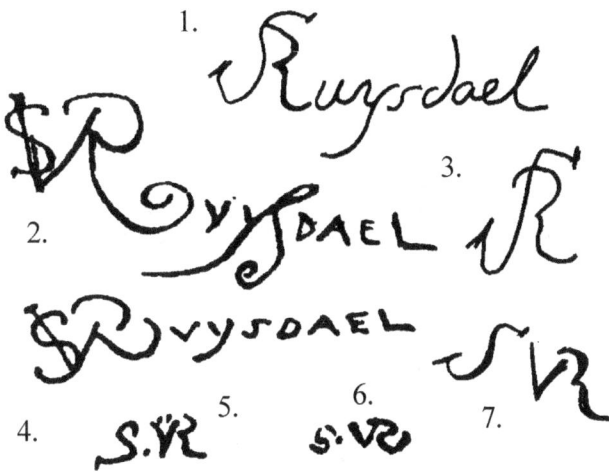

SALOMON JACOBSZ VAN RUIJSDAEL
(Also Ruisdael) 1600-1670
Dutch Landscape, Old Master $4,752,000

PHILIP RUMPF 1821-1896
German Portraits, Genre $4,500

CARL RUNGIUS 1869-1959
American N.A. Cowboys, Genre, Landscape $50,000

FERDINAND RUNK 1746-1834
Austrian Landscape $1,500

S. Rusiñol

SANTIAGO RUSIÑOL 1861-1931
Spanish Landscape, Genre $1,092,000

1.   2.   4.

CMR   *CMRussell*

3.

Cm Russell

CHARLES M. RUSSELL 1864-1926
American Cowboys $1,432,000

1. *M·R*   2. *M·R.*

3. *Morgan Russell*

MORGAN RUSSELL 1886-1953
American Synchromist $500,000

1. *L Russolo*

2. *LRussolo*

LUIGI (also Guido) RUSSOLO 1885-1947
Italian Futurist, Genre, Compositions $420,000

CARL RUTHART 1630-1703
German Landscape, Animal Painter $30,000

RACHEL RUYSCH 1664-1750
Dutch Still Life $500,000

ALFRED RUYTINX 1871-
Belgian Painter, Still Life , Genre $15,000

1.   2.

ANNE RYAN 1889-1954
American Painter, Contemporary $6,500

ISSACHAR BER RYBACK 1897-1935
Russian Painter, Genre, Landscape $10,000

D. Ryckaert

DAVID RYCKAERT 1612-1661
Dutch Genre $20,000

B de Rycke

BERNARD DE RYCKERE 1535-1590
Dutch Portraits $10,000

A P Ryder

ALBERT PINKHAM RYDER 1846-1912
American N.A. Landscape, Genre $25,000

P.P.R yder

PLATT POWELL RYDER 1821-1896
American A.N.A. Painter, Genre $9,000

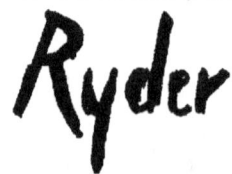

SUSAN RYDER 1900's
British Still Life $6,000

HENRY RYLAND

HARRY RYLAND 1859-1924
British Illustrator, Genre $15,000

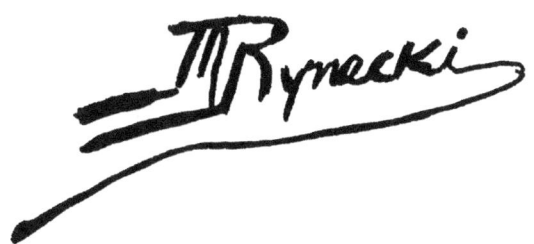

MOSES RYNECKI 1885-1943
Polish Genre, Portraits $2,000

PEETER RYSBRACK 1655-1729
Dutch Landscape $30,000

1.

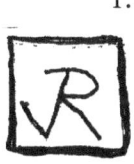

2.

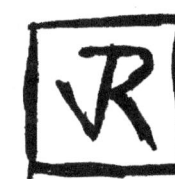

3.

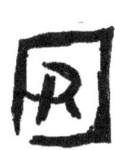

THEO VAN RYSSEL BERGHE 1862-1926
Belgian Landscape, Allegory $3,152,000

Artists starting with the letter "S"

A Sacchi

ANDREA SACCHI 1600-1661
Italian Painter $10,000

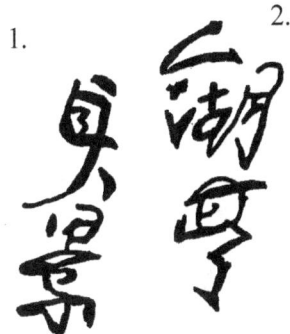

1.   2.

SADAKAGE 1825-1835
Japanese Woodblocks $4,000

E. S.

EGIDIUS SADELER 1570-1629
Flemish Old Master, Allegory, Genre $45,000

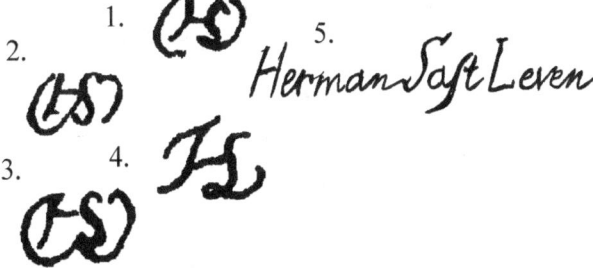

1.   5.
2.
3.   4.

HERMAN (the younger) SAFTLEVEN 1609-1685
Netherlandish Landscape Genre $120,000

CORNELIS SAFTLEVEN 1607-1681
Netherlandish Allegorical Interiors, Landscape, Genre $90,000

HENRI DE SAINT DELIS 1878-1949
French Landscape $70,000

EMILIO GRAU SALA 1911-1975
American Illustrator, Genre $65,000

PAOLA SALA 1859-1929
Italian Landscape, Genre $20,000

EMILIA SALA Y FRANCES 1850-1910
Spanish Illustrator, Genre $15,000

PORFIRIO SALINAS 1910-1972
American Landscape, Genre $7,500

FERDINAND SALKIN 1862-
French Seascape $1,500

LEONARD SALUIS 1874-1949
Painter

PAUL SAMPLE 1896-1974
American N.A. Abstract $15,000

EDGAR SANCHEZ 1939-
Venezualan Painter $10,000

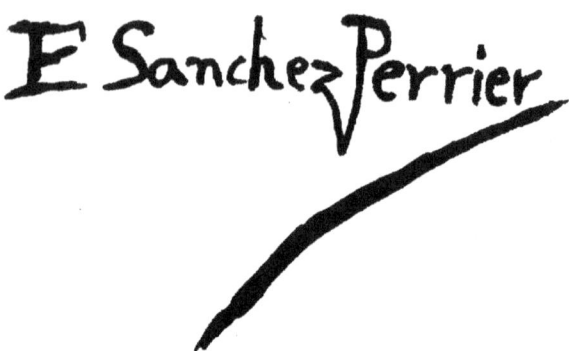

EMILIO SANCHEZ-PERRIER 1855-1907
Spanish Painter, Genre, Landscape $30,000

1.   2.

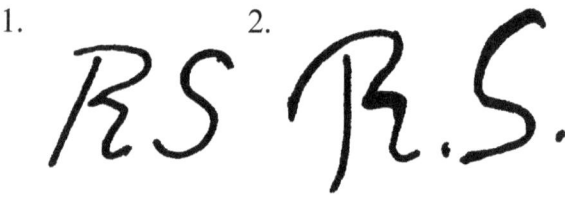

RAGNAR SANDBERG 1902-1972
Swedish Landscape, Genre $70,000

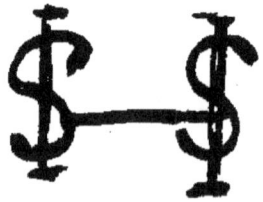

JOACHIM SANDRART 1606-1688
German Genre, Portraits $7,000

Birger Sandzen

SVEN BIRGER SANDZEN 1871-1954
American Impressionist, Landscape $7,000

1.

2.

3.

ANTONIO SANT ELIA 1888-1916
Italian Architect

1.

2.

JEAN BAPTISTE SANTERRE 1658-1717
French Genre $125,000

GIUSEPPE SANTOMASO 1907-1990
Italian Painter, Landscape $150,000

RUBENS SANTORO 1859-1942
Italian Canals, Genre $60,000

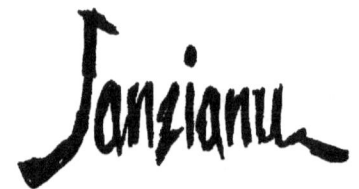

MICHEL SANZIANU 1944-
Swiss Painter, Portraits $12,000

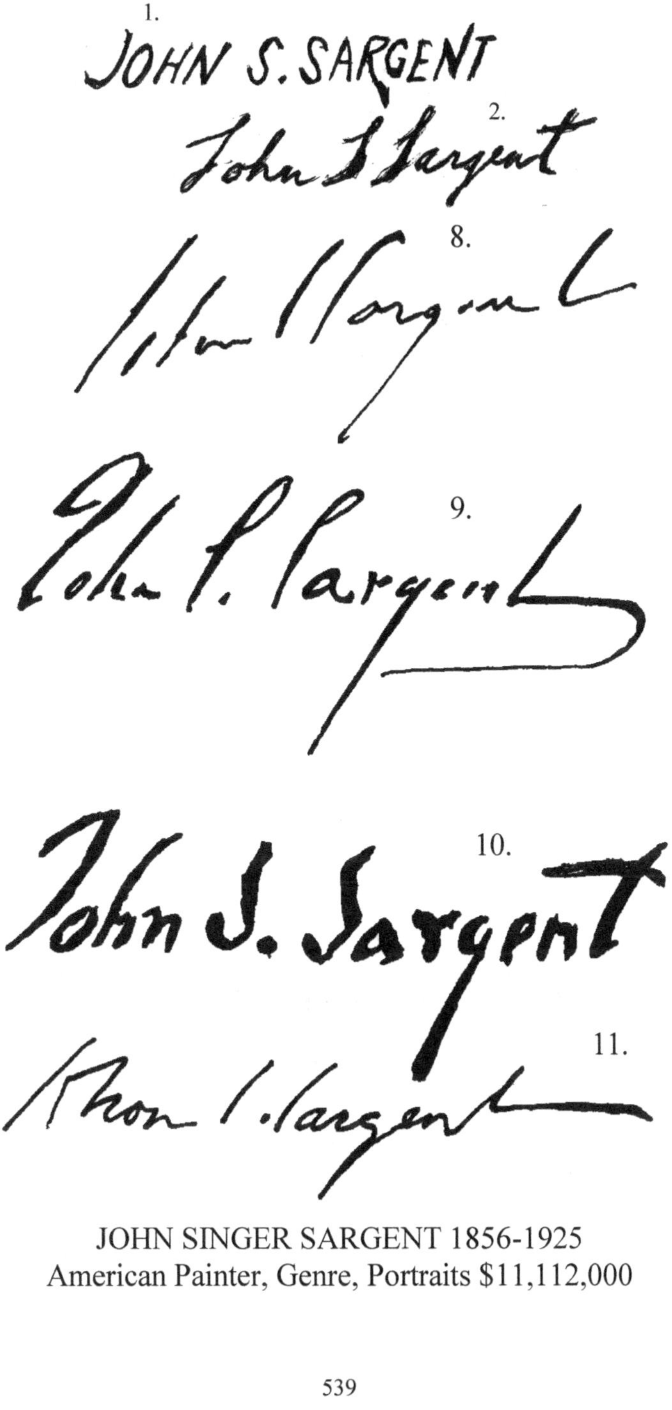

1. *JOHN S. SARGENT*

2. *John S Sargent*

8. *John Sargent*

9. *John S. Sargent*

10. *John S. Sargent*

11. *Khon S. Sargent*

JOHN SINGER SARGENT 1856-1925
American Painter, Genre, Portraits $11,112,000

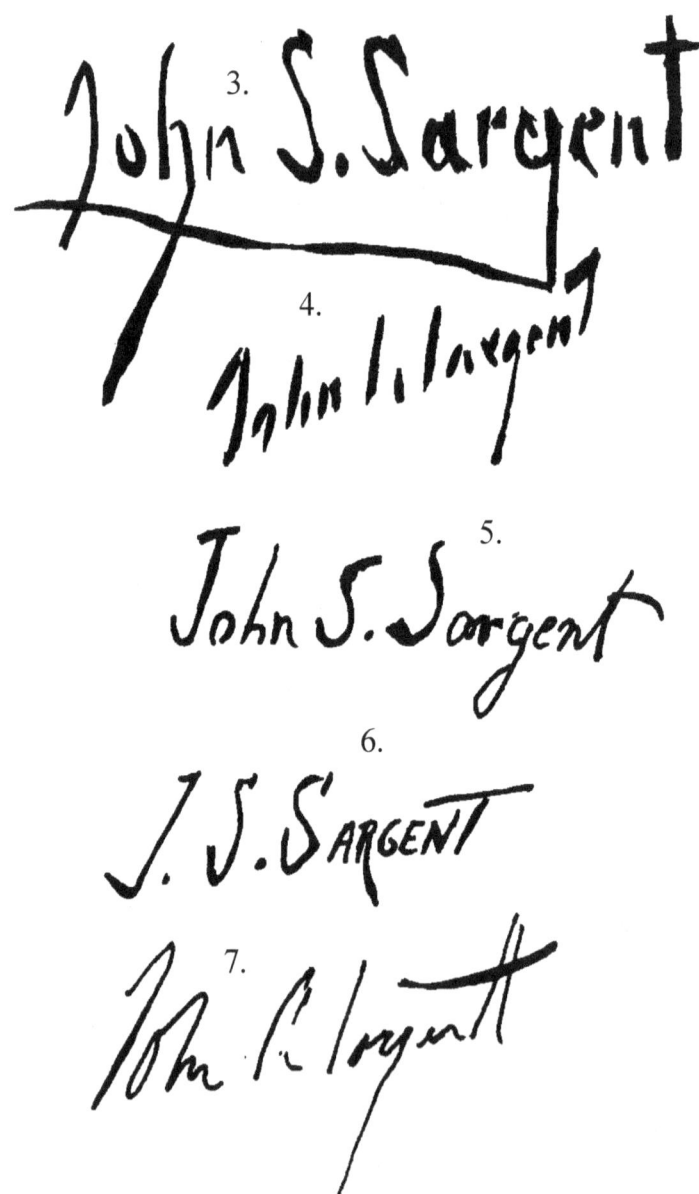

3.

4.

5.

6.

7.

JOHN SINGER SARGENT 1856-1925
American Painter, Genre, Portraits $11,112,000

AN DSART 1.

2. *Andrea del Sarto*

ANDREA DEL SARTO 1486-1531
Italian Landscape $25,000

Saurfelt

LEONARD SAURFELT 1800's
French Painter, Genre $5,000

Roelaent Savery

ROELAND I.))) SAVERY. FE

ROELANT SAVERY 1576-1639
Netherlandish Still Life Landscape, Genre $2,650,000

Savinio

ALBERTO SAVINO 1891-1952
Italian Painter, Genre, Landscape $800,000

F.W. SCARBROUGH

FREDERICK WILLIAM SCARBROUGH 1863-1945
British Seascape, Landscape $6,000

ROLPH SCARLETT

ROLPH SCARLETT 1899-1985
American Design, Painter, Abstract $20,000

Schabelitz

RUDOLPH FREDERICK SCHABELITZ 1884-1959
American Illustrator, Genre, Portraits $2,000

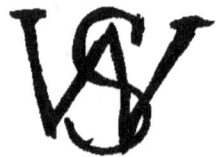

FRIEDRICH WILHELM SCHADOW 1789-1862
German Portraits $25,000

H. Schäfer

HEINRICH SCHAFER 1815-1884
German Painter $1,500

F. Schafer

FREDERICK F. SCHAFER 1841-1917
American Indians $7,500

1. *G. Schalcken* 3. *gs*

2. *gs.*

GODFRIED SCHALCKEN 1643-1706
Dutch Genre, Religious, Portraits $100,000

LOUIS SCHANKER 1903-1981
American Landscapes $10,000

HANS LEONHARD SCHAUFELIN 1489-1540
German Painter, Portraits, Religious $175,000

Ary Scheffer

ARY SCHEFFER 1797-1858
French Portraits, Religious, Genre $200,000

Scheiber

1. *H*   2. *Scheiber*

HUGO SCHEIBER 1872-1950
Hungarian Genre, Landscape $25,000

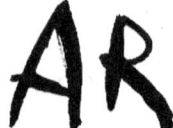

ANTON RAEDER SCHEIDT 1892-1970
German Abstract $10,000

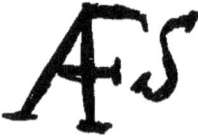

MATHIAS SCHEITS 1640-1700
Dutch Genre, Religious $2,000

AUGUST FRANZ SCHELVER 1805-1844
German Genre, Animals, Landscape $4,500

JOHANN SCHERREWITZ 1868-1951
Dutch Landscape $12,000

JULIUS SCHEURER 1859-1913
German Landscape $12,000

ANDREA SCHIAVONE 1521-1582
Italian Painter, Mythology, Religious, Genre $25,000

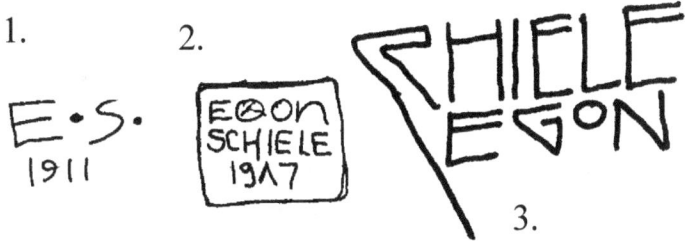

1.   2.

3.

EGON SCHIELE 1890-1918
German Painter, Landscape, Nudes $23,287,000

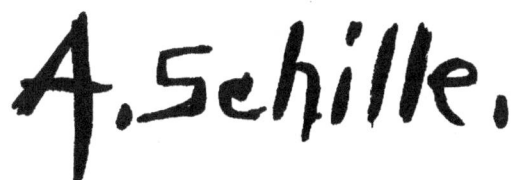

ALICE SCHILLE 1869-1955
American Portrait, Genre, Landscape $6,000

1.   2.

JOHANN W. SCHIRMER 1807-1863
German Painter, Landscape, Genre $100,000

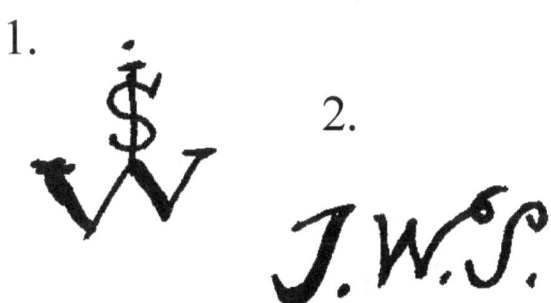

ADOLF SCHLABITZ 1854-1943
German Painter, Landscape $1,500

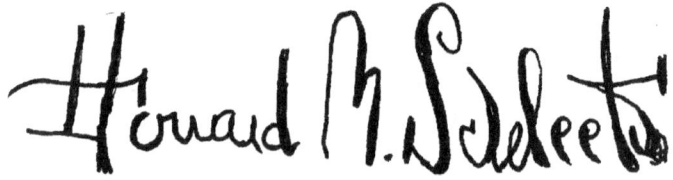

HOWARD B. SCHLEETER 1903-
American Western, Abstract $1,000

ROBERT SCHLEICH 1854-1934
German Landscape, Genre $30,000

AUGUSTE SCHLEISSNER 1810-1882
Danish Landscape, Portraits $5,000

1.

2.

FELIX SCHLESINGER 1833-1910
German Painter, Genre $75,000

RUDOLF SCHLICHTER 1890-1955
German Collage, Genre, Landscape $400,000

THEODOR SCHLOEPKE 1812-1878
German Genre

JULES SCHMALZIGAUG 1886-1917
Belgian Compositions, Genre, Landscapes, Portraits $200,000

MATTHIAS SCHMID 1835-1923
Austrian Painter, Landscape, Portraits $30,000

ALBERT SCHMIDT 1883-1970
Swiss Landscape, Genre $5,000

1.

2.

LEOPOLD SCHMUTZLER 1864-1941
German Painter, Genre $25,000

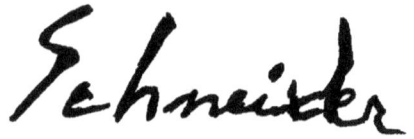

GERARD SCHNEIDER 1896-1986
Swiss, Painter, Abstract $70,000

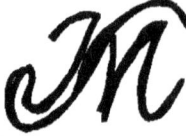

MICHAEL SCHNITZLER 1782-1861
German Animal Painter $3,000

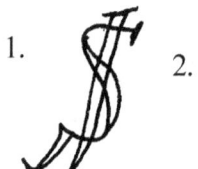

VON KAROLFELD SCHNORR 1794-1872
German Landscape, Religious, Genre $30,000

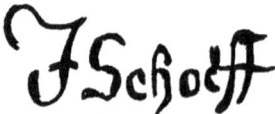

JOHANNES PIETERSZ. SCHOEFF 1608-1666
Dutch Landscape $15,000

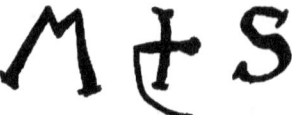

WERNER SCHOLZ 1898-1963
German Painter, Landscape $5,000

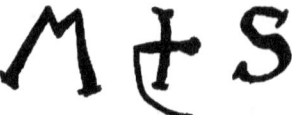

MARTIN SCHONGAUER 1445-1491
German, Old Master, Painter $1,779,000

FRANK EARLE SCHOONOVER 1877-1972
American, Illustrator, Landscape, Genre $35,000

KARL SCHORN 1800-1850
German Painter, Portraits $1,000

JULIUS (also Anton) SCHRADER 1815-1900
German Painter, Genre, Portraits, Religious $40,000

KARL SCHRAG 1912-
German Illustrator, Landscape $1,500

GEORGES SCHREIBER 1904-1977
American, Illustrator, Landscape, Genre $4,000

ADOLPH SCHREYER 1828-1899
German Landscape $75,000

Chas Schreyvogel.A.N.A.

CHARLES SCHREYVOGEL 1861-1912
American, A.N.A., Cowboys, Landscape, Genre $1,047,000

LOUIS DE Schryver

1.

DE,Schryver

2.

LOUIS MARIE DE SCHRYVER 1862-1942
French, Painter, Still Life, Genre $100,000

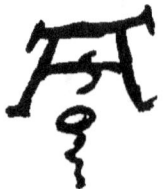

ADOLF SCHRODTER 1805-1875
German Genre, Portraits $1,000

P - S h BKVCK -

PIETER SCHUBRUCK 1570-1607
German Landscape Shepherds

Schumacher

EMIL SCHUMACHER 1912-
German Painter, Landscape $150,000

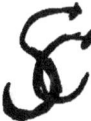

CARL SCHUMACHER 1797-1860
German Painter

WILLIAM S. SCHWARTZ 1896-1977
American, Abstract, Landscape, Genre $20,000

ALBERT SCHWENDY 1820-1903
German Painter $15,000

1. 2. 3.

KURT SCHWITTERS 1887-1948
German, Assemblage, Genre, Abstract, Landscape $170,000

1. 2.

GIUSEPPE SCIUTI 1835-1911
Italian Painter, Stage, Genre $1,500

*F*RANK *E*DWIN *S*COTT

FRANK EDWIN SCOTT 1863-1929
American Painter, Genre $4,000

Peter Scott

SIR PETER SCOTT 1909-1989
British, Painter, Landscape $10,000

Tom Scott

TOM SCOTT 1854-1927
British Watercolour, Landscape $4,500

Edward Seago   1.

Seager   2.

EDWARD SEAGO 1910-1974
British Landscape $50,000

1. *Ronald Searle*

2. *Ronald Searle*

RONALD SEARLE 1920-
British Illustrator Watercolour, Genre $9,000

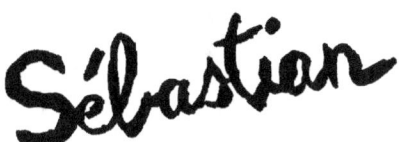

SEBASTIAN
$2,000

K.S̃R.

KARL SEEGER 1808-1866
German Landscape $3,500

L Seehas

CHRISTIAN LUDWIG SEEHAS 1754-1802
German Portraits $1,000

L. Seel

LOUIS SEEL 1880-1958
American Painter $1,000

A segal

ARTHUR SEGAL 1875-1944
German Painter, Genre, Landscape $70,000

George Segal

GEORGE SEGAL 1924-
American, painter, Portraits $600,000

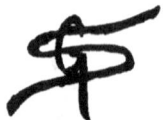

GIOVANNI SEGANTINI 1858-1899
Italian Genre, Portraits $9,500,000

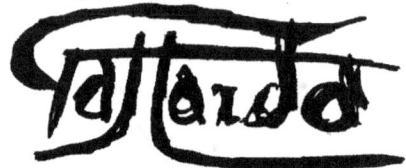

GOTTARDO SEGANTINI 1881-1974
Italian, Landscape, $20,000

1. *Daniel Seghers*

D. Seghers 3. *DS*

2.

DANIEL SEGHERS 1590-1661
Netherlandish Still Life, Allegory, Portraits $50,000

enemel

EUSTAQUIO SEGRELLES 1936-
Ecuador Painter $7,000

Segui

ANTONIO SEGUI 1934-
Argentinian Abstract $25,000

CHRISTIAN SEIBOLD 1697-1768
German Portraits

1.

2.

GUILLAUME SEIGNAC 1870-1924
French, Allegory, Genre $100,000

GUSTAV SEITZ 1906-1969
German Painter, Genre $3,000

GEORGE SEITZ 1810-1870
German Still Life $10,000

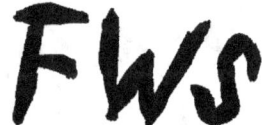

FRANZ WILHELM SEIWERT 1894-1933
German Painter, Still Life, Genre $20,000

1. *Seligmann* 2. **KS**

KURT SELIGMAN 1900-1962
American, Costume, Stage Design, Genre, Indians $50,000

J. SELMERSHEIM·Desgrange

JEANNE SELMERSHEIM-DESGRANGE 1877-1958
French Painter, Still Life $30,000

1.
O.C.SELTZER. 2. (S)

OLAF CARL SELTZER 1877-1957
American, Cowboys, Landscape $80,000

Eisman · Semenowsky

EISMAN SEMENOWSKY-1911
French Portraits, Genre $7,500

SEN
TI ERI

SENTIERI 1900's
French Painter $1,000

1. *zoltan, Sepeshy* **DS.**

2.
ZOLTAN SEPESHY 1898-1934
American Painter, Genre, Landscape $3,000

CS

CAROLYN SERGEANT 1900's
American Still Life $1,000

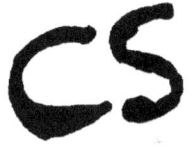

1. P.S. 2. PSerusier 3. SER

PAUL SERUSIER 1863-1927
French, Nabis Style, Genre, landscape $400,000

a. Servaes

ALBERT SERVAES 1883-1966
Belgian Landscapes, Genre $80,000

SERVRANCKX

VICTOR SERVRANCKX 1897-1965
Belgian Sculptor, Painter $55,000

Seurat

GEORGES SEURAT 1859-1891
French Impressionist, Genre, Landscape $35,200,000

1. G. Severini

2. G. Severini

GINO SEVERINI 1883-1966
Italian Futurist, Landscapes $3,300,000

PINCHAS SHAAR 1900's
Belgian Painter, Genre $1,500

FELIX SHADOW 1819-1861
German Genre

1.

2.

BEN SHAHN 1898-1969
American Illustrator, Genre $100,000

DOROTHY SHAKESPEAR
Painter

FRED SHANE 1906-
American Painter $1,000

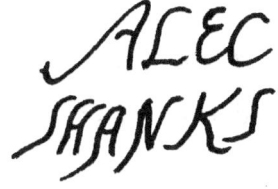

ALEC SHANKS 1900's
British Stage Costume Design $1,000

JJ SHANNON

JAMES J. SHANNON 1862-1923
American, A.N.A. Painter, Portraits $75,000

CNS

CHARLES HAZELWOOD SHANNON 1863-1937
British, Genre, Landscape, Portraits $15,000

F.H Shapleigh

FRANK HENRY SHAPLEIGH
$1,000

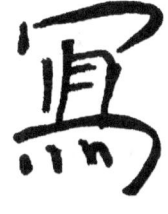

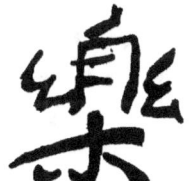

SHARAKU -1795
Japanese Woodblock $1,000

JHSHARP

JOSEPH HENRY SHARP 1859-1953
American, Indians, Landscape, Genre $85,000

1. *Charles Sheeler*

Sheeler 2. Sheeler. 3.

CHARLES SHEELER 1883-1965
American Painter, Abstract, Photo, Landscape, Realist $300,000

Millard Sheets

MILLARD OWEN SHEETS 1907-1989
American, N.A. Illustrator $30,000

David Shepherd

DAVID SHEPHERD 1931-
British Animals, Landscape $60,000

WARREN SHEPPARD

WARREN W. SHEPPARD 1858-1937
American Seascape $10,000

AMRITA SHER GIL 1913-1941
Hungarian Painter $35,000

DANIEL SHERRIN 1868-1915
British Landscape $5,000

1. *T. W. SHIELDS*

2. *Thos. W. Shields*

THOMAS W. SHIELDS 1850-1920
American Painter, Genre $7,500

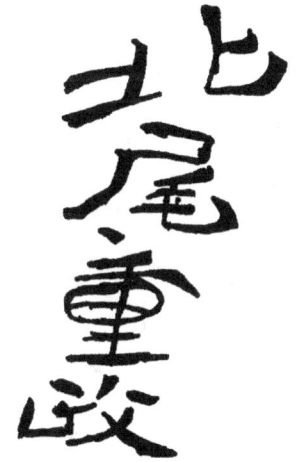

KITAO SHIGEMASA 1739-1820
Japanese Woodblocks $5,000

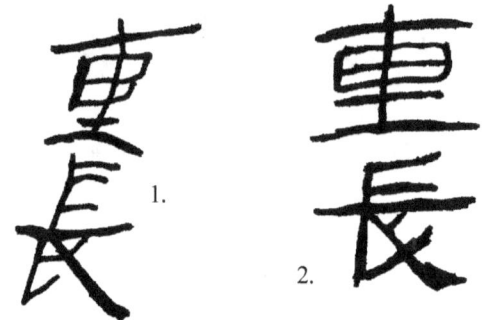

NISHIMURA SHIGENAGA 1697-1756
Japanese Woodblock $3,000

SHIH KE
Chinese Watercolour

ALUSH SHIMA 1942-
Indian Modern $6,000

EVERETT SHINN 1876-1953
American N.A. Painter, Genre $3,300,000

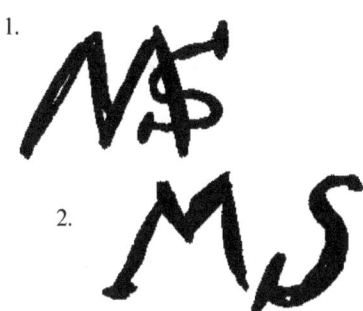

1.

2.

MARTIN SHONGAUER 1445-1488
German Portraits

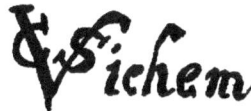

1.

2.

3.

JAN SIBERECHTS 1627-1697
Belgian Genre, Landscape $1,100,000

CRISTOPH VAN SICHEM 1546-1624
Dutch, Painter, Old Master $3,000

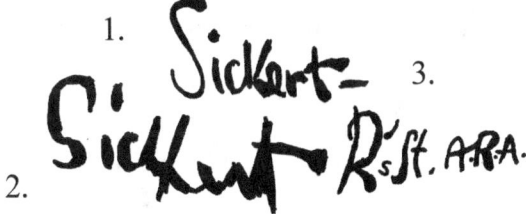

1.

2.

3.

WALTER RICHARD SICKERT 1860-1942
British A.R.A. Painter, Genre $85,000

Le Sidaner

HENRI LE SIDANER 1862-1939
French Landscape $450,000

Aug Siegen

AUGUSTE SIEGEN 1800's
German Landscape $8,000

Fred Sieger

FRED SIEGER 1902-
Dutch Still Life $1,500

X. Sigalon

XAVIER SIGALON 1788-1837
French Genre, Portraits, Landscape $3,500

P.S 1. *P. Signac* 2.

PAUL SIGNAC 1863-1935
French Neo-Impressionist $2,692,000

F.A. Silva.

FRANCIS A. SILVA 1835-1886
American, Seascape, Landscape $1,472,000

JULIUS SIMMONS 1843-1924
German Genre, Interiors, Painter $2,500

1. 2.

LUCIEN SIMON 1861-1945
French, Landscape, Genre $10,000

MAX SINCLAIR -1911
British Harbors, Landscape $3,000

MITCHEL SIPORIN 1910-1976
American, Illustrator, Portraits $1,000

DAVID ALFARO SIQUEIROS 1898-1974
Mexican, Landscape, Genre $150,000

1. 2.

GIOVANNI ANDREA SIRANI 1610-1670
Italian Painter, Religious, Allegory $12,000

SIRONI

MARIO SIRONI 1885-1961
Italian Painter, Genre, Landscape $450,000

Sisley

ALFRED SISLEY 1839-1899
French Impressionist, Landscape $3,000,000

F. Skarbina

FRANZ SKARBINA 1849-1910
German Painter, Genre $70,000

KAREL   S L

KAREL SLABBAERT 1619-1654
Netherlandish Portraits Genre $2,500

I le vojT

MAX SLEVOGT 1868-1932
German Impressionist $250,000

1.   2. P.V.Slingeland

PIETER CORNELISZ VAN SLINGELAND
(alsoSlingelandt) 1640-1691
Netherlandish Genre, Old Master, Portraits $75,000

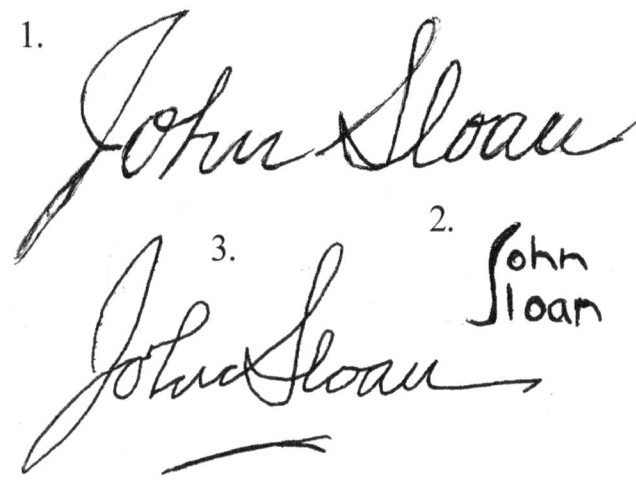

1.

2.

3.

JOHN SLOAN 1871-1951
American N.A. Ash Can, Landscape, Genre $2,205,000

JAN SLUIJTERS 1881-1957
Dutch, Painter, Portraits, Landscape,Impressionist $140,000

FRANS SMEERS 1873-1960
Belgian Painter, Genre $30,000

GUSTAVE DE SMET 1877-1943
Belgian, Landscape $150,000

GEORGE H. SMILLIE 1840-1921
American N.A. Landscape $10,000

FRANCIS HOPKINSON SMITH 1938-1915
American, Watercolour, Landscape $15,000

HARRY KNOX SMITH 1879-1934
American Painter $1,000

HELY AUGUSTUS MORTON SMITH 1862-1941
American, Watercolour, Genre $2,000

JACK WILKINSON SMITH 1873-1949
American Impressionist $15,000

LAURENCE BEALL SMITH 1909-
American, Illustrator, Genre, Landscape $35,000

1.

Leon Polk Smith

2.

LPS

LEON POLK SMITH 1906-
American Abstract $40,000

Russell Smith

RUSSELL SMITH 1812-1896
American Landscape $9,000

S. Smith

GEORGE SMITH 1870-1934
British Animals $3,000

MS

SIR MATTHEW SMITH 1879-1959
British Painter, Still Life, Landscape $40,000

Jacob Smits

JACOB SMITS 1856-1928
Belgian Painter, Landscape, Portraits $70,000

1. *F·Snijders*
2. *F·Snijders*
3. *F.Sneyders*
4. *F Snyders*

FRANS SNIJDERS (also Snyders) 1579-1657
Flemish, Still Life, Old Master, Landscape, Animals $100,000

Snowman

ISAAC SNOWMAN 1874-
Israeli Portraits, Genre $30,000

P Snyers

PEETER SNYERS 1681-1752
Flemish Portraits, Genre, Landscape, Still Life $40,000

Zoust

GERARD VAN (Zonst) SOEST 1600-1681
German Painter, Portraits $7,500

SOFFICI

ARDENGO SOFFICI 1879-1964
Italian Cubist, Compositions, Landscape, Portraits $55,000

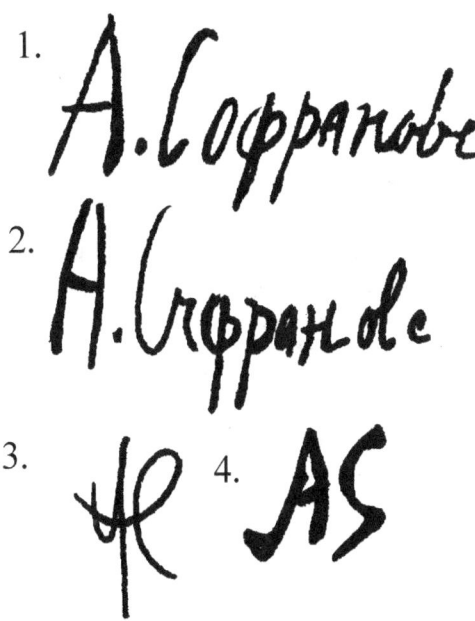

1. A.Софранове
2. А.Сфраноle
3. 4. AS

ANTONINA SOFRONOVA 1892-1966
Russian, Cubist, Genre

N Soggi

NICCOLO SOGGI 1480-1551
Italian Religious $150,000

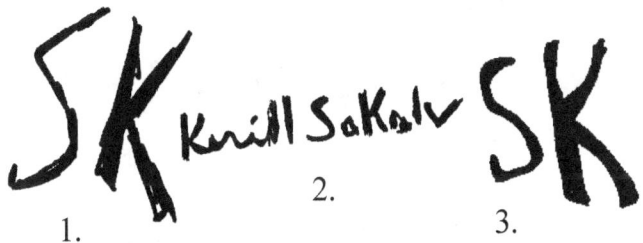

1. SK   2. Kirill Sakolv   3. SK

KILL (also Kirill) SOKOLOV 1900's
Russian, Scottish $1,500

J. Solana

JOSE GUTIERREZ SOLANA 1885-1953
Italian, Abstract, Seascape, Landscape $75,000

SOLDATI

ATANASIO SOLDATI 1896-1953
Italian Abstract, Seascape, Landscape $75,000

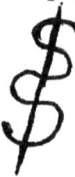

SIMEON SOLOMON 1840-1905
British Genre $50,000

Somerscales

THOMAS J. SOMERSCALES 1842-1928
British, Seascape, Landscape $15,000

1. *J. VAN·SON*

2. *J. VAN·SON*

3. *J. VAN·SON·f*

JORIS VAN SON 1623-1667
Netherlandish Still Life $200,000

FRITZ SONDERLAND 1836-1896
German Painter, Genre $10,000

WILLIAM LOUIS SONNTAG JR. 1870-1898
American Seascape, Genre, Landscape $10,000

RAFFAELLO SORBI 1844-1931
Italian, Landscape, Genre $100,000

HENDRIK MAERTENSZ SORGH 1611-1670
Netherlandish Allegorical, Genre $175,000

RAYA SORKINE 1936-
French Painter, Genre $10,000

JOAQUIN SOROLLA Y BASTIDA 1863-1923
Spanish, Landscape, Genre $3,173,000

1.

2. SOUDEIKINE

3.

SERGEI SOUDEIKINE 1883-1940
American, Costume Stage Design, Landscape, Genre $4,500

FREDERIC SOULACROIX 1825-1879
French, Painter, Genre $100,000

PIERRE SOULAGES 1919-
French Abstract $1,537,000

JOHN BULLOCH SOUTER 1890-1972
American, Landscape, Genre $15,000

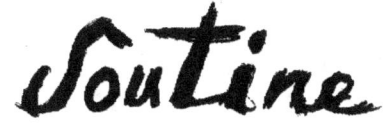

CHAIM SOUTINE 1894-1943
Russian Landscape, Genre $9,449,000

FRANCIS NEWTON SOUZA 1924-
India Modern $1,360,000

MOSES SOYER 1898-1974
American, N.A. Portraits, Genre $20,000

RAPHAEL SOYER 1899-1987
American N.A. WPA Painter, Genre, Landscape $50,000

ISAAC SOYER 1907-1981
American Painter, Genre $12,000

RUSKIN SPEAR 1911-1990
British Painter, Landscape, Genre $25,000

arthur Spear -

ARTHUR P. SPEAR 1879-1959,
American, A.N.A. Landscape, Genre $2,000

Eugene Speicher

EUGENE SPEICHER 1883-1962
American N.A. Landscape $10,000

Francis Speight

FRANCIS SPEIGHT 1896-1989
American Painter, Genre, Landscape $3,000

Robert Spencer

ROBERT SPENCER 1879-1931
American A.N.A. Landscape, Genre $100,000

L. Spilliaert

LEON SPILLIAERT 1881-1946
Belgian, Landscape, Seascape $100,000

B Sprangers

BARTHOLOMEUS SPRANGER 1546-1627
Flemish Portraits, Mythology, Religious $50,000

CORNELIS SPRINGER 1817-1891
Dutch Painter, Genre $150,000

LEONARD R. SQUIRRELL 1893-1979
British Landscape $5,000

LOUIS VAN STAATEN 1835-1909
Dutch Landscape $4,000

GEORGE STAINTON -1890
British Seascapes, Landscape $6,000

ADRIAEN VAN STALBEMT 1580-1662
Flemish Landscape, Religious, Allegory, Genre $80,000

THEODOROS STAMOS 1922-
American Painter, Abstract $150,000

JACK GAGE STARK 1882-1950
American, Landscape, Genre $1,000

ANNA STAUB 1944-
Swiss Genre, Landscape $1,500

1.

2.

JAN ADRIAENSZ VAN STAVEREN 1625-1668
Netherlandish Allegory, Genre, Landscape $10,000

RALPH IDRIS STEADMAN 1936-
American Abstract, Landscape, Genre, Cartoons $3,000

JUNIUS BRUTIUS STEARNS 1810-1985
American, N.A. Indians, Genre $20,000

T.C. STEELE 1847-1926
American A.N.A. Landscape $15,000

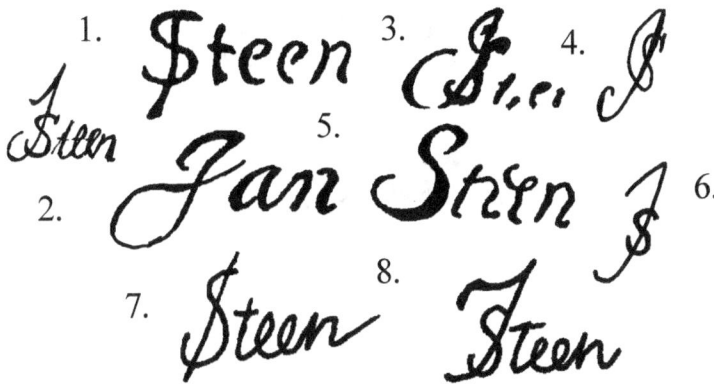

JAN STEEN 1626-1679
Dutch Old Master, Landscape, Genre $500,000

HENDRIK VAN (the younger) STEENWIJCK
(also STEENWYCK
Netherlandish Architecture Interiors, Old Master $80,000

HENDRIK VAN STEENWYCK (Elder) 1550-1604
Flemish Architectural Painter, Religious $70,000

PHILIP WILSON STEER 1860-1942
British Painter, Genre, Portraits, Landscape $35,000

1. *[signature: Ron Stefan]*

2. *[signature: Ross Stefan]*

ROSS STEFAN 1934-
American Landscape, Genre $2,500

[signature: Georges Stein]

GEORGES STEIN 1870-
French Paris Streets $25,000

[signature: STEINBERG]

SAUL STEINBERG 1914-
American Painter, Genre, Landscape $100,000

[signature: Est]

EMMANUEL STEINER 1778-1831
Swiss Painter, Still Life $3,500

[signature: 7 Steinhardt]

JACOB STEINHARDT 1887-1968
Israeli, Landscape, Genre $6,500

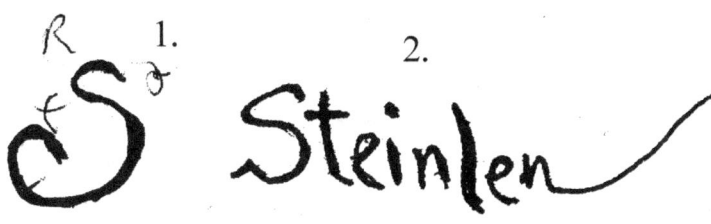

THEOPHILE ALEXANDRE STEINLEN 1859-1923
French, Illustrator, Landscape, Genre $40,000

1. *Jos. Stella*

2. *Joseph Stella*

JOSEPH STELLA 1880-1946
American Modernist, Genre, Abstract, Landscape $35,000

1. 2. *Stella*

JACQUES STELLA 1595-1657
French Painter, Mythology, Religious $30,000

Alice Barber Stephens

ALICE BARBER STEPHENS 1858-1932
American, Illustrator, Genre $5,500

STERN

ERNST STERN 1876-
German Painter, Landscape $1,000

1.

2.

MAURICE STERNE 1878-1957
American, N.A. Muralist, Genre, Still Life $10,000

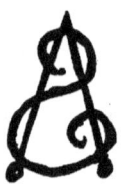

ALFRED STEVENS 1823-1906
Belgian Seascapes, Genre, Portraits $1,625,000

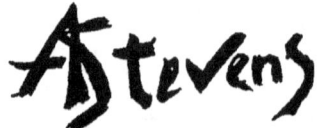

GEORGE W. STEVENS 1866-1926
American Painter, Landscape $1,000

ALFRED STEVENS 1887-
British Landscape $20,000

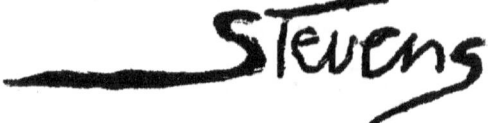

WILL HENRY STEVENS 1887-1949
American, Painter $1,000

1.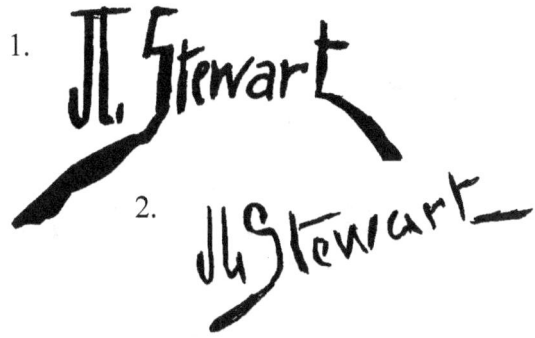

2.

JULIUS L. STEWART 1855-1919
American Painter, Genre $800,000

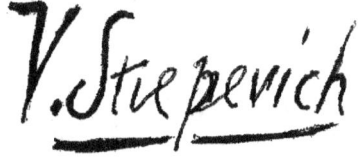

VINCENT STIEPEVICH 1841-1910
Russian Arab Scenes, Genre $40,000

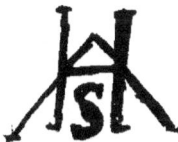

HERMANN STILKE 1803-1860
German Painter, Genre $20,000

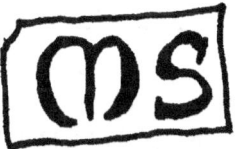

MARIANNE STOKES 1855-1927
British Young People, Genre $60,000

MAERTEN STOOP 1618-1647
Netherlandish Genre $10,000

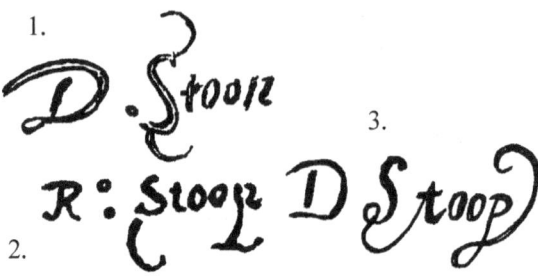

1.

3.

2.

DIRK (also Dirck, Daniel) STOOP 1610-1686
Dutch Genre, Seascapes, Hunts, Landscape, Portraits $50,000

1. **A ¯Storck**

2. A . Storck

ABRAHAM JANSZ STORCK (Also Stork) 1635-1710
Netherlandish Seascapes, Landscapes $175,000

G H Story.

GEORGE HENRY STORY 1835-1923
American A.N.A. Genre, Portraits $20,000

T. Stothard

THOMAS STOTHARD 1755-1834
British Illustrator, Portraits, Genre $10,000

Stradanus

JAN VANDER STRAET DIT STRADANUS 1523-1605
Flemish Old Master, Genre $45,000

STRANG

RAY C. STRANG 1893-1957
American Cowboy, Genre $5,000

Van Straten

VAN STRATEN 1900's
Belgian Painter, Genre $1,000

Strecker

PAUL STRECKER 1900-1950
German Painter, Genre, Landscape $1,000

1.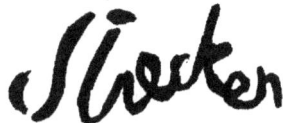

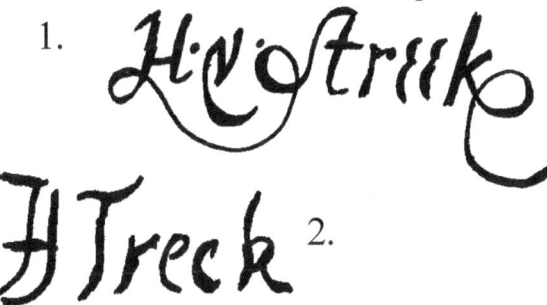 2.

JURIAAN VAN STREEK (also Jurian Streeck) 1632-1678
Dutch Still Life, Portraits $300,000

R.Street

ROBERT STREET 1796-1865
American Landscape $20,000

Philip E Stretton

PHILIP EUSTACE STRETTON-1919
British Animals Dogs, Genre $10,000

A Van Stry

ABRAHAM VAN (Elder) STRY (Also Strij) 1753-1826
Dutch Genre, Animals, Portraits, Landscape $65,000

J-E-STUART

JAMES EVERETT STUART 1852-1941
American Landscape $5,000

Geo: Stubbs

GEORGE STUBBS 1724-1806
British, Sporting, Landscaper $4,700,000

FRANZ STVCK

FRANZ VON STUCK 1863-1928
German Painter, Portraits, Genre, Nudes $200,000

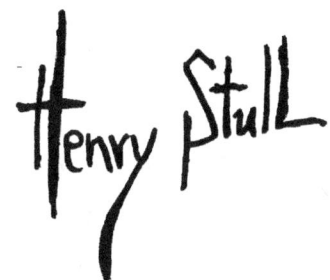

HENRY STULL 1851-1913
Canadian Sporting, Landscape, Genre $15,000

MARK STUPAR 1936-
Belgian Painter $6,500

FRITZ STURM 1834-1906
German Seascape, Landscape $1,000

HELMUT STURM 1932-
German, Landscape, Genre $20,000

KARL STURMER 1803-1881
German Painter

H.St.

HANS STURZENEGGER 1875-1943
Swiss, Landscape, Genre $3,500

蘇東坡

SU TUNG P'O 1035-1101
Chinese Watercolour Flowers Birds

P.SUBLEYRAS

1.

2. *P.Subleyras*

PIERRE SUBLEYRAS 1699-1749
French Painter, Religious, Genre, Portraits $125,000

R.Suhrlandt

RUDOLF SUHRLANDT 1781-1862
German Portraits $1,000

I H.Suhrlandt

HEINRICH SUHRLANDT 1742-1827
German Portraits, Landscape, Still Life, Animal

1. 2.

THOMAS SULLY 1783-1872
American Portrait $100,000

MAUD SUMNER 1902-1985
South African, Landscape, Genre $6,500

1.

2.

3.

LEOPOLD SURVAGE 1879-1968
French Landscape, Genre, Abstract $150,000

GRAHAM VIVIAN SUTHERLAND 1903-1980
British Landscape $45,000

1.

2.

JOSEPH BENOIT SUVEE 1743-1807
Flemish Portraits, Religious, Genre, Landscape $20,000

A. Suzor-Cote

MARC AURELE SUZOR-COTE 1869-1937
Canadian Painter, Genre, Landscape $275,000

Svend Svendsen

SVEND SVENDSEN 1864-1915
Norwegian Landscape $2,500

N-a Swertchkow

NIKOLAI GRIGOREVICH SVERCHKOV 1817-1898
Russian Landscape, Genre $40,000

IACOMO
SWANEN
BVRGH

JACOB ISAACZ SWANENBURGH 1571-1638
Netherlandish Genre, Portraits, Seascape $50,000

1.

Hs

2.

HSWANEVELT

HERMAN SWANEVELT 1600-1655
Dutch Landscape, Mythology, Portraits $15,000

1.

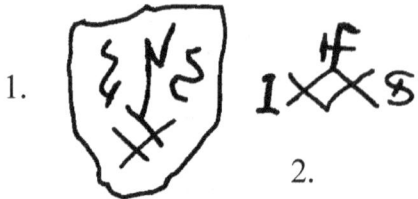

2.

JAN SWART 1469-1535
Dutch Landscape, Religious $4,000

signature

JACQUES FRANCOIS J. SWEBACH 1769-1823
French Genre, Animals, Landscape $75,000

signature

JAMES BRADE SWORD 1839-1915
American Landscape, Genre $8,000

signature

ANTAL SZIRMAI 1860-1927
Austrian Painter $20,000

signature

FERNANDO DE SZYSZLO 1925-
Peruvian Abstract, Genre $25,000

Artists starting with the letter "T"

TAGE 1900's
Swiss Painter $1,000

ARTHUR FITZWILLIAM TAIT 1819-1905
American, N.A. Cowboys, Still Life $600,000

REUBEN TAM 1916-
American Landscape $1,000

RUFFINO TAMAYO 1900-1991
Mexican, Painter, Portraits, Genre $2,587,000

ARNOLDO TAMBURINI 1843-
Italian, Painter, Genre $6,000

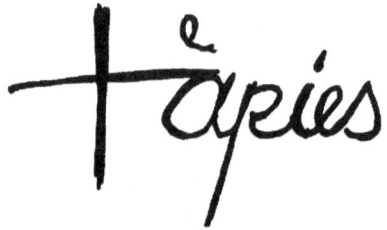

ANTONI TAPIES 1923-
Spanish Contemporary, Abstract $850,000

GEORG TAPPERT 1880-1957
German Landscape, Genre $250,000

EDMUND C. TARBELL 1862-1938
American, N.A. Portraits, Genre $400,000

NICOLAS TARKHOFF 1871-1930
Russian Landscape Fauvist, Genre $25,000

FREDERIC TAUBES 1900-1981
American Allegorical, Abstract, Genre, Landscape $5,000

1. *Taunay*

TAUNAY
2.

3. *Taunay*

NICOLAS ANTOINE TAUNAY 1755-1830
French Landscape. Animals, Genre $35,000

AVERNIER

ANDREA TAVERNIER 1858-1932
Italian Landscape, Genre $25,000

H Weston Taylor

H. WESTON TAYLOR 1881-
American, Illustrator, Painter $1,000

P. Tchelitchew

PAVEL TCHELITCHEW 1898-1957
Russian Costume Stage Design, Genre $35,000

A Tempesta

ANTONIO TEMPESTA 1555-1630
Italian Battle Painter, Religious, Animals, Genre $30,000

Juliaen Teniers

JULIAEN TENIERS 1616-1679
Netherlandish Genre, Old Master $20,000

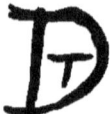

DAVID TENIERS (Elder) 1582-1649
Flemish Genre, Landscape, Religious $20,000

1. *D·F* 2. *D·F*

3. *Teniers* 5. *D* 6. *D*

4. *Dteniers*

DAVID TENIERS (Younger) 1610-1690
Flemish Genre, Landscape, Allegory,Portrait,Religious $5,700,000

Ter Meulen

FRANS PIETER TER MUELEN 1843-1927
Dutch Landscape $5,000

R.

ROUBEN TER-ARUTUNIAN 1900's
Dutch Costume Stage Design $1,000

GJBorch 1. 2.
HB *GB* *G Terburg*
3. 4.

GERARD TERBOURG (Terborch) 1613-1681
Dutch Genre, Portraits $400,000

WLADIMER DE TERLIKOWSKI 1873-1951
French, Painter, Genre $2,500

LOUIS ADOLPHE TESSIER 1855-1911
French Painter, Genre $30,000

PIETRO TESTA 1611-1650
Italian Painter, Religious, Still Life $50,000

1.

2.

HENRI TESTELIN 1616-1695
French Portraits, Genre $30,000

1.   2.

JANOS MATTIS TEUTSCH
Hungarian

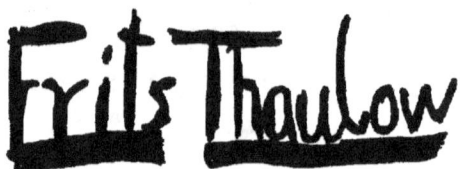

FRITS THAULOW 1847-1906
Norwegian, Landscape $120,000

ABBOTT HANDERSON THAYER 1849-1921
American Landscape, Animals, Religious $30,000

THIAIS-LOUBRIS

THIAIS-LOUBRIS
Painter

1.

2.

JOHANN ALEXANDER THIELE 1685-1752
German Landscape $12,000

1.

2.

JAN PHILIP VAN THIELEN 1618-1667
Flemish Floral, Religious, Still Life $100,000

1.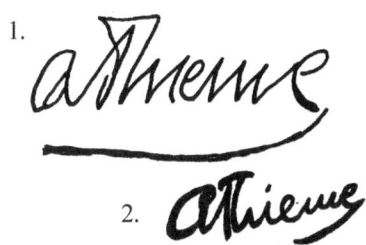

2. *[signature: Athieme]*

ANTHONY THIEME 1888-1954
American Landscape, Genre $15,000

[monogram: Hh]

HANS THOMA 1839-1924
German Landscape, Genre $100,000

[signature: Isa Thompson]

ISA THOMPSON 1850-1926
British Genre $15,000

1. *[signature: Archibald Thorburn]*

2. *[signature: A. Thorburn]*   3. *[signature: A.T.]*

ARCHIBALD THORBURN 1860-1935
British Watercolour, Landscape $90,000

[signature: Francis Throop]

FRANCIS HUNT THROOP 1800's
American Floral $7,000

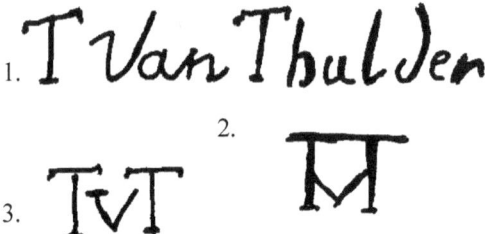

1. *T Van Thulden*

2.

3.

4.

THEODORUS VAN THULDEN (also Thulen) 1606-1676
Flemish Genre, Landscape, Religious, Mythology $40,000

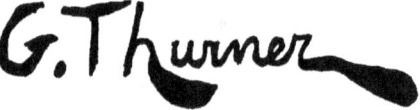

GABRIEL EDOUARD THURNER 1840-1907
French Painter, Genre $1,500

PIERRE THURNER 1799-1958
French Landscape $6,500

PEETER THYS (also Pieter Thijs) 1624-1677
Flemish Portraits, Allegory $12,000

1.

2.

3.

DOMENICO TIBALDI 1541-1583
Italian, Portraits $2,000

1.

2.

3.

4.

GIOVANNI BATTISTA TIEPOLO 1696-1770
Italian Painter, Religious, Portraits, Allegory $2,202,500

LAJOS TIHANYI 1885-1938
Hungarian Portraits $1,000

1.

2.

3.

GILLIS VAN EGIDIUS TILBORGH (Also Tilborch, Younger)
Netherlandish Genre, Portraits, Landscape $100,000

JAN TILENS (also Hans Tielens) 1589-1630
Flemish Landscape, Religious, Genre $15,000

A. Tischbein

AUGUST A. TISCHBEIN 1805-1867
German Genre $3,500

1. *JB*   2. *Tischbein*

JOHANN HEINRICH TISCHBEIN 1722-1789
German Portraits, Mythology, Genre $55,000

1. *J.J. Tissot*   *J. Tissot* 2.

JAMES JACQUE JOSEPH TISSOT 1836-1902
French Painter, Genre $5,282,000

1. **F. Titian**   2.

TITIANUS EQUES

Tiziano Vecellio TITIAN 1477-1576
Italian Painter, Mythology, Religious, Portraits $13,555,000

AM de Tobar

ALONSO MIGUEL DE TOBAR 1678-1758
Spanish Painter, Religious, Genre $9,000

1. *Tobey* 2. *Tobey*

3. *Tobey*

4. *Tobey*

MARK TOBEY 1890-1976
American, Abstract, Landscape $741,660

1. *Theo Tobiasse*

2. *Tobiasse*

THEO TOBIASSE 1927-
Israeli Painter, Genre, Landscape $40,000

L. Tocque

LOUIS TOCQUE 1696-1772
French Portraits $40,000

H.G. Todd

HENRY GEORGE TODD 1847-1898
British Landscape, Still Life $8,000

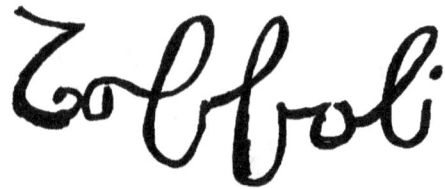

LOUIS TOFFOLI 1906-
French Painter, Genre, Landscape $35,000

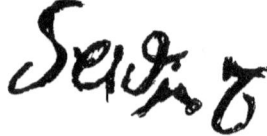

SEIJI TOGO
Painter

VIRGILIO TOJETTI 1851-1901
American Painter, Genre $20,000

1.
2.

DOMINICUS VAN TOL 1631-1676
Dutch Genre, Portraits $7,500

FRANCISCO TOLEDO 1940-
Mexican Painter, Sculptor $250,000

BRADLEY WALKER TOMLIN 1899-1953
American Abstract $150,000

LUDOVICO TOMMASI 1866-1941
Italian Landscape, Portraits, Genre $10,000

J.V. TONGEREN
JAN VAN TONGEREN CIRCA 1900'S
Dutch Still Life $4,000

JACOB (also Jason) TOORENVLIET 1641-1719
Dutch Genre, Portraits, Religious $12,000

JAN TOOROP 1859-1928
Dutch, Landscape, Genre $150,000

MORRIS TOPCHEVSKY 1900-1947
American Painter $1,000

GIOVANNI BATTISTA TORRIGLIA 1858-1937
Italian, Painter, Genre $75,000

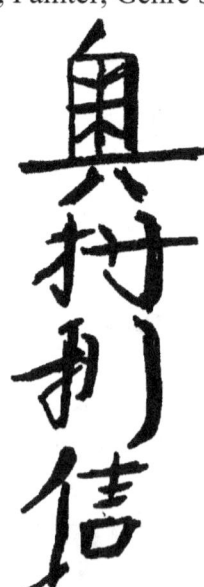

OKUMURA TOSHINOBU 1717-1750
Japanese Woodblock $4,000

EDOUARD TOUDOUZE 1848-1907
French Floral $10,000

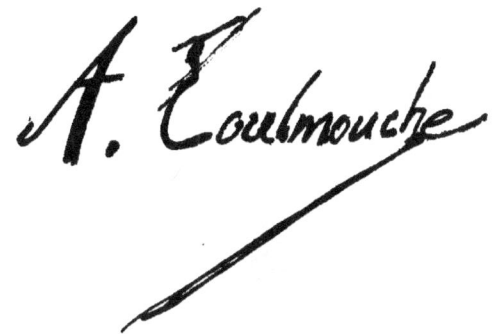

AUGUSTE TOULMOUCHE 1829-1899
French, Painter, Genre $30,000

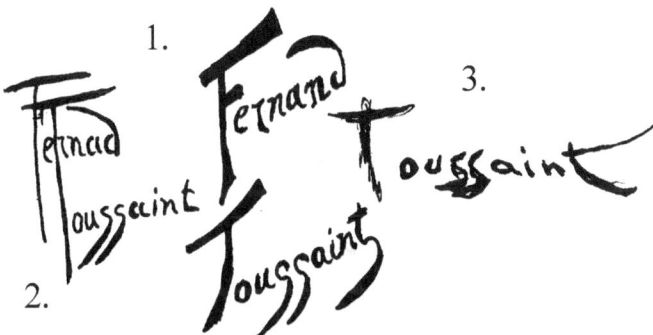

ROBERT LEVRAC TOURNIERES 1668-1752
French Portraits, Genre $3,000

FERNAND TOUSSAINT 1873-1955
Belgian Landscape, Portraits, Still Life $100,000

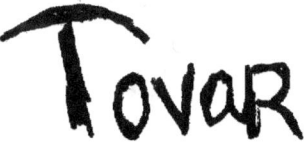

IVAN TOVAR 1942-
Latin American Painter, Genre $30,000

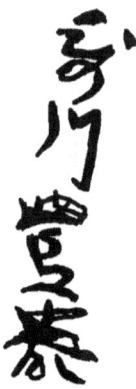

UTAGAWA TOYOHARU 1735-1814
Japanese Woodblocks $8,000

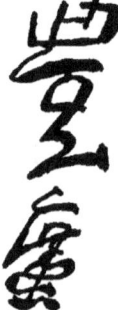

UTAGAWA TOYOHIRO 1773-1828
Japanese Woodblocks $4,000

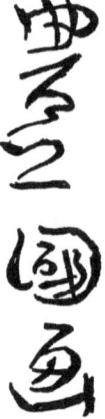

UTAGAWA TOYOKUNI 1769-1825
Japanese Woodblocks $30,000

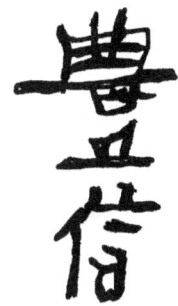

ISHIKANA TOYONOBU 1711-1785
Japanese Woodblocks $20,000

MARIO TOZZI 1895-1979
Italian Painter $40,000

ALBERT TRACHSEL 1863-1929
Swiss Landscape $1,500

JOHN M. TRACY 1843-1893
American, Indians $40,000

1.

2.

3.

PIERRE CHARLES TREMOLLIERE 1703-1739
French Genre, Mythological, Religious, Landscape $9,000

JULIAN TREVELYAN 1910-1988
British Watercolour, Landscape, Genre $10,000

SHIRLEY TREVENA 1900's
British Still Life $1,000

JAN ZOETELIEF TROMP 1872-1947
Dutch Painter, Genre $30,000

HECTOR TROTIN 1894-1966
French, City Scenes, Genre $1,500

PAUL DESIRE TROUILLEBERT 1829-1900
French Painter, Genre $20,000

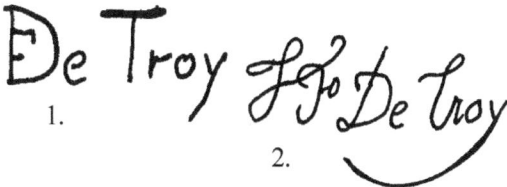

1. 2.

JEAN FRANCOIS DE TROY 1679-1752
French Genre, Allegory, Religious, Portraits $50,000

C. TROYON

CONSTANT TROYON 1810-1865
French Landscape, Genre $70,000

W. Trübner

WILLIAM TRUBNER 1851-1917
German Painter, Genre, Landscape $30,000

Trunk

HERMAN TRUNK 1894-1963
American Architectural Painter $1,000

Tschacbasov

NAHUM TSCHACBASOV 1899-1984
American Abstract, Genre $1,500

Fv Tscharner

JOHANN WILHELM VON TSCHARNER 1886-1946
Swiss Abstract, Landscape, Genre $7,500

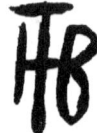

HERBERT BOLIVIER TSCHUDY 1874-1946
American Watercolour, Landscape $1,000

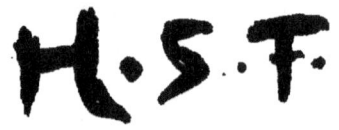

HENRY SCOTT TUKE 1858-1929
British Seascapes, Genre $80,000

TUMARKIN

YGAEL TUMARKIN 1932-
Israeli Painter, Portraits $2,000

C.F.Tunnicliffe

CHARLES FREDERICK TUNNICLIFFE 1901-1979
British Animals, Genre, Landscape $7,500

AM Turner

ALFRED M. TURNER 1851-1932
American Painter, Genre $2,000

LEON TUTUNDJIAN 1906-1968
French Abstract $18,000

JOHN HENRY TWACHTMAN 1853-1902
American Impressionist, Landscape, Genre $500,000

CY TWOMBLY 1929-
American Contemporary, Landscape $7,968,000

JACK TWORKOV 1900-1982
American Abstract $70,000

1.   2.

JAMES GALE TYLER 1855-1931
American Seascape $15,000

EDGARD TYTGAT 1879-1957
British Genre, Illustration, Genre, Allegory $90,000

Artists starting with the letter "U"

MARIA VON UCHATIUS 1882-1958
Austrian Abstract, Designer, Avant Garde $10,000

LUCAS VAN UDEN 1595-1672
Flemish Landscape, Genre, Religious, Animals $60,000

WALTER UFER 1876-1936
American N.A. Taos Painter, Genre $100,000

JACOB VAN DER ULFT 1627-1688
Dutch Landscape, Architectural, Genre, Mythology $12,000

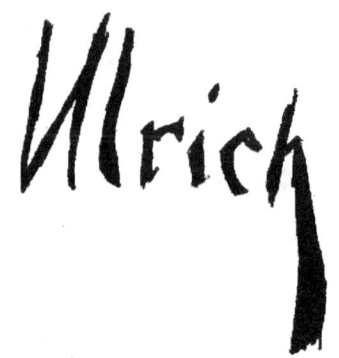

CHARLES FREDERIC ULRICH 1858-1908
American A.N.A. Castles, Genre $25,000

FRANZ RICHARD UNTERBERGER 1832-1902
Belgian Landscape, Genre $60,000

HUMBERTO URBAN
Painter

LESSER URY 1862-1931
German Landscape, Genre $100,000

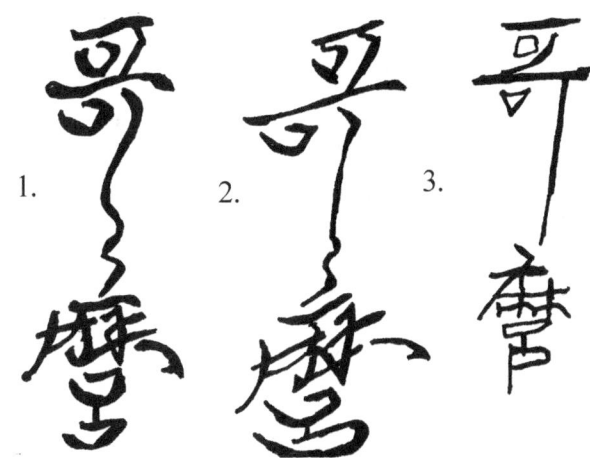

1. 2. 3.

KITAGAWA UTAMARO 1754-1806
Japanese Woodblocks $25,000

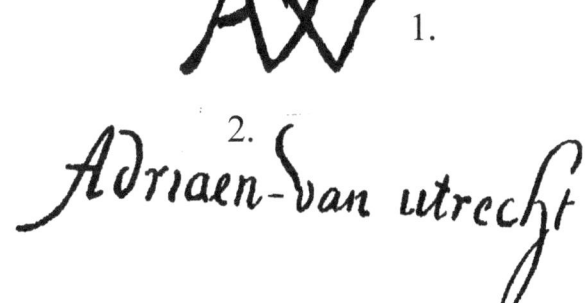

1.

2.

ADRIAEN VAN UTRECHT 1599-1653
Netherlandish Still Life, Landscape, Genre $100,000

MAURICE UTRILLO 1883-1955
French Street Scenes, Paris $1,454,000

MOYSESZ VAN UYTTENBROECK 1590-1648
Netherlandish Allegory, Portraits, Landscape $100,000

Artists starting with the letter "V"

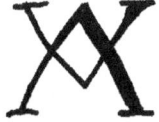

ANDREA VACCARO 1598-1670
Italian Painter, Allegory, Religious $35,000

LODEWYCK DE VADDER 1605-1655
Flemish Landscape, Animals $20,000

EUGENE VAIL 1857-1934
American Water Scenes, Genre $10,000

WALLERANT VAILLANT 1623-1677
Flemish Portraits, Still Life, Allegory $40,000

SUZANNE VALADON 1867-1938
French Landscape $175,000

1. 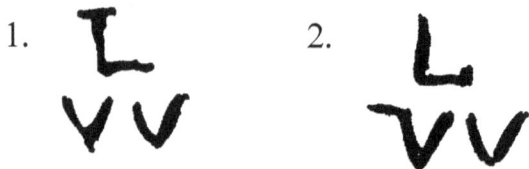 2.

LUCAS VAN VALCHENBORCH 1535-1597
Netherlandish Landscapes, Genre, Old Master $70,000

M.V.Valckenborg

MARTEN VAN VALCKENBORCH 1533-1612
Flemish Genre, Landscape, Portraits $12,000

Valenciennes

PIERRE HENRI DE VALENCIENNES 1750-1819
French Landscape $400,000

1. *M. valentin*

2. *Valentin*

LE JEAN DE VALENTIN 1591-1634
French Genre, Mythology $85,000

1. 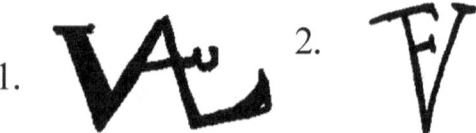 2.

FRANCESCO VALESIO 1500's
Italian, Painter

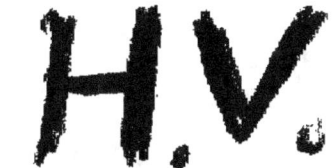

HENDRIK VALK 1897-1986
Dutch Genre $10,000

DIRK VALKENBURG 1675-1721
Netherlandish Still Life Hunt Scenes $75,000

LUDOVIC VALLEE 1864-1939
French Painter, Genre, Landscape $8,000

ANTONIO VALLEJO-1784
Mexican Painter, Religious $30,000

JONAS JOSEPH LA VALLEY 1857-
American Landscape, Still Life $1,500

1.
F.VALLOTTON.
2. F.VALLOTTON

FELIX VALLOTTON 1865-1925
Swiss Illustrator, Portraits, Still Life $1,388,000

L.V   2. L.V.
1.

LOUIS VALTAT 1869-1952
French Impressionist, Genre, Landscape $175,000

1.   2.

HENDRIK VAN BALEN 1623-1661
Flemish Painter, Religious, Landscape $1,921,000

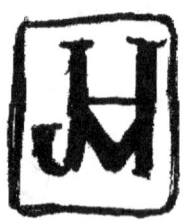

JACOBA VAN HEEMSKERCK VAN BEEST 1828-1894
Dutch Painter $5,000

My Van Bree

MATTHEUS I. VAN BREE 1773-1839
Flemish Painter, Genre, Allegory $4,500

1. *Antony Mor*

2. *Antoniuy Mor*

ANTONIS VAN D. MOR 1512-1578
Dutch Portraits

J.F.V. Dael

JAN FRANS VAN DAEL 1764-1840
Flemish Floral, Still Life, Genre $300,000

1. **E.V.VEL**

2. **DE II.**

3. **E·V·VELDE**

4. **E·V·VELDE**

5. **E·Y VELDE**

6. *E·V·VELDE*

E SAIAS VAN DE VELDE 1590-1630
Dutch Old Master $40,000

P.VANDERHEM

PIET VAN DER HEM 1885-1961
Dutch Painter $5,000

1.

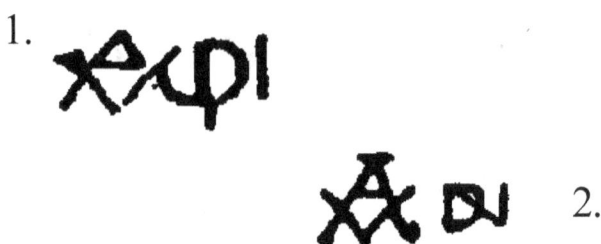

2.

AART VAN DER NEER 1603-1677
Dutch Landscape, Genre $900,000

EGLON HENDRIK VAN DER NEER 1643-1703
Dutch Landscape, Genre, Portraits, Religious $1,000,000

1.

2.

EGBERT VAN DER POEL 1621-1664
Dutch Genre, Landscape $20,000

VINCENT LAURENSZ VAN DER VINNE 1629-1702
Dutch Portraits, Landscape, Animal Painter $8,000

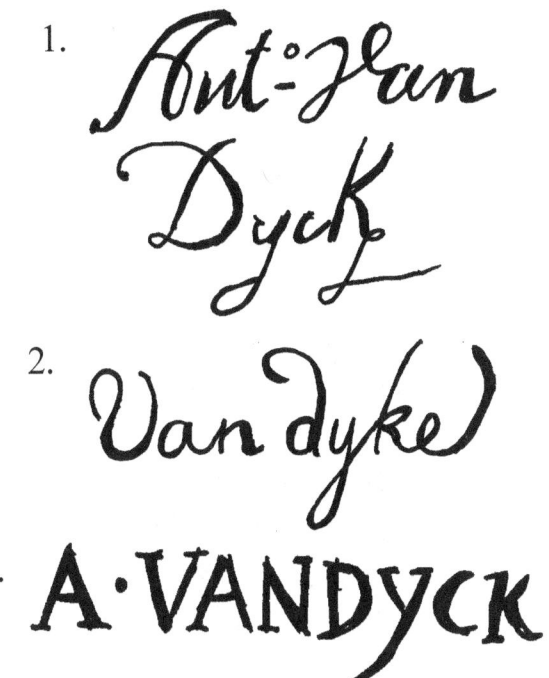

1.

2.

3.

SIR ANTHONY (also Anton) VAN DYCK 1599-1641
Flemish Old Master, Portraits, Religious $3,100,000

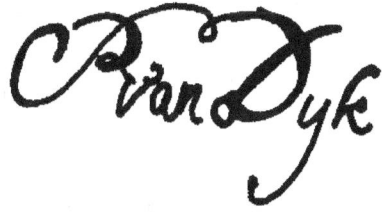

PHILIP VAN DYCK 1681-1753
Dutch Genre, Portraits, Religious $30,000

JAN VAN EYCK 1381-1440
Dutch Painter, Portraits, Genre, Religious $100,000

1.

2.

VINCENT VAN GOGH 1853-1890
Dutch Impressionist $82,500,000

JAN VAN GOOL 1690-1765
Dutch Landscape, Animal Painter $15,000

CORNELIS VAN LEEMPUTTEN 1841-1902
Belgian Animals, Landscape $20,000

JOHAN VAN NECK 1636-1714
Dutch Portraits, Religious, Landscape $15,000

ISAAC VAN NICKELE 1630-1703
Dutch Architectural $25,000

Gvil ᵐᵒ VAN NIEVLANT

WILLEM VAN NIEULANT 1584-1635
Flemish Painter, Engraver , Landscape, Religious $35,000

L VOort

LAMBERT VAN NOORT 1520-1570
Flemish Religious $3,500

A V. Noort

ADAM VAN NOORT 1562-1641
Flemish Painter, Religious $10,000

J. V oost

JACOB (younger) VAN OOST 1639-1713
Flemish Painter, Portraits, Religious, Genre $15,000

J Van oost

JACOB (elder) VAN OOST 1600-1671
Flemish Portraits, Genre, Religious, Landscape $15,000

Maria Oosterwyc/)

MARIA VAN OOSTERWYCK 1630-1693
Dutch Floral, Still Life $60,000

V. opstal

CASPAR JACOBUS VAN OPSTAL 1654-1717
French Portraits, Allegory $45,000

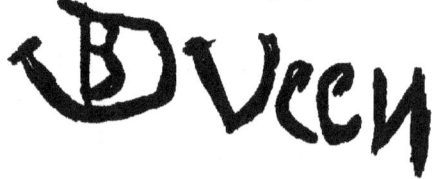

BALTHASAR VAN DER VEEN 1596-1657
Dutch, Genre, Landscape $20,000

1.   2.

ADRIEN VAN DE VEEN 1589-1680
Dutch, Painter

P van Veen

PIETER J.L. VAN VEEN 1875-1961
American Painter $1500

J.G. van Velde

BRAM VAN VELDE 1910-1981
Dutch Landscape $80,000

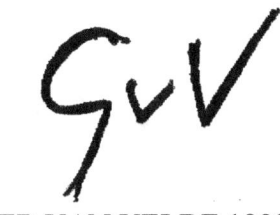

GEER VAN VELDE 1898-1978
Dutch Abstract $20,000

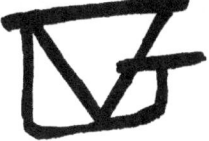

GEORGES VANTONGERLOO 1886-1965
Belgian Abstract $60,000

GEORGE VARION 1865-1923
American Illustrator $1,000

VICTOR VASARELY 1908-
Hungarian Abstract $100,000

MARIE VASSILIEFF 1884-1957
Russian Painter $7,500

GEZA VASTAGH 1866-1919
Hungarian Landscape, Animals $25,000

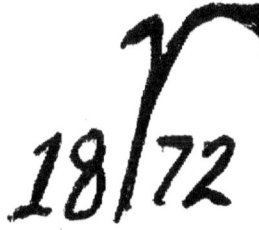

ELIHU VEDDER 1836-1923
American N.A. Illustrator, Genre, Landscape $30,000

JOSE MARIA VELASCO 1840-1912
Mexican Landscape $100,000

LUIS DE VELASCO -1606
Spanish Religious Painter $7,500

1.

2.

DIEGO RODRIGUEZ DE VELASQUEZ 1599-1660
Spanish Painter, Still Life, Genre, Portraits $50,000

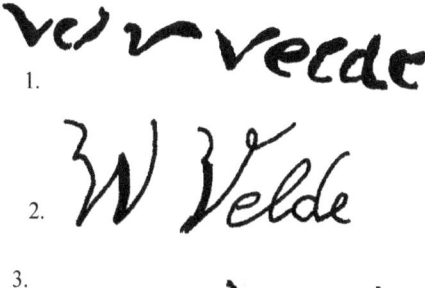

1.

2.

3.

WILLEM VAN DE VELDE 1633-1707
Netherlandish Marines, Boats, Landscape $200,000

EVANDEVELDE

ESAIAS VAN DE VELDE 1590-1630
Netherlandish Landscapes, Portraits, Allegory $185,000

A W Velße

ADRIAEN VAN DE VELDE (also Adriaan) 1636-1672
Netherlandish Landscapes Animals, Genre $60,000

Ga VENARD

2. C. VENARD

1.

CLAUDE VENARD 1913-
French Abstract, Landscape, Compositions $45,000

1. Veni

2. Veni

3. Veni

GLIGOROVA-SMITH VENI 1900's
Russian Watercolour $1,000

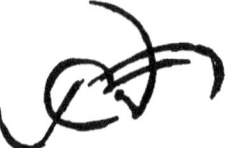

ADRIAEN PIETERSZ VAN DE VENNE 1589-1662
Netherlandish Genre, Allegory, Portraits $90,000

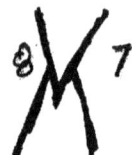

GUILLERMO MUNOZ VERA 1956-
Chilian Genre $30,000

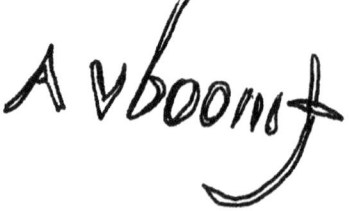

EUGENE JOSEPH VERBOECKHOVEN 1799-1881
Belgian Animal Painter, Landscape $50,000

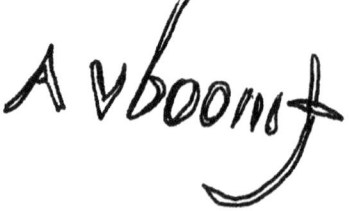

ADRIAEN HENDRIKSZ VERBOOM 1628-1670
Netherlandish Genre, Landscape $20,000

ABRAHAM VERBOOM 1657-
Dutch Landscape

FRANCOIS VERDIER 1651-1730
French Painter, Religious, Mythology $2,000

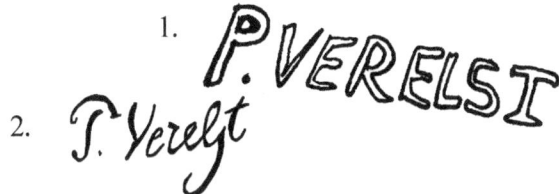

1.
2.

PIETER HARMANSZ VERELST 1618-1686
Netherlandish Genre, Still Life, Portraits $200,000

TOBIAS VERHAEGT 1561-1631
Flemish Landscape, Architectural, Genre, Religious $80,000

FRANZ VERHAS 1827-1897
Belgian Painter, Portraits $10,000

ISIDORE VERHEYDEN 1846-1905
Belgian Landscape $18,000

JAN VERKOLJE 1650-1693
Netherlandish Allegory, Genre $15,000

NICOLAAS VERKOLJE 1673-1746
Netherlandish Allegory, Genre $25,000

1.

2.

CHARLES MICHEL MARIA VERLAT 1824-1890
Belgian Portraits, Animal Painter, Genre, Landscape $3,500

1.

2.

JAN (van der meer) VERMEER 1656-1705
Netherlandish Landscape Animals $50,000

J. Vermeer

JOHANNES(van der meer) VERMEER 1632-1675
Dutch Genre, Still Life, Portraits, Landscape $3,000

H. Vernet

HORACE VERNET 1789-1863
French Genre, Portraits, Animals $480,000

1. *Joseph Vernet*
J. Vernet 3.
2. *J Vernet*

CLAUDE JOSEPH VERNET 1712-1789
French Seascape, Genre, Landscape $1,540,000

Carle Vernet

CHARLES VERNET 1758-1836
French Animal Painter, Landscape, Portraits $20,000

1. 2.
E Vernon
E Vernon

EMILE VERNON 1900's
French Painter Genre, Portraits, Seascape $60,000

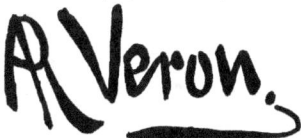

R Veron

ALEXANDRE RENE VERON 1826-1897
French Landscape, Genre $20,000

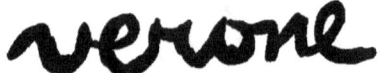

BIENENFELD VERONE 1900'S
Swiss Painter $4,000

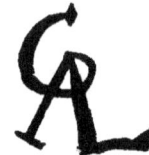

PAOLO VERONESE 1528-1588
Italian Painter, Portraits, Costume, Religious $2,700,000

1. *H.V.g*

2. *H.Verschuring*

HENDRICK (also Hendrik) VERSCHURING 1627-1690
Netherlandish Genre Landscapes, Military Painter $15,000

C.Verschuur

C. VERSCHUUR
Dutch Painter $1,000

Johan Verspronck

JAN (also Johannes Cornelisz) VERSPRONCK 1597-1662
Dutch Portraits $1,652,000

1. *Daniel Vertanghen*

D Vertangen 2.

DANIEL VERTANGEN (also Vertanghen) 1598-1684
Netherlandish Genre,Allegory, Landscape $15,000

636

MARCEL VERTES 1895-1961
Hungarian Stage Costume Design $12,000

FRANCOIS VERWILT 1620-1691
Netherlandish Nymphs, Genre, Landscape $20,000

JAN VETH 1864-1925
Dutch Portraits $6,500

JEAN GEORGES VIBERT 1840-1902
French Painter, Genre $35,000

JACOMO (Jacobus) VICTOR 1640-1705
Netherlandish Birds, Landscape, Still Life $7,500

A. · VICTORYNS

ANTHONI VICTORIJNS 1620-1656
Netherlandish Genre Allegorical $6,500

1. **Jan Victoors**

2. **Jan·bictors**

3. **Jo San·Victor**

4. **7 Victors**

5. **Jan Victons**

JAN VICTORS 1620-1676
Netherlandish Genre Allegorical Portraits, Landscape $55,000

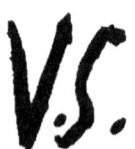

MARIA ELENA VIEIRA DA SILVA 1908-1992
Spanish Landscape $250,000

1. **J.V** 2. **Vien**

JOSEPH MARIE VIEN 1716-1809
French Painter, Portraits, Religious, Allegory $30,000

1.

2.

FELIX DE VIGNE 1806-1862
Belgian Painter, Genre $1,000

VICTOR PAUL VIGNON 1847-1909
French Landscape, Impressionist, Still Life $55,000

MIGUEL VILADRICH 1889-
Spanish Painter, Religious $1,000

JAVIER VILATO 1921-
Spanish Genre, Portraits $2,000

ARMANDO VILLEGAS 1928-
Peruvian Portrait, Genre $15,000

Villegas

JOSE VILLEGAS Y CORDERO 1848-1922
Spanish Painter, Genre $300,000

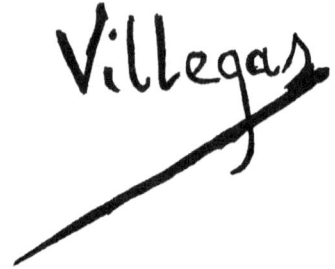

EMMANUEL DE LA VILLEON 1858-1944
French Landscape, Genre $15,000

1.

Villon

2.

JOSEPH MARIE VIEN 1716-1809
French Painter, Portraits, Religious, Allegory $30,000

1.

2.

FELIX DE VIGNE 1806-1862
Belgian Painter, Genre $1,000

M. Vinogradoff-

VICTOR PAUL VIGNON 1847-1909
French Landscape, Impressionist, Still Life $55,000

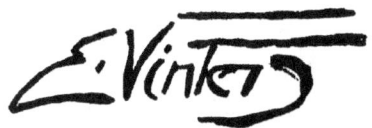

MIGUEL VILADRICH 1889-
Spanish Painter, Religious $1,000

CORNELIS VISSCHER 1629-1658
Dutch Old Master, Genre $2,000

1.

2.

JOSEPH VIVIEN 1657-1735
French Portraits, Landscape, Seascape $70,000

2.

1.

MAURICE DE VLAMINCK 1876-1958
French Painter, Landscape, Still Life, Portraits $10,721,000

3.

1.

2.

4.

SIMON DE VLIEGER 1600-1653
Netherlandish Marines Boats, Landscape, Genre $2,300,000

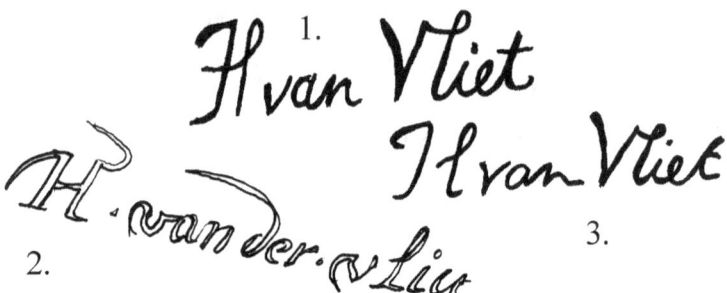

HENDRICK CORNELISZ VAN VLIET 1611-1675
Netherlandish Portrait, Genre, Seascape, Architectural

GOTTFRIED WILHELM VOELCKER 1775-1849
German Painter, Still Life, Floral $15,000

FRITZ G. VOGT 1841-1893
American Painter $2,500

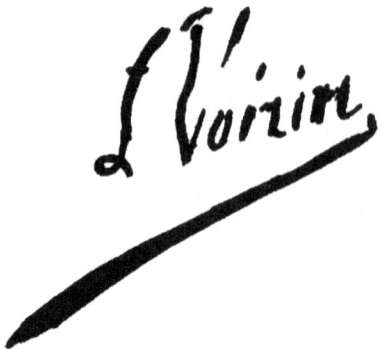

LEON VOIRIN 1833-1887
French Painter, Genre $10,000

1.
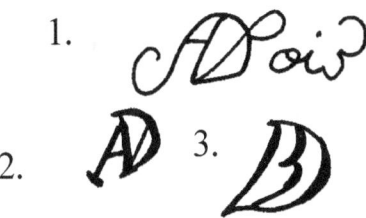

2. 3.

ADRIAN DE VOS 1631-1680
Dutch, Painter

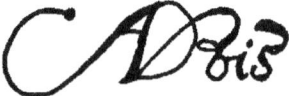

ARIE VOIS 1641-1698
Dutch Portraits, Landscape, Genre $10,000

1. 2.
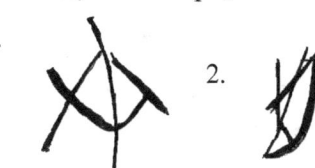

ADALBERT JOHN VOLCK 1828-1912
German Sporting $2,500

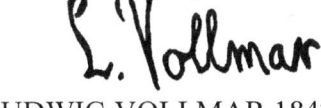

LUDWIG VOLLMAR 1842-1884
German Painter, Genre $40,000

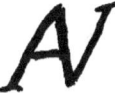

ADOLF VOLLMER 1806-1875
German Landscape, Seascape $1,500

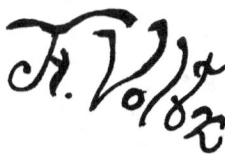

FRIEDRICH VOLTZ 1817-1886
German Landscape $45,000

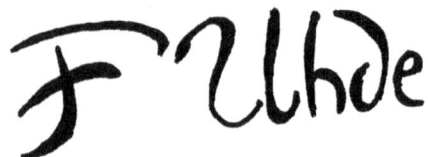

FRITZ KARL HERMANN VON UHDE 1848-1911
German Painter $40,000

ELIAS VONCK 1605-1652
Netherlandish Still Life, Portraits $30,000

ROBERT WILLIAM VONNOH 1858-1933
American N.A. Landscape $160,000

MAREVNA VOROBIEFF 1892-1984
Russian Genre, Landscape $30,000

WILHELM VORTEL 1793-1844
German Painter

PAULUS DE VOS 1590-1678
Flemish Animal Painter, Landscape, Animal, Still Life $45,000

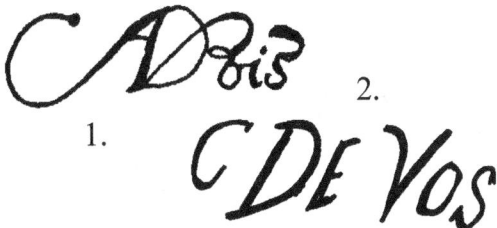

1.   2.

CORNELIS DE VOS 1585-1651
Flemish Portraits, Children, Mythology, Religious $50,000

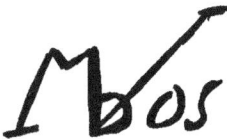

MARTEN DE VOS 1532-1603
Flemish Portraits, Mythology, Religious $60,000

S. De Vos

SIMON DE VOS 1603-1676
Flemish Portraits, Genre, Allegory, Religious $45,000

2.   3.

1.

Simon Vouet

SIMON VOUET 1590-1649
French Portraits, Religious, Allegory $400,000

1.   3.

2.

ROELOF (also Roelant) JANSZ VAN VRIES 1631-1681
Netherlandish Castles Landscape, Portraits $30,000

1.

2.

ADRIAAN DE VRIES 1601-1643
Dutch Portraits $3,000

2.

VROOM

1.

dROOM

HENDRIK CORNELISZEN VROOM 1566-1646
Dutch Seascape, Landscape $40,000

1. *E. Vuillard*

2. *E. V* 3. *EV*

EDOUARD VUILLARD 1868-1940
French Impressionist, Seascape, Genre $7,481,000

Yuillefroy

FELIX DE VUILLEFROY 1841-1910
French Landscape, Animal Painter $2,000

Artists starting with the letter "W"

HENRY WABEL 1889-1981
Swiss Landscape, Genre, Still Life $1,500

CORNELIS DE WAEL 1592-1662
Flemish Military Painter, Religious, Genre $60,000

1.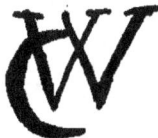

2.

MAX JOSEF WAGENBAUR 1774-1829
German Landscape, Animal Painter $35,000

OTTO ERICH WAGNER 1895-1975
German Designer, Avant Garde, Abstract $2,000

LOUIS WAIN 1860-1939
British Genre, Animals $10,000

William Walcutt

WILLIAM WALCUTT 1819-1882
American Sculptor, Painter, Portraits $1,000

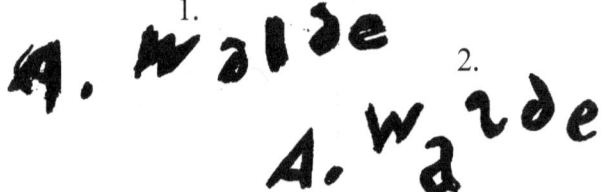

ALFONS WALDE 1890-1958
Austrian Landscape, Genre $60,000

NW

NELL WALDEN 1887-1975
Swedish Landscape $1,000

WAWalker.

WILLIAM AIKEN WALKER 1838-1921
American Black People $90,000

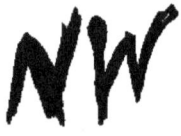

ABRAHAM WALKOWITZ 1880-1965
American Abstract, Landscape $10,000

WILLIAM GUY WALL 1792-1862
American Landscape, Genre $10,000

ALFRED S. WALL 1801-1896
American Painter $1,000

SAMUEL EDMUND WALLER 1850-1903
British Painter, Genre, Horses $12,000

ALFRED WALLIS 1855-1942
British Seascapes $15,000

JAN WALRAVEN 1827-
Dutch Painter, Genre $10,000

JACOB VAN WALSCAPELE 1644-1727
Dutch Floral, Still Life Painter $200,000

_J.W.W._

J.W. WALSHAW-1906
British Street Scenes $1,000

Martha Walter

MARTHA WALTER 1875-1976
American Children, Genre, Seascape $40,000

L. Ward,

JOHN WARD OF HULL 1798-1849
British Painter, Seascape, Genre $50,000

ARTHUR.WARDLE

ARTHUR WARDLE 1864-1949
British Sporting, Landscape, Genre $80,000

1.

2.

3.

Andy Warhol

ANDY WARHOL 1928-1987
American Pop Art $71,700,000

Melvin C. Warren

MELVIN C. WARREN 1920-
American Cowboys $80,000

q. G. Warshawsky

ABRAHAM GEORGE WARSHAWSKY 1883-1967
American Painter, Genre, Landscape $6,000

Ch. J. Watelet

CHARLES JOSEPH WATELET 1867-1954
Belgian Painter, Genre $5,000

J.W. Waterhouse

JOHN WILLIAM WATERHOUSE 1849-1917
British Genre, Portraits $10,000,000

1. *AW* 2. *AW*

ANTHONIE WATERLOO 1609-1690
Dutch Landscape, Allegory, Genre $10,000

Watrous

HARRY W. WATROUS 1857-1940
American N.A. Painter, Genre $20,000

1. *Wa* *ant Watteau* 2.
3. *Watteau* 4. *Watt*

ANTOINE WATTEAU 1684-1721
French Genre, Landscape, Portraits $3,185,000

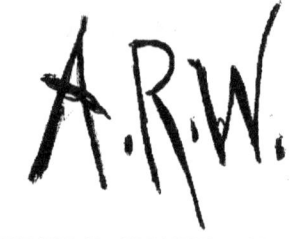

ALFRED R. WAUD 1828-1941
American Illustrator, Portraits $5,000

JOHN WEBBER 1750-1793
British Landscape, Genre $17,000

ALFRED CHARLES WEBER 1862-1922
French Painter, Genre $5,500

THEODORE ALEXANDER WEBER 1838-1907
French Seascape $10,000

MARIA WEBER 1800's
French Painter, Genre $2,000

MAX WEBER

1.

2. **Max Weber**

MAX WEBER 1881-1961
American Portraits, Genre, Cubist, Still Life $442,500

E.A.WEBSTER

E. AMBROSE WEBSTER 1869-1935
American Painter, Genre $5,000

S Webster

STOKELY WEBSTER 1912-
American Landscapes, Portraits $10,000

W. Weekes

WILLIAM WEEKES 1800's
British Animals $5,000

1. **E.L Weeks**   2. **E.L.WEEKS**

3.

E.L Weeks

EDWIN LORD WEEKS 1849-1903
American Illustrator, Landscape, Genre $1,570,000

1.

2.

3.

JAN (younger) WEENIX 1640-1719
Netherlandish Hunt Still Life, Landscape $200,000

JAN BAPTISTA (elder) WEENIX 1621-1664
Dutch Genre, landscape, Animal Painter $80,000

J.J. WEERTS

JEAN JOSEPH WEERTS 1847-1927
French Portraits, Genre, Still Life $1,000

ADOLF WEGELIN 1810-1881
German Landscape, Architectural Painter $1,200

GERDA WEGENER

GERDA WEGENER 1885-1940
Danish Painter, Portraits $30,000

1.

2.

ZACHARIAS WEHME 1550-1606
German Painter

WEISGERBER

ALBERT WEISGERBER 1878-1915
German Portrait, Expressionist $15,000

Jos. Weiss

FRANZ JOSEF WEISS 1735-1790
Swiss Painter, Portraits, Allegory $6,500

R. Weisse

RUDOLF WEISSE 1846-1933
Swiss Painter, Genre $50,000

J. Hendrik. Weissenbruch

HENDRIK JAN WEISSENBRUCH 1824-1903
Dutch Landscape $70,000

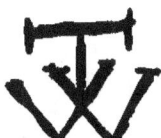

THEODOR LEOPOLD WELLER 1802-1880
German Genre $25,000

William Wells

WILLIAM PAGE ATKINSON WELLS 1872-1923
British Landscape $10,000

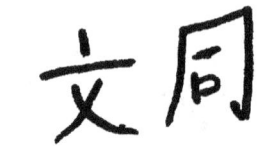

WEN T'UNG 11th Century
Chinese Watercolour

1.

WILLIAM WENDT

2.

WILLIAM WENDT

WILLIAM WENDT 1865-1946
American A.N.A. Plein Aire, California, Landscape $50,000

P. vd Werff

PIETER VAN DER WERFF 1665-1718
Dutch Genre, Religious, Allegory, Mythology $10,000

ADRIAAN VAN DER WERFF 1659-1722
Dutch Genre, Portraits, Mythology, Landscape $100,000

THEODOR WERNER 1886-1969
German Painter, Landscape $5,000

JOHN WESLEY 1928-
American Painter, Genre $1,500

1.

2.

BENJAMIN WEST 1738-1820
American R.A. Portrait, Religious $100,000

JACOB WILLEMSZ DE (the elder) WET 1610-1672
Netherlandish Allegory, Portraits $50,000

GERRIT DE WET 1615-1674
Netherlandish Genre, Allegory $3,000

GEORGE F. WETHERBEE 1853-1920
American Painter, Genre, Landscape $4,000

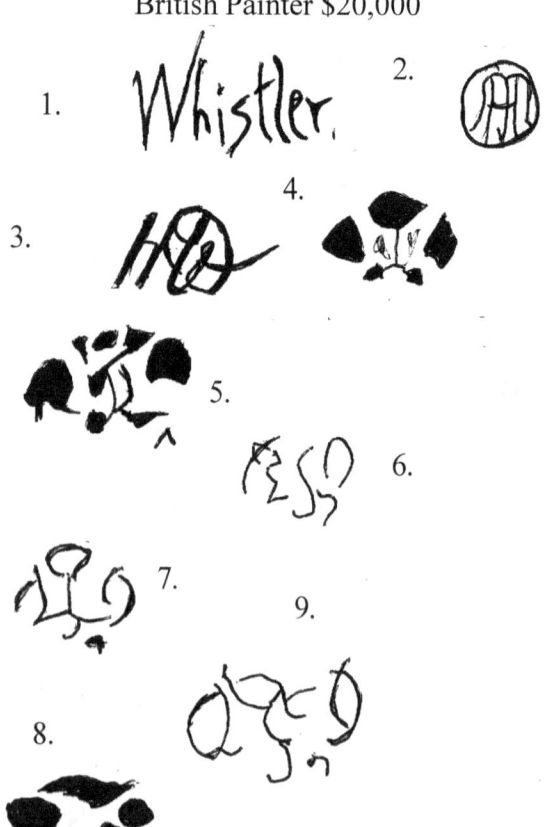

STEFAN WEWERKA 1928-
Turkish Painter, Genre, Compositions $1,000

ROLAND WHEELWRIGHT 1870-1956
British Painter $20,000

1.   2.

3.   4.

5.

6.

7.   9.

8.

JAMES ABBOTT MCNEILL WHISTLER 1834-1903
American Landscape, Impressionist, Seascape $2,866,000

WMJ. WHITTEMORE

WILLIAM J. WHITTEMORE 1860-1955
American A.N.A. Painter $5,000

W.Whittredge

WORTHINGTON WHITTREDGE 1820-1910
American N.A. Landscape, Genre $1,700,000

John Whorf

JOHN WHORF 1903-1959
American N.A. Landscape, Genre, Seascape $30,000

J.B. Wicar

JEAN BAPTISTE WICAR 1762-1834
French Portraits $15,000

1. *O-Wieghorst*

2. *O-Wieghorst ℞*

OLAF CARL WIEGHORST 1899-1975
American Cowboys $60,000

H·B·Wieland

HANS BEAT WIELAND 1867-1947
Swiss Painter, Landscape, Genre $7,500

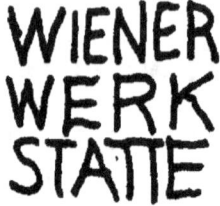

Wiener Werk Statte

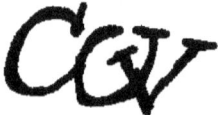

CORNELIS CLAESZ VAN WIERINGEN 1580-1633
Dutch Painter, Religious, Landscape $20,000

$$\text{HE W}$$

HIERONYMUS WIERIX 1553-1619
Flemish Painter, Genre $1,000

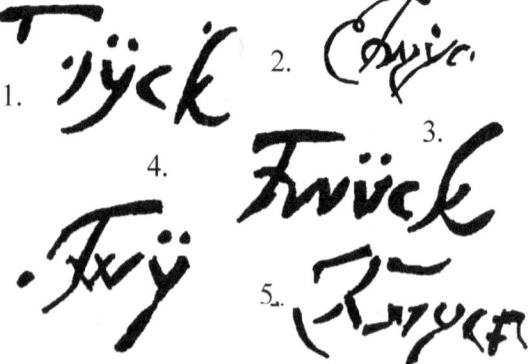

THOMAS WIJCK (also Wyck) 1616-1677 (See page 843)
Netherlandish Genre, Landscape $40,000

JAN WIJNANTS 1620-1684
Netherlandish Landscapes $50,000

CHARLES WILDA 1854-1907
Australian Painter, Genre $55,000

JAN WILDENS 1586-1653
Flemish Landscape, Animals $50,000

J.C. WILDER 1783-1838
German Painter

IRVING RAMSAY WILES 1861-1947
American Portrait, Landscape, Genre $90,000

CARL WILHELMSON 1866-1928
Sweden Painter, Genre, Landscape $300,000

1.   2.

SIR DAVID WILKIE 1785-1845
British Painter, Portraits, Landscape, Genre $100,000

1. *FRANK-WILL*

2. *FRANK-WILL*

FRANK WILL 1900-1951
French Painter $25,000

1. *ſBW*

2. **A Willaerts**

ABRAHAM WILLAERTS 1613-1671
Dutch Seascape, Portraits, Genre $35,000

Adam W

ADAM WILLAERTS 1577-1662
Dutch Landscape, Seascape, Genre $100,000

1. *Willink*

2. *A. C. Willink*

CAREL WILLINK 1900-1979
Dutch Landscape, Portraits $40,000

J·F·W

JENS FERDINAND WILLUMSEN 1863-1958
Danish Painter $40,000

Rich Wilson

RICHARD WILSON 1713-1782
British Landscape, Animals, Portraits $150,000

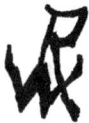

RUDOLF WIMMER 1849-1915
German Painter, Portraits, Genre $1,500

Tye

J.W. WINDTER 1696-1765
German Painter

HWF ¹ ²JaW

JEREMIAS VAN WINGHE 1578-1645
German Painter, Mythology, Still Life $300,000

Joduus d Winghe

JODOCUS VAN WINGHE (Wingen) 1544-1603
Flemish Portraits $12,000

1. *Fwinter*

2. *CWinter*

FRITZ WINTER 1905-1976
German Abstract $75,000

ANDREW WINTER 1892-1958
American N.A. Landscape, Seascapes $10,000

STANISLAW IGNACY WITKIEWICZ (Witkacy) 1885-1939
Polish Portraits, Landscape $10,000

KARL WITKOWSKI 1860-1910
American Painter, Genre, Portraits $20,000

EMANUEL DE WITTE 1607-1692
Dutch Architectural Painter $150,000

MICHAEL WOHLGEMUTH 1434-1519
German Painter, Religious $17,000

FRANZ XAVER WOLF

1.

X. Wólfle 2.

FRANZ XAVIER WOLF 1896-1989
Austrian Landscape, Genre $5,000

LONE 🐺 WOLF

LONE WOLF 1882-1970
American Cowboys $10,000

Erick Wolfsfeld

ERICH WOLFSFELD 1884-1956
Austrian Painter, Genre $7,500

WOLS

OTTO WOLS (WOLFGANG SCHULTZE) 1913-1951
German Abstract $60,000

1.   2.

PCW P.C.W

PIETER C. WONDER 1780-1852
Dutch Genre $20,000

GRANT WOOD 1892-1942
American Murals, Genre, Landscape $6,960,000

1.

2.

THOMAS WATERMAN WOOD 1823-1903
American N.A. Black Portraits, Genre $100,000

LAWSON WOOD 1878-1957
British Watercolour, Genre, Landscape $5,000

BEATRICE WOOD 1893-
American Painter, Portraits $8,500

ROBERT WOOD 1889-1979
American Landscape $7,500

G.B.Wood Jr.

GEORGE BACON WOOD Jr. 1832-1909
American Painter, Genre, Landscape $2,500

Henry Woods

HENRY WOODS 1846-1921
British Landscape, Genre $25,000

M. Woodward

MABEL WOODWARD 1877-1945
American Landscape, Genre $25,000

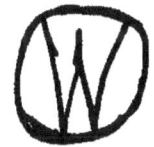

RAYMOND WOOG 1875-
French Portraits $4,000

A. Woolf

ANNETTE WOOLF 1889-
American Painter $1,000

Jos. Wopfner

JOSEPH WOPFNER 1843-1927
Austrian Painter, Landscape $30,000

J. W.

THOMAS WORLIDGE 1700-1766
British Etcher $7,500

F. W. P

FRANS WOUTERS 1612-1659
Netherlandish Allegorical, Animals, Landscape $6,500

GW

GOMAER WOUTERS 1600's
Flemish Painter

Wouwerman

PIETER WOUWERMANS 1623-1682
Netherlandish Landscapes City Scenes, Genre $20,000

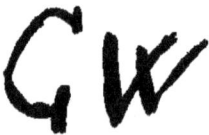

PHILIPS WOUWERMANS 1619-1668
Netherlandish Genre Hunt Scenes, Landscape $1,267,000

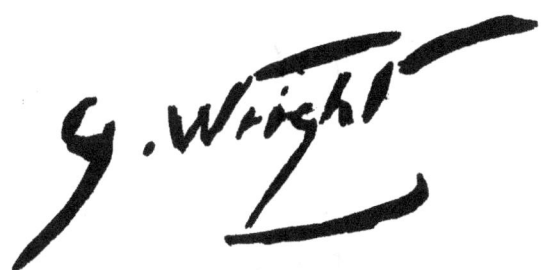

GEORGE WRIGHT 1860-1942
British Sporting, Genre $15,000

JOACHIM ANTHONISZ WTEWAEL 1566-1638
Netherlandish Allegory, Landscape $650,000

FRANS WULFHAGEN 1624-1670
German Religious Painter $5,500

PAUL WUNDERLICH 1927-
German Landscape, Genre $15,000

ALEXANDER WUST 1837-1876
American Landscape $10,000

ALEXANDER H. WYANT 1836-1892
American N.A. Landscape $30,000

1. 2. 3. *[signatures of Thomas Wyck]*

THOMAS WYCK (also Wijck) 1616-1677 (See page 830)
Dutch Landscape, Seascape, Genre $40,000

1. 2. *[signatures of N.C. Wyeth]*

N.C.WYETH

NEWELL CONVERS WYETH 1882-1945
American Illustrator $75,000

1. *[signature]* 2. ANDREW

3. *[signature]* 4. AW

5. **AW** 6. AW

7. AW 8. *[signature Andrew Wyeth]*

9. *[signature A. Wyeth]* A.W. 10.

11. *[signature Andrew Wyeth]*

ANDREW WYETH 1917-
American Landscape $7,000,000

_J.W._

JAMIE WYETH 1946-
American Landscape $30,000

W.Wyld

WILLIAM WYLD 1806-1889
British Landscape $10,000

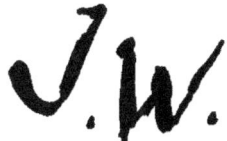

JAN WYNANTS 1615-1679
Dutch Landscape, Animals $50,000

DOMINICUS VAN WYNEN 1661-
Dutch Painter, Genre, Allegory $40,000

M.Wytman

MATHEUS WYTMAN 1650-1689
Dutch, Landscape, Genre, Still Life $5,000

Artists starting with the letter "Y"

YANG PU-CHIH
Chinese Watercolour Plum Tree Flowers

JACK B. YEATS

1. *Yeats J.B.* 2.

JACK BUTLER YEATS 1871-1957
Irish Painter, Genre, Landscape $1,500,000

R.D. Yelland

RAYMOND YELLAND 1848-1900
American Landscape $50,000

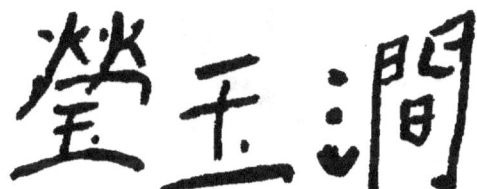

YING YU CHIEN
Chinese Watercolour

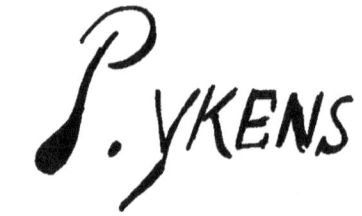

PEETER YKENS 1648-1695
Flemish Portraits, Allegory $2,500

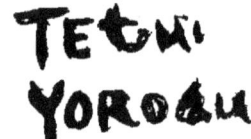

TETSUGORO YOROZU

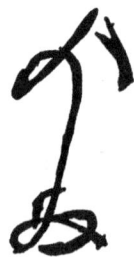

HIROSHI YOSHIDA 1876-1950
Japanese Woodblocks, Landscape, Portraits $60,000

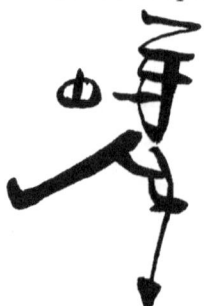

TAISO YOSHITOSHI 1839-1892
Japanese Woodblocks $10,000

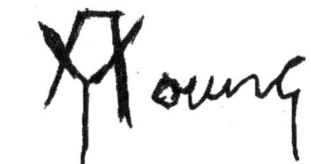

ALEXANDER YOUNG 1882-1920
British Landscape, Genre $5,000

WILLIAM YOUNG-1784
Painter

MA YUAN 1190-1224
Chinese Watercolour

ADOLPHE YVON 1817-1893
French Genre $20,000

Artists starting with the letter "Z"

RZabaleta

RAFAEL ZABALETA 1907-1960
Spanish Painter, Genre, Landscape $70,000

Léon Zack

LEON ZACK 1892-1980
Russian Portraits, Landscape $6,500

ZADKINE

OSSIP ZADKINE 1890-1967
French, Painter, Genre, Landscape $45,000

EugZak

EUGENE ZAK 1884-1926
Polish Genre $50,000

E Zampighi

EUGENIO ZAMPIGHI 1859-1944
Italian Landscape, Genre $50,000

1. *Zandomeneghi*

2. *Zandomeneghi*

FEDERICO ZANDOMENEGHI 1841-1917
Italian Landscape, Genre $900,000

1. *M* 2. *Ab*

ANTONIO M. ZANETTI 1680-1757
Italian Allegory $2,000

A. Zanieri

ARTURO ZANIERI 1870-
Italian Landscape, Genre, Still Life $10,000

RZATKOVA

ROUGENA ZATKOVA
Painter

Ilia Zdanevich

ILIA ZDANEVICH 1900's
Russian Landscape, Theatre $1,500

R. Zeeman

REINTER ZEEMAN 1612-1663
Dutch Seascape $5,000

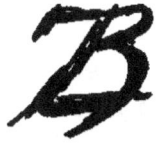

BARTHOLOME ZEITBLOOM 1455-1518
German Painter, Religious $5,000

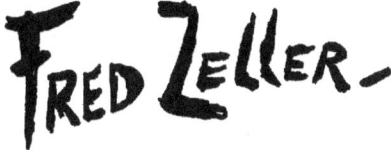

FRED ZELLER 1912-
Swiss Genre, Landscape $6,000

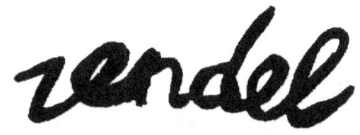

GABRIEL ZENDEL 1906-
German Painter, Landscape, Still Life $4,500

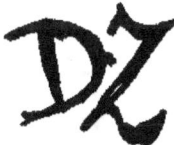

DOMENICO ZENONI -1580
Italian Painter, Genre $1,000

J. Ziegler

JULES ZIEGLER 1804-1856
French Portraits

Ziem.

FELIX FRANCOIS GEORGES PHILIBERT ZIEM 1821-1911
French Landscape, Genre $60,000

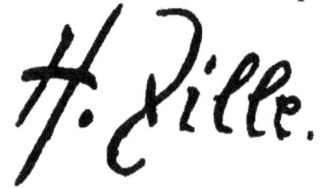

GIUSEPPE ZIGAINA 1924-
Italian Painter, Still Life, Landscape $20,000

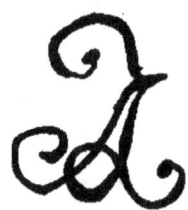

HEINRICH ZILLE 1858-1929
Danish Graphics, Genre, Portraits $20,000

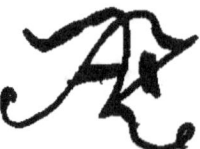

FRANZ ZIMMERMAN 1864-
Swiss Painter, Genre $3,000

JOSEPH A. ZIMMERMAN 1705-1795
German Painter

ZINNOGGER LEOPOLD

LEOPOLD ZINNOGGER 1811-1872
Austrian Painter, Still LIfe $20,000

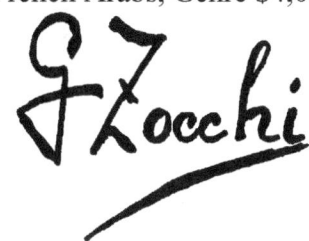

BENJAMIN ZIX 1772-1811
French Painter, Children $6,000

ACHILLE ZO

ACHILLE ZO 1826-1901
French Arabs, Genre $4,000

GUGLIELMO ZOCCHI 1874-
Italian Portraits, Genre $20,000

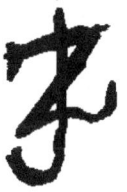

JOHN ZAUFFELY ZOFFANY 1733-1810
British Painter, Landscape, Genre, Mythology, $300,000

1. R.F. Zogbaum

2. Rufus F. Zogbaum

RUFUS FAIRCHILD ZOGBAUM 1849-1925
American Cowboys $2,500

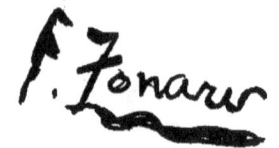

FAUSTO ZONARO 1854-1929
Italian Genre $10,000

W.ZORACH

WILLIAM ZORACH 1887-1965
American Painter, Genre, Landscape $50,000

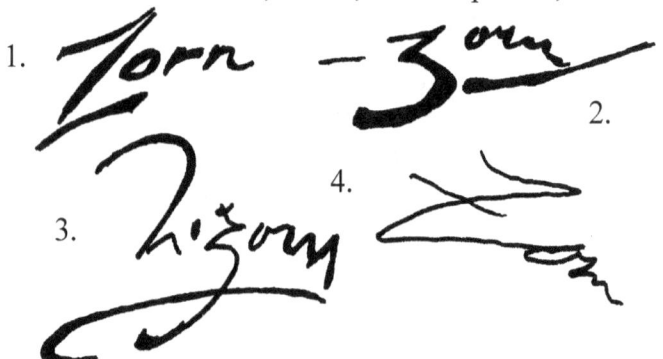

ANDERS LEONARD ZORN 1860-1920
Swedish Painter, Nudes, Landscape, Genre $3,000,000

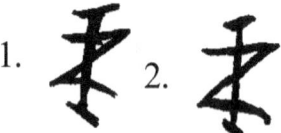

JACOB ZUBERLEIN 1556-1607
German Painter

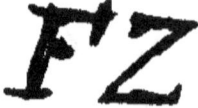

FREDRICO ZUCCARO 1542-1609
Italian Painter, Religious, Portraits, Allegory, $100,000

L.Z VCCHERI

LUIGI ZUCHERRI 1904-1974
Italian Landscape $3,000

93.

JOE ZUCKER 1941-
American Painter, Genre, Still Life $7,500

H Zügel

HEINRICH JOHANN ZUGEL 1850-1941
German Landscape, Impressionist $100,000

I. Zuloaga

IGNACIO ZULOAGA Y ZABALETA 1870-1945
Spanish Dancers $400,000

F. v. Züllow

FRANZ VON ZULOW 1883-1963
Austrian Abstract, Landscape, Portraits $9,000

R. Zünd

ROBERT ZUND 1827-1909
Swiss Landscape $125,000

Zğa

FRANCISCO ZUNIGA 1911-
Latin American Portraits, Sculptor $3,712,000

WU ZUOREN 1908-
Chinese Scrolls, Animals $20,000

F Zurbaran 2.
1. *F. DZVRBAN*
3. *f Zurbaran*

FRANCISCO DE ZURBARAN 1598-1663
Spanish Monks, Genre, Religious $2,095,000

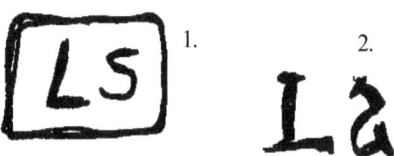

LAMBERT SOETE ZUTMAN 1510-1567
Flemish Painter

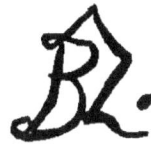

BERNARDUS ZWAERDECROON 1617-1654
Dutch Painter, Landscape, Portraits $15,000

GERARD P. ZYL 1607-1665
Dutch Painter, Genre $8,000

ANTON ZYLVELT 1600's
Dutch Painter

www.ingramcontent.com/pod-product-compliance
Lightning Source LLC
Chambersburg PA
CBHW071245220526
45468CB00001B/2